Family and Filiality

SUNY series, Translating China
———
Roger T. Ames and Paul J. D'Ambrosio, editors

Family and Filiality
An Intercultural Perspective

ZHANG XIANGLONG

Translated by
KEVIN J. TURNER

Cover calligraphy by Peimin Ni.

Published by State University of New York Press, Albany

© 2025 State University of New York

All rights reserved

Printed in the United States of America

Originally published as *Jia yu xiao* 家与孝 by Zhang Xianglong
(SDX Joint Publishing, 2017). Translated and published with the permission of the author's estate.

No part of this book may be used or reproduced in any manner without written permission. No part of this book may be stored in a retrieval system or transmitted in any form or by any means including electronic, electrostatic, magnetic tape, mechanical, photocopying, recording, or otherwise without the prior permission in writing of the publisher.

Links to third-party websites are provided as a convenience and for informational purposes only. They do not constitute an endorsement or an approval of any of the products, services, or opinions of the organization, companies, or individuals. SUNY Press bears no responsibility for the accuracy, legality, or content of a URL, the external website, or for that of subsequent websites.

EU GPSR Authorised Representative:
Logos Europe, 9 rue Nicolas Poussin, 17000, La Rochelle, France
contact@logoseurope.eu

For information, contact State University of New York Press, Albany, NY
www.sunypress.edu

Library of Congress Cataloging-in-Publication Data

Names: Zhang, Xianglong, author. | Turner, Kevin J., 1989– translator.
Title: Family and filiality : an intercultural perspective / Zhang Xianglong ; translated by Kevin J. Turner.
Description: Albany : State University of New York Press, [2025] | Series: SUNY series. Translating China. | Includes bibliographical references and index. | Text in English. Translation from Chinese.
Identifiers: LCCN 2024042775 | ISBN 9798855802184 (hardcover : alk. paper) | ISBN 9798855802191 (ebook)
Subjects: LCSH: Filial piety—China. | Families—Cross-cultural studies. | Parent and child—Cross-cultural studies. | Parent and child—Philosophy. | Confucian ethics.
Classification: LCC BJ1533.F5 Z436613 2025 | DDC 173.0951—dc23/eng/20250103
LC record available at https://lccn.loc.gov/2024042775

Contents

Preface		vii
Chapter 1	Between Confucianism's "Treating Family Affectionately" and Kierkegaard's "Abraham's Sacrifice of Isaac"	1
Chapter 2	Is Human Nature Related to the Family and the Way of Filial Reverence? Critiquing the New Culture Movement on the Family	11
Chapter 3	Anthropology and the Temporality of the Way of Filial Reverence	27
Chapter 4	Imagination and Historical Memory: The Stratification of Internal Time Consciousness	51
Chapter 5	Incest Taboos and the Way of Filial Reverence	69
Chapter 6	Incest and Plato's *Republic*	77
Chapter 7	Who Should Care for the Elderly?	97
Chapter 8	Parents, Children, and the Confucian Classics	103
Chapter 9	Toward a Confucian Special Zone by Way of an Intercultural Dialogue with the Amish	109

Chapter 10 Can Confucianism Accept a Matriarchal Family?
            Learning from the Matriarchal Mosuo
            of Southwestern China   127

Chapter 11 Family Relations and the Way of Filial Reverence
            in *Harry Potter*   149

Notes   179

Works Cited   193

Index   199

Preface

The history of Western philosophy is a history without family (jia 家), and traces of family are rare sights in modern Chinese philosophy, which has followed the way of Western philosophy. Western philosophy has searched for origins, numbers, existence, principles, universal and particulars, form and matter, and knowledge and virtue. In modern and contemporary times, Western philosophy has also paid attention to subjects and objects, perception and rationality, logic and experience, mind and matter, analysis and totality, meaning and reference, language and reality, intentionality, temporality, embodiment, and more. These are all related to human beings' feelings, thoughts, and the existential experience of being in the world; however, that part most directly related to human beings has been left out. This philosophical principle of the most intimate experience is represented by the word "family."

Human beings first and foremost receive their lives from the coming together of their parents, following an indistinct experience in the womb. Sensation of the outer world begins at birth; how to act and how to speak are learned while under the care of one's parents, grandparents, guardians. Mature emotions, a sense of measure, relationships, morality, and all kinds of capabilities are learned from the relations one has with brothers, sisters, friends. Once able to leave their parents, one's sexual maturity has been reached, consciousness has sharpened, the world is more alive and abundant, and philosophical thinking is within reach. A person throws themselves into society and the world, establishing their own family, reciprocating with their parents, while at the same time caring for their own children, and ultimately settling down under the care of their children and perhaps grandchildren. When human beings look back on their lives, they self-consciously believe they have never let down their ancestors, nor do they feel shame in front of later generations; thereupon an ultimate consciousness of being able to die without regrets is produced and those without families can obtain this kind of tranquility only by relying on religion. For the vast majority of human beings, their most sincere, most passionate emotions and experiences are related to homes and families. The reason why a photograph of a three-year-old (Alan Kurdi) who has drowned can change the fate of a million refugees is because it moves people's innate moral knowledge and capacities for loving their children and others through the juxtaposition of adorability and suffering.

However, for more than two thousand years, Western philosophy has ignored the earliest experiences of life, nibbling only at the part sliced off from its living body. To put it nicely is to say "logic comes first;" for example, how can people perceive external phenomenon in pure neutrality? How do we turn these perceptions into objects for reason? How do people find absolute certainty within their consciousness of self? And even (for the philosophers of cognitive science in recent years), why can all conscious activities be reduced to neural networks in the brain? Or in order to raise the problem of an eternal substance or essence to harden the continuous experience of the family that transcends the individual. Not until the relatively late wave of phenomenological thought did philosophers like Heidegger and Levinas begin paying attention to the problem of the family. They became aware that the family has an entire living problematic, vocabulary, and mode of thought to itself, that it cannot be simply seen as a sociological object, and that it must be faced directly from the perspective of "existential hermeneutics" or "the other." This is the experience of pure intuition that turns toward things themselves and in it finding within an energetic life before it is dismembered a method to give meaning to the world. What phenomenological reduction sets aside first is not the attachment to existence but instead the impoverishment and conceptual analysis of existential experience. Actually, the most intimate and complete experience that humanity can have is *a priori* experience, one yet to be divided into before and after.

This book wants to use the new philosophical meaning brought about by the phenomenological turn within Western philosophy, especially that living analytic method undertaken in philosophical thought, or that is to say, a way of thinking that is a Western-style pulse-taking and needling. Nevertheless, it will not be limited to that, because this method itself has not allowed even thought as profound as Heidegger's finally to enter into the true lifeblood of the home and the family; the Way of Filial Reverence (*xiaodao* 孝道) need not even be mentioned. The philosophy of ancient China is another never-ending source, using the method of *yin* and *yang* mutually supplementing each other and generating ceaselessly to think profoundly about life and the world. The trigrams in the *Book of Changes*, the transformations directly entering into the "familied" thought of heaven as father, earth as mother, and *qian* 乾 and *kun* 坤 as birthing the six children. The Confucians adopted this way of thinking and developed into a naturally intuitive, ethically familial, and artistically opportunistic philosophical realm, making this way of living the mainstream of Chinese civilization. The author of this book has been situated between these two traditions for a long time and has born the grinding tension of being situated between "others," and I hope that I can use my writing to express my "feelings and profound comprehension" of my contingent fate. In order to do this, I am expending great effort in thinking and writing, and in anticipating when I will be able to present something complete to the reader.

Following Meng Shuwei's 蒙舒炜 kind suggestion, I have gathered together different essays on "family" and "filial reverence" that I have written in recent years that pay special attention to East–West comparisons or that are related to Western philosophy and culture into a collection to present to everybody and hope that readers find it worthwhile. Among these, some are yet to be published, and some are immature, such as *Incest Taboo and the Way of Filial Reverence* (which is more or less an outline), but because this way of thinking is necessary, I have included it. Incest taboos and the founding of families have a profound connection and have been viewed by the academic world as being the origin of marriage systems, but what is the relation between incest taboos and the relationships among parents and children? This chapter tries to explore this question, and moreover to lead up to the following chapter discussing the philosophical king in the classical West.

To give this book a clear direction, I have worked further on all of the essays collected within so as to improve coherence. Because the main theme is relatively focused and each essay was originally written separately, readers will note some redundancies. I ask readers for their understanding, or to be sympathetic and perhaps view the redundancies as a kind of melody.

Among modern Chinese research, there is my friend's Xiao Si's 笑思 *Jia Zhexue—Xifangren de Mangdian* 家哲学—西方人的盲点 ("Philosophy of Family—the Westerners' Blind Spot"), which appeared in recent years and opened up and broke through the unphilosophical condition of research on the family. This has had profound significance. I have received much benefit from a long friendship with Xiao Si, and we agree on many things; for example, we both think that the family is the source of human subsistence and virtue and that the Western model is greatly flawed at this point. However, our research methods, academic backgrounds, and points of attention differ. Of course, this is no more than the diversity of individuals. I have been influenced the most by phenomenology when it comes to Western philosophy, and my thought resonates with the analytic philosophy of Wittgenstein and Kuhn's philosophy of science. I am also interested in contemporary anthropology, psychology, and even cognitive science. I am even more passionately interested in the philosophical import of the Way of Filial Reverence. In my view, the phenomenon and consciousness of filial reverence is probably one of the keys to understanding the uniqueness of humanity and the family. It is also essential to understanding Confucianism and its future. As for a definite path of exploration, readers will gain their own sense after reading this book.

I am grateful for the encouragement of my friends at SDX Joint Publishing, for without them this book would not be. I would also like to thank the philosophy department at Shandong University for providing me with a tolerant environment. When I went to their department to discuss my research plan, I promised to write a book about the Way of Filial Reverence. This book, although not large, is nonetheless the result of many years of thinking and research, and has provided me with new meaning.

Chapter 1

Between Confucianism's "Treating Family Affectionately" and Kierkegaard's "Abraham's Sacrifice of Isaac"

Abraham submitted to the request of Yahweh—the supreme God of Judeo-Christian religious belief—and went to sacrifice his only son by his true wife. This is section 22 of Genesis in the Old Testament that takes the relationship between God and man as its main theme. However, if we give this story more consideration, we can deepen our understanding of the human relationship between parent and child as well as its temporal philosophical and religious existential connotations. This is a different kind of understanding. Actually, key parts of the Bible often reveal the constitutive power of parent–child relationships in religious faith and thought. If this is not understood, it cannot be considered a living theology.

The discussion below centers on the case of Abraham sacrificing his son Isaac. This sound of Yahweh hammering on the parent–child relationship is perhaps the most capable of startling people. Here, we want to make use of Kierkegaard's creative analysis in his 1843 *Fear and Trembling*; its inspirational power is also startling. In appropriate places, we will also touch upon other essential materials regarding the parent-child relation in the Bible.

Why Was There a Need for This Kind of Sacrifice?

"And it came to pass after these things, that God did tempt Abraham, and said unto him, Abraham: and he said 'Behold, [here] I [am]'"

(Genesis 22:1).[1] Why did God want to test Abraham? Was it that God did not understand him? Abraham was already over one hundred years old at that time and had always submitted to the will of God. He had withstood previous tests; however, God still wanted to test, examine, and put him to trial, otherwise how could He be at ease. Why? Was it because God's promise to him was too grand and distant? "Neither shall thy name any more be called Abram, but thy name shall be Abraham; for a father of many nations I have made thee. And I will make thee exceedingly fruitful, and I will make nations of thee, and kings shall come out of thee. And I will establish my covenant between me and thee and thy seed after in their generations for an everlasting covenant, to be a God unto thee, and to thy seed after thee" (Genesis 17:5–7). Did God need this ultimate test in order to guarantee that his counterpart would not leave his part of the contract unfulfilled and because of the tendency of Adam and Eve's descendants to fall? (note that due to this tendency occurred both the flood that destroyed humanity and the fire that burned Sodom). Or perhaps it was that even the "omniscient and omnipotent" God could not relax when dealing with this kind of person or could not distinguish his deepest tendencies, especially his tendency to change over a long period of time?

Now, then, what kind of sacrifice was it? "And he said, Take now thy son, thine only [son] Isaac, whom thou lovest, and get thee into the land of Moriah; and offer him there for a burnt offering upon one of the mountains which I will tell thee of" (Genesis 22:2). Why was it this kind of sacrifice? Was it because it was frightening beyond what people could accept stabbing most deeply to the heart and marrow and therefore could reveal this person's true nature? Abraham waited seventy years before he saw his own son at the age of one hundred; placing his hopes for generational transmission in him, he was "whom [he] lovest," the adorable Isaac. Yet, God wanted Isaac through a fire sacrifice; he even wanted Abraham to kill his own son with his own two hands! Who can think of a request more painful, more terrifying? Therefore, at least for this kind of person, it was an ultimate request. For this kind of person living in this kind of generational temporality who takes this temporality as the origin of the meaning of life, it was an ultimate request. If Abraham was able to fulfill this request, was able to bear this "test," then he not only would be "buried in a good old age" (Genesis 15:15) without breaking his contract a single time throughout his entire life, but moreover, his "seed after in their generations" would also not betray this "everlasting covenant." Everything depended on whether Abraham was capable of turning his knife on his own son Isaac, and then placing his son's dead body on the burning burial pyre.

However, without Isaac, how could God fulfill his promise to Abraham? Without this only son, how could He "make [him] exceedingly fruitful"? Would he perform another miracle and make the aging Sara become pregnant again? But after accepting this kind of sacrifice, after killing the "Isaac whom [he] lovest," could Abraham and Sara, as human beings, also accept the pregnancy and birth of another child? Yes, God is omnipotent, but from the necessity of this test it can be seen that God must also do battle with the sense of time (human beings' source of knowledge) in the deepest place of human nature, and Isaac was the time soul of his parents. More important, if Abraham believed God would use someone else instead of Isaac to instantiate the contract when he faced this trial, then he would still have something to rely and deliberate on. Would sacrificing Isaac then still be an ultimate test? Therefore, no matter what we say, as far as Abraham was concerned, there was only one Isaac, and God could only offer his promise through him. And nevertheless, Abraham could only sacrifice him according to the word of God.

According to Kierkegaard, what Abraham had to perform was not a normal test (*Anfoegetlse*, temptation, trial) but rather a paradox that neither Abraham nor we can understand the conceptual or causal meaning of. Relying on the powers of absurdity that transcends all mediators, Abraham was able to become the "knight of faith," and God was able to establish a universally ethical, tragic, and even an "infinite resignation" between him and humanity.

"What I intend now is to . . . see how monstrous a paradox faith is, a paradox capable of making a murder into a holy act well pleasing to God, a paradox which gives Isaac back to Abraham, which no thought can grasp because faith begins precisely where thinking leaves off"(*Fear and Trembling*, 82).[2] Of course, the "thought" noted by Kierkegaard here is just that thought that depends on the "universal" or concepts and ideas but does not include all of humanity's rational modes of thought. Otherwise, what he himself wanted to transmit with his book, and what we are trying to do here, are just illusions.

However, regardless of whether it is paradoxical faith or absurdity, or if it is the divine in a murder, or a murder desired by the divine, their understandability all revolves around a single focal point: the relationship between Abraham and Isaac. The relationship between parent and child is so fundamental and fatal to people like us that God *can only use it* to implement his test. Can you imagine this kind of trial being undertaken amongst the Gods or superhumans? As if the Greek gods, Christian angels, or Buddhist arhats had a test like this? Can you imagine a test like this taking place between two lovers? As if God had requested Romeo to sacrifice Juliet to determine the purity of his faith? There would be many kinds of interpretations, including some impure ones. It is only within familial affection that the "most frightening and absurd" is not an insipid paradox, that it is not just a tragedy or a comedy, that it can excite a passion or feeling like an aurora, and that "a murder [is made] into a holy act well pleasing to God."

"Venerable Father Abraham! Second father to the human race! You who first saw and bore witness to that tremendous passion . . . you needed a hundred years to get the son of your old age, against every expectation, that you had to draw the knife before keeping Isaac" (*Fear and Trembling*, 56).

The Temporality of This Sacrifice (1): Generational Time and Living Time

This sacrifice is not a trial that happens just once, as it penetrates into existential temporality and can happen anywhere with a certain unpredictability. It is also not an entirely clear problem that is just waiting for a ready-made answer.

First, the text surrounding this sacrifice is filled with the perspective of humanity's life in time. A large part of Genesis is composed of a "family genealogy" that spans generations: this is "genesis." It is also the shadow of the "Heavenly Father" who created the world and the creatures in it. "So God created man in his [own] image, in the image of God created he him; male and female created he them. And God blessed them, and God said unto them, Be fruitful and multiply, and replenish the earth, and subdue it: and have dominion over the fish of the sea, and over the fowl of the air, and over every living thing that moveth upon the earth" (Genesis 1:27–28) Of course, God is not the real father of humankind not only because he has no wife to have offspring with but also because he created humankind in just one day, with no full-term pregnancy, and those whom he created apparently had no periods of infancy or childhood (the situation after being expelled from Eden is another story). Regardless, the "generation" created by God, in addition to being the "world," also has the meaning of "era."[3] And the relationship between God and Abraham is thoroughly connected by the promise and expectation of "thy seed after in their generations." Isaac represents a key generation among them.

Next, Abraham's whole life was a struggle with that treacherous and illusory time within which he won a kinship and loving genealogical time: "He had fought with that subtle power that invents everything, with that watchful opponent that never takes a nap, with that old man who outlives everything—time itself" (*Fear and Trembling*, 52). To pass God's trial, he had to kill the one thing this genealogical time is dependent upon—Isaac—thereby leading to Abraham's total failure in the struggle against time: "For what meaning could there be in it if Isaac was to be sacrificed!" (53). However, Abraham did not hesitate for a moment to do that thing which would bring about his failure: "And they came to the place which God had told them of, and Abraham built an altar there, and laid the wood in order, and bound Isaac his son, and laid him up the altar upon the wood. And Abraham stretched forth his hand, and took the knife to slay his son" (Genesis 22:9–10). At the moment when he "took the knife to slay his son," he had overcome time: "And he said, Lay not thine hand upon the lad, neither do thou anything unto him: for now I know that thou fearest God, seeing how thou has not withheld thy son, thine only [son] from me . . . That in blessing I will bless thee, and in multiplying I will multiply thy seed as the stars of heaven, and as the sand which [is] upon the sea shore" (22:12–18).

It is easy for people to say that Abraham won God's promise of generational time through faith. This saying is not bad. However, the problem is what kind of faith is capable of winning but not transcending time? Very few people are able to follow up with this question and understand the internal temporality of this sacrifice. This is where the key lies. Was it that he raised the knife because he believed God would "bear [him] up?" (Gospel of Matthew 4:6). Or did he perform this sacrifice because he respected universal ethical laws and possessed the courage and devotion of a tragic hero? Or was it because of the "infinite resignation," the abandonment of all life that he did not hold onto his son? Or was it that he was a zealous believer with a strong conviction who confusedly went to kill his son upon hearing the voice of God? No, none of these are the faith that can win time. The focal point of Kierkegaard's discussion is entirely about this.

Kierkegaard differentiates this sacrifice from others by revealing its temporal course. Other sacrifices seem to simply be a process of "determination" or "making a decision" and can be completed in a single moment. Moreover, as soon as one is decided, there is only a linear path with no remaining turns or detours. "They praise God's mercy for giving him Isaac once again, the whole thing was just a trial. A trial—that can say a lot or little, yet the whole thing is as quickly done with as said. One mounts a winged horse, that very instant one is on the mountain in Moriah, the same instant one sees the ram. One forgets that Abraham rode on an ass, which can keep up no more than a leisurely pace, that he had a three-day journey, that he needed time to chop the firewood, bind Isaac, and sharpen the knife" (*Fear and Trembling*, 80). What is the difference between a single moment and three days? The difference is that conceptualization and universalization can be completed within a single moment; or, with the nod of Agamemnon's head, others will go on his behalf to complete the heroic undertaking of the tragic sacrifice of his daughter. But our Abraham, who is pitiful yet remarkably magnificent, was requested to go forth and sacrifice his own son. Every moment of these three days was a test; each moment could change (61), every step could be "making the movement of the infinite" (69), each moment could allow for the mistakes of "excess" and "insufficiency" (58–59, 74–75). Therefore, "a single moment" is just the present moment, what is completed through it is just the flat serialization and eternalization of the present; but "three days" is full of memories (e.g., the memory of his own and Sara's life, of Isaac's birth), hope (e.g., God's promise and its imminent evaporation), and observation (e.g., the observance of Isaac's naïve cuteness and the arising associations) that are fresh and makes people crazed and despaired; it is an originary time full of all kinds of possibilities for change.

"The older he [Kierkegaard] became the more often his thoughts turned to that tale [of Abraham], his enthusiasm became stronger and stronger, and yet less and less could he understand it. Finally it put everything else out of his mind; his soul had but one wish, actually to see Abraham, and one longing, to have been witness to those events. . . . What he yearned for was to accompany them on the three-day journey, when Abraham rode with grief before him and Isaac by his side. He wanted to be there at that moment when Abraham raised his eyes and saw in the distance the mountain in Moriah, the moment he left the asses behind and went on up the mountain alone with Isaac. For what occupied him was not the finely wrought fabric of imagination, but the shudder of thought" (*Fear and Trembling*, 44). Therefore, the preface of *Fear and Trembling* goes along the path of Abraham four times: from when he set out to the three days spent traveling, all the way to the mountain top, the binding, the lifting of the knife . . . and even the return home afterward (45–48). From all of these, from the experiences realized from different perspectives, we can begin to understand the unusualness of this affair. What is terrifying is that it shares nothing with any moral principle. From this we also know the difficulties and subtleties of phenomenologists: they think in step with originary experience and tremble in unison along with he who experiences when they think. Thought that does not begin to tremble, that does not make outsiders dizzy, is not a true thought that can enter timeliness to create a spectacle, and instead is just a re-productive imagination and conceptual construction. True thought and what is thought is the relationship between parent and child; this is where understanding paradoxes and living time is possible.

The Temporality of This Sacrifice (2): The Time That Despair and Paradox Point To

The temporality of Abraham's faith is revealed through the paradoxicality of this faith. This paradox itself is a phenomenological and transcendental reduction. It necessarily uncovers the pure faith that is prior to all intentional action. And this paradox is able to take shape within the most absurd, desperate, and passionate relationship between parent and child.

Abraham's sacrificing his own son is different from those child sacrifices undertaken for the benefit of the people and puts him in the company of tragic heroes. This is because his sacrifice has nothing to do with moral commands or any universal principles, it is purely "private" and "individual." The sacrifice of the tragic hero makes people cry, but Abraham's sacrifice does not lead people to shed a tear (*Fear and Trembling*, 89). The tragic hero sacrifices one thing that is certain for another thing that is certain, but the meaning of Abraham's actions hangs in the air and is unthinkable (89). Actually, Abraham *is not able* to perform this sacrifice *for anything*—ethical purposes have entirely ceased—otherwise, he would be unable to achieve the nakedness and sincerity of this sacrifice. All external explanations find their end here with nothing to say. In order to do this, he must have a fundamental relationship with he whom is being sacrificed, must have a love for he whom is being sacrificed that is passionate and profound, which goes beyond his own life values, and which has no goals outside of pure time itself. Moreover, this most precious thing (Isaac) also cannot be killed in sacrifice for anything (God commands only that the sacrifice be initiated, but this does not constitute a real teleological cause). How absurd! How dazzling! How paradoxical! It makes those who are not "knights of faith" lose more sleep and experience more "fear and trembling" the more they think about and imagine it. It is only the love between parent and child that can connect he who sacrifices and he who is sacrificed, otherwise it would just be an ultimate evil. He who has experienced the great love between parent and child is he who is able not to simply hate and despise it. Regarding this, familial affection is the resting place of humanity; it is the highest point of the human spirit and originary imagination. From this perspective, in Kierkegaard's interpretation of Gospel of Luke 14:26 in the New Testament that says "If any man come to me, and hate not his father, and mother, and wife, and children, and brethren, and sisters, yea, and his own life also, he cannot be my disciple" (*Fear and Trembling*, 99), he opposed changing the word "hate" to the softer phrase "has little love for" because God demanded the absolute love of humanity that cannot be replaced by the act of degrading the original love between parents and their child into something else (how can those who have no great love for their parents have absolute love for God?) (101). As far as Kierkegaard is concerned, this "hate" can be understood only as the love God demands, which has an internal dizzying paradoxicality (101).

Kierkegaard sometimes says that the meaning of "paradox" or "faith" is that "the single individual as the particular is higher than the universal" (*Fear and Trembling*, 84). But actually, these special individuals just point to "parent and child." Abraham, on the road, was a lonely individual on the surface, but from top to bottom and inside and out, he was living with the life and death of Isaac through his relationship with him. This includes when he "stretched forth his hand, and took the knife to slay his son." Otherwise, he would just have been a murderer and not a believer at all. Therefore, the relationship between parent and child is of originary time. It must live and die along with this time, and cannot go beyond this time at all to know, think, and plan. This is to say that when Abraham stretched out his hand to take up the knife, he could not think or imagine that God would in the next moment call for him to stop but was indeed about "to slay his son." However, this "want to slay" is not the same as holding some intention to murder so that he could not even hear the call of God to stop or not see the ram "caught in a thicket by his horns" (Genesis 22:13). The first half of this experience sought the separation from temporality: the present is absolutely different from the future. The present's movement toward the future is an unthinking and imageless leap; the second half of this experience sought some kind of temporal continuity where the future can change, turn back, and even negate the present where it is not separated from the present and where that leap does not necessarily lead to fragmentation. Abraham certainly wanted to kill his son in sacrifice; however, he did not want to do so for anything—he wanted to be able to kill him with no reservations. He was dancing a strange dance, that "stable leaping" dance—"stand[ing] there in it in the leap itself" (*Fear and Trembling*, 70)—that is able to take the fatalistic leap of faith and come safely to the ground (70, 74–75), the dance that "is at every moment making the movement of infinity" (69). It is, in other words, that dance which dances on the sharp edge (paradox) between the infinite and the finite, the personal and the public, love and murder, without getting hurt and conversely uses its cutting momentum to move up and down. Therefore, after the infinite resignation, it is still possible to prepare for the acceptance of miracles within the world of the finite, for example, "the return of Isaac," so that he could happily face Isaac and Sara with no gloomy embarrassment at all. This Judeo-Christian doctrine of the mean that totally connects the infinite and the finite "does not force it yet is in the middle, does not think it yet obtains it, is carefree and easy in the middle of the way" (*Liji—Zhongyong* 禮記・中庸). Even those knights of the infinite resignation are unable to do this (66–67). This is a bottomless and infinite abyss of faith, a faith that cannot be understood by a consciousness already formed. It can be only originary time, prior to any comprehensive conceptual or objective associations. It freely relies on the meaning constituted by the differences of the past, the present, and the future (it is the faint connection in absolute separation). Perhaps it is not as good to say that it is a realm of meaning.

Abraham's sacrifice cannot be imitated in any sense at all. It is an absolute "particular" or the temporalization of the parent–child relationship. A priest preaching on Sunday tells the listening audience: "Abraham loved God like this, loved him to the point that he was willing to give what was most precious to him in sacrifice." Regarding the content, this could not be said any better—there is nothing wrong with it. Thereupon, there is a sincere believer who hearing the sermon and going home "wants to do just like Abraham [sacrificing his son to God]; for the son is certainly the best thing he has" (*Fear and Trembling*, 58). That preacher must have known this because he hurried to the scene where "[t]he comic and the tragic converge on each other in absolute infinity" to rebuke and scold that sincere believer (59). He was correct to do so. However, this single-minded person scolded as one of the "dregs of society . . . [who] wanted to murder [his] own son" (59) would find it confusing, telling the priest, "It was in fact what you yourself preached on Sunday" (59). Here Kierkegaard leaves a comment, changing an already popular saying—"What a shame things in the world don't go in the way the priest preaches"—to "How fortunate that things in the world don't go in the way the priest preaches" (59, see footnote).

Why is it the case that what Abraham was capable of doing and what the priests were capable of preaching was not something that believers were capable of doing? It is because what Abraham did was more than it appeared to be, and what the priest said was not actually what Abraham did. Abraham's sacrifice was created through the most passionate and uninhibited emotion in the world; those who truly understand and experience it under most circumstances (where one has not yet become a knight of faith) will feel fear, anxiety, and insomnia (*Fear and Trembling*, 58–59). They will even begin to behave in certain ways but be unable to put into words that truly summarize it—they will also not turn it into a classic model to emulate. If there happens to be a person who after truly understanding or experiencing it does something similar to what Abraham did (although the possibility of this is small to the degree that people cannot imagine it), then this is the fate of that event itself, and is not the same as the tragic-comedic act being talked about here.

This passion is the love between parent and child; it allows the sacrifice of one's child to become the ultimate, that is, to become completely internal time. And living internal time can only generate and cannot be emulated. Is it that there is only the particular and not the universal within it? Or is it that the particular and the universal therein are intertwined as originary consciousness and originary meaning?

Chapter 2

Is Human Nature Related to the Family and the Way of Filial Reverence?

Critiquing the New Culture Movement on the Family

Over one hundred years ago, in 1915, the journal *Xin Qingnian* 新青年 (New Youth) was first published under the title *Qingnian Zazhi* 青年雜誌 (Youth Magazine). From then on, the New Culture Movement gradually gained in momentum, riding on the winds of the times and transcending the left–right divide to form the entirety of modern Chinese ideology. This movement can thus be called important, even profound, although many of its theories have serious problems from the perspective of rigorous thought. There were nine volumes of the *Xin Qingnian*, and beginning with the eighth volume it became a journal published by the communist organization in Shanghai. From this it can be seen that even this journal had the shared focal point of criticizing Chinese culture. It included writers from many schools of thought and eventually achieved fame over its contemporaries. But it certainly did move from rapid cultural change to rapid political change, and then created even greater thought on rapid cultural change. That is to say it raced from being anti-tradition to that kind of special political party, body, and leadership that can truly establish the new and break the old. Afterward, in 1966, there began the most thorough anti-tradition cultural movement, which proclaimed of all things old that "there is a reason for revolution." The "new" of the *Xin Qingnian* led China through the twentieth century, making it so radical that many revolutionaries eventually wanted to "say goodbye to revolution." Another aspect is that those rightists like Hu Shi 胡適

(1891–1962) and Fu Sinian 傅斯年 (1896–1950) and those right-wingers who followed them in being anti-tradition actually participated in the creation of this radicality. These were the kind of people who complained of the cold without reflecting on being outside in the wind.

Within the past ten years or so, there has appeared a new left-wing wave of thought in mainland China. This wave has startled people by raising the slogan of "Confucian socialism" (particularly Gan Yang 甘陽). The revolution of the twentieth century remains respected, but its cultural direction must be fundamentally altered so people can partake in the process of the rise of Chinese ethnicity. However, the opposition between revolution and tradition from the past century is as present as ever. How we should talk about it and how to explain it remain problems, even more so when touching on the deep-level issues currently being dealt with.

In conclusion, regardless of whether it is the left wing or the right wing and Confucianism, they all must directly reflect on this New Culture Movement and thereby recognize their own identity within China, be it the past or the future. Within modern China, Confucius's spirit is dead. Using Nietzsche's saying from *Thus Spoke Zarathustra*, we can ask: who killed him? The clear voice of a madman shouts: all of us killed him together! There are people today who publicly confess their behaviors from the time of the "cultural revolution," but will there be those who confess on behalf of the cultural movement for the havoc it wreaked? Will there be people who confess to sullying the Chinese family? Even the human family?

What follows will reveal the basic view on the family and the parent–child relationship of the New Culture Movement, discussing the consequences effected by its thought. Our discussion will expend great effort to directly respond to the New Culture Movement in order to make both it and our response to it more profound and to show how the view of the New Culture Movement on family is fundamentally incorrect.

The Predecessors and Influence of the Anti-Family Thought of the New Culture Movement

After the Opium War, Western influence on China gradually created a tendency to oppose the Chinese-style family, and even the human family. By the time of the New Culture Movement, this had reached its most brilliant and self-aware stage. Under the influence of missionaries, Hong Xiuquan (洪秀全, 1814–1864), the leader of the Taiping rebellion, believed that when facing the heavenly father God there was no difference in familiarity between people created through the family: "the many men underneath Heaven are all brothers; the many women underneath Heaven are sisters" (*Yuandao Xingshi Xun* 原道醒世訓). Therefore, in his *Taiping Tiaogui* 太平條規, he made it a regulation for officials and soldiers that "men camp together and women camp together," strictly forbidding husbands and wives to live together. During the long period of time that this regulation was in effect, it actually negated the marriages and family lives within the Taiping army. An important element of Kang Youwei's 康有為 *Datongshu* 大同書 was the destruction of family lineage (Liang Qichao's 梁啟超 words), and in its imagined highest state of society, there was no family at all. Tan Sitong's 譚嗣同 *Renxue* 仁學 went even further. By the late Qing dynasty, revolutionary activities went along with the agitation of the revolution in the family.

In the first publication of *Xin Qingnian*—that is, the first essay in the first volume published of the *Qingnian Zazhi*—Chen Duxiu 陳獨秀 wrote: "There is not a single ethics, law, learning, or custom that is not an inheritance from a feudal system" (*Qingnian Zazhi* 1, no. 1: 3).[1] Thereupon, in *Wuren Zuihou zhi Juewu* 吾人最後之覺悟 ("My Last Enlightenment"), he believed that:

> We should establish a republic with a constitution that takes independence, equality, and freedom as its principles and which cannot have anything at all to do with the traditional class system. We must preserve one and abandon the other. If the government rejects this opting for despotism in favor of preserving the old power of the familial society, then the principles of equality in the eyes of the law and the economic independence will be destroyed without remainder and then where will there be left to go? (*Qingnian Zaizhi* 1, no. 6: 4)

Chen believed the family or family ethics of China was completely an inheritance of the feudal system, and because he wanted to establish a new republic and constitution, he thus needed to abolish this kind of familial society. He labeled this family system a "traditional class system," confounding the Chinese ethical roles such as father and son, husband and wife, with the class distinctions of the West. And later, it was the party newly establish by Chen that believed the most in the theory of class struggle.

Closely related to this is Wu Yu's 吳虞 call in his *Jiazu Zhidu wei Zhuanzhizhuyi zhi Genju Lun* 家族制度為專制主義之根據論 ("On the Family System Being the Foundation of Authoritarianism"), published in *Xin Qingnian* (vol. 2, no. 6) and later called *Chiren yu Lijiao* 吃人與禮教 ("Cannibals and Rituals"). Wu wrote: "Today we should be clear! Cannibals are those who talk about rituals! Those who talk about rituals are cannibals!" (*Xin Qingnian* 6, no. 6: 580). The famous author Tang Si (Lu Xun 魯迅) argued strongly that "there is no compassion between father and son" in his *Women Xianzai Zenyang Zuo Fuqin* 我們現在怎樣做父親? ("How Should We Be Fathers Now?"). His reason was that: "The result of food and drink is the nourishment of the self, there is no compassion for oneself; the result of copulation is the birth of sons and daughters, in regard to them there is also nothing to be considered compassion" (556). Moreover, Fu Sinian, in his essay *Wan'e zhi Yuan* 万恶之源 ("The Root of All Evil") in the first publication of *Xinchao* 新潮 ("New Wave"), points to the "Chinese family" as the root of all evil because it oppresses the personalities of young people: "Ai! This slavish life, is there anything left to bury?" (*Qimeng Sichao* 啟蒙思潮, 68)[2]

This attack on, denigration of, and even cursing of the Chinese family, the human family, and the parent–child relationship—Fu Sinian: "If you want to know the situation of the Chinese family, then just draw a pigpen" (*Qimeng Sichao*, 69)—is not simply the voice of a few overly passionate literary figures. They brought about a long-lasting and irreversibly historical consequence. A great deal of essays and novels (Ba Jin's 巴金 *Jia* ["Family"], *Chun* ["Spring"], and *Qiu* ["Autumn"] are the most well-known) criticizing the so-called old-style family encouraged hotblooded youth to join the revolution; and the marriage laws of the Republic and post-1949 era at least partially embodied the appeals of the "new youth." At the time of the "cultural revolution" in 1966, the anti-family thought of the New Culture Movement had reached its sharpest point. It is unknown how many families were ripped apart, husbands and wives thrown into disarray by their class struggle; they are found everywhere. Even if the opening up and reformation of the commercialization and globalization of the economy used a different method to mutilate the family, we cannot say there is no relation between the New Culture Movement and the phenomena of the missing "way of filial reverence" and the high divorce rate of today's China.

From Criticizing the Chinese Family to the Denial of the Rationality of the Human Family Itself

The many figures of the New Culture Movement were almost all people who praised the West and disparaged China. Therefore, in their criticism of the Chinese family, they more often than not brought up the Western family composed of individual contracts as a comparison. They thought that the latter respects the individual and therefore it is substantially better. They also said of the former that it oppressed the development of individual freedom and thus deserved more than death. Today, the situation is already relatively clear: the individual freedom they believed in would not stop at the freely established *family*—instead they wanted to go further and realize a freedom that surpassed the true form of the family. For example, they wanted freedom for homosexuals to start families and to even destroy the freedom of the family by allowing divorce at will—this at the same time implies harm done to the freedom of sons and daughters—they wanted freedom for single-parent families, unmarried cohabitees, and freedom for those who want no children. Obviously, the denigration of the Chinese-style family is not simply a question of cultural criticism. Neither is it only a question of allowing the shape of the family to change with society into something new. Instead, it is a question of necessarily falling into an attack on the rationality of the family itself. Regarding this, the predictions of those "stubborn" conservatives of that time were not wrong. Therefore, it was inevitable that essays and thought like that in Lu Xun's essay mentioned above would appear. Such thinkers denied the compassion of parents for their children and maintained that the family and child rearing are only the results of released sexual impulses. In other words, the family and parent–child relations do not have their own basis or a basis in human nature because sexual desires are traits that we share with other animals. This way of thinking also opened a space within which to accept Marxist theories of the family—there is no family in the beginning and end of human history. Because Marxism argues that human nature in the very beginning and at the highest stage of its realization has nothing to do with the family, it actually determines that human nature is not familial or is homeless. Although Marxism believes that human beings are constituted of social relations and lack an abstract human nature, the social system of the family nevertheless has to change with changes in the modes of production. But because in communism the modes of production have reached their highest stage and hence have achieved the greatest rationality, Marxism thus ultimately perceives human nature in terms of the family negatively.

This theory became a national ideology after 1949 all the way up to today. It is obvious that the anti-family thought of the New Culture Movement rushed into all places. Due to it and the Westernized modernity it relied on as its model, the Confucianism that took family as its source and the culture of parent–child relationships that had thrived for thousands of years in China necessarily declined. Moreover, the rapidity of this decline surpassed the normal speed and degree that Western modernization usually has on tradition and the family. That a one child policy could suddenly exist across the country, where it was once considered to be the greatest act of unfilial behavior and even the most tragic affair to be "without descendants" (*wuhou* 無後), is clear evidence of the success of the New Culture Movement. China has been made "new" by the movement to no small degree!

Is There Any Compassion and Morality to the Parent–Child Relationship?

Therefore, the primary question now is not whether the Chinese-style family should exist or not. Instead, it is whether the family itself and parent–child relations have a basis in human nature that go beyond specific time periods. What *is* the family? The basic meaning of the word "family" used here is the basic existential unit composed of a formal binding of husband and wife and the subsequent birthing and raising of their children and its generational continuation. It can take many different forms including adoption, bigger families such as those families composed of several generations living under one roof, and even those family lineages composed of many families. Lu Xun and the others maintained the "truth of biology" (*Xin Qingnian* 6, no. 6: 557) that the parent–child relation is created through the sexual desires of the parents, and therefore there is no compassion to speak of regarding parents toward their children and there is no obligation of the child to be filial to them in anyway. This ignores a basic fact and element of the parent–child relationship: that is, for children, the parents did not just give them birth, they also raised them. Therefore, since there are adoptive parents, this raising, caring, and educating surely cannot be reduced to the impulses of sexual desire.

Is it the case that there is no compassion of parents toward their child? This touches on the issues of whether parents giving birth to and raising a child was determined by biological or other external forces and whether it can be considered compassionate for the parents to give birth to and raise children before obtaining their agreement.

Let's first consider the situation of raising children. Even if it is the biological parents, is it that they were driven by biology to raise their children? No. If we can say that the nurture other animals give their offspring is determined by instinct, then for animals like humans who possess a profound temporal consciousness and ability to choose, although there certainly is an instinct to care for one's own children and even those of others, it is not always the case they will provide such care. Historically, when a problem appears or when due to the influence of a male chauvinistic culture, there have been the phenomena of abandoning female babies or giving them over to the care of others. And today in an economic and cultural atmosphere not conducive to the family, we see many people who do not raise their own children and do things such as leaving them in their parents' care, being a surrogate mother without raising the child, abandoning females, and not raising sick children. Steve Jobs was a child abandoned by his parents. There is thus a choice in whether parents raise their children, and the life and living condition of the child is related to this choice. Other than this, when there is a common and reliable method to avoid pregnancy there are some people who choose not to raise children in order to avoid the trouble and all kinds of costs associated with it. In other instances, people raise few or no children and yet are able to satisfy their sexual desires. We can therefore see that raising children is a conscious expenditure and contribution of the parents on behalf of their children, so how can we say there is no compassion? It cannot be that because "when a village wife breastfeeds her child, she never thinks of herself as extending compassion" (*Xin Qingnian* 6, no. 6: 557). To claim that this breastfeeding is without compassion is the same as saying that the rapist who does not see himself as doing violence does not actually do violence.

Can the historical generation of children only be reduced to a biological instinct? It appears not. Different from other animals, humans are able to engage in sexual activities and get pregnant in old age.

But during the long process of the formation of human nature—this is by far the largest portion of human history—because humans were primarily hunter-gatherers, they needed four or five years between each child, otherwise it would be hard to raise them. If this fact discovered by anthropology can hold its ground, then there must be a choice of whether or not to raise children. It does not matter if this choice is realized through contraception or child abandonment. Obviously, the reproductive descendants of humanity were never entirely passive; a single person has life, and this is not a so-called coincidence—there is certainly something received from one's parents and grandparents.

Another popular Western concept can serve as a comparison to the above idea that thinks that parents producing children is entirely passive. It is based on the passivity of the child's own birth and rejects the compassion of parents for their children. Let us stick with Lu Xun's essay. Lu Xun was quoting a saying from one of Ibsen's plays. It came from the mouth of a sufferer of syphilis who had inherited it from his father. When his illness acted up, he wanted his mother to give him a large dose of morphine so he could commit suicide. Thereupon he said to his mother: "I never told you to give birth to me. What kind of life did you ever give me? I don't want it! Why don't you take it back!" (*Xin Qingnian* 6 no. 6: 558). In regard to the question that we are discussing, this saying can have two levels of meaning. The first is that because when you gave birth to me or when parents give birth to their children they do not obtain their agreement, therefore, children should not be grateful to their parents for giving them life. The second is that the life which you gave me is not healthy, but instead full of suffering, therefore not only do you not have compassion for me, but you have a debt to pay. Regarding the second level of meaning, we can respond by saying that, on the one hand, if parents know they will transmit something that will create a fundamental problem for their child, they have a responsibility to avoid giving birth or to correct the problem beforehand. On the other hand, in most situations, parents do not know or are not clear on what they will transmit to their children. Thus the parents cannot be blamed. Almost all parents want their children to be healthy and fortunate; however, there are a few who are not so healthy, or there are some who, later in their life, are not so fortunate according to a general standard, especially those people who are born in a chaotic world. But who can provide an absolutely effective definition of what health and fortune are? Ever since ancient times, Eastern and Western philosophers have all observed that human fortune and suffering is not ready-made; it changes in accordance with the times or personal cultivation, and one can even take the place of the other. "Oh disaster, it is that which fortune relies on, Oh fortune, it is that which disaster relies on. Who knows their limits? There is nothing regular about them" (*Laozi* 58). I was born into the family of a learned person who had opened an architecture company. When I was a young child and during my adolescence, because of my father's "problematic" social status as a business owner, I was always discriminated against. But because of this, should I blame my parents? After the reform and opening up, I attended college and was able to undertake the career that I enjoyed, and so on. Should I at that time, because of all this, go thank my parents? Blaming our parents is not right because they only think to give us a good life. Thanking our parents is always right because our appreciation is not dependent on whether we are fortunate. Instead, we should thank them for our being alive at all, for being conscious, for having free will. We should thank them for the fundamental perspective of this life's temporality and historicity, for our own meaningful judgment that we are not just this single life and that we are connected to the future world and the past world. Even if we are born into a chaotic world and live tragic lives, or are slaves or children of a class enemy, because we are not simply this living moment but live in the future through our wishes and hopes we will still be able to experience the meaning of life by ensuring the continuation of the family lineage.

  The profound form of the first level of meaning has received even more theoretical attention. In his *Metaphysics of Morality*, Kant maintained that because parents did not get the agreement of their children before giving birth to them, they are thus responsible for bringing them to adulthood until they possess free will and a complete personality. Afterward, there is no natural parent–child connection but only a contractual relationship if they want to stay in touch. Therefore, parents raising their children into adulthood have no moral reason for compensation.[3] The modern American scholar Jane English, in her 1979 article *What Do Adult Children Owe their Parents*, pointed out a similar argument. She differentiated "favors that can create debt" and "friendships that cannot create debt."[4] If person A does something beneficial for person B, for example, when person B's car breaks down and person A uses their own car's battery to restart it, then afterward, when person A encounters the same or similar trouble, does person B have a moral debt or duty to help person A in return? English claims this is determined by whether or not person B sought help from person A at the time. If person A helped at the time of person B's request, then person B has a sense of moral indebtedness to person A and thereafter has a moral obligation to help person A when the time comes. However, if person B did not request person A's help, but instead person A did something of their own volition for person B, then person B has no moral obligation to fulfill. If person B chooses to repay person A, this only comes out of the friendship established between these two through this affair. Neither does person B choosing not to repay person A result in a moral debt. English uses this distinction to argue that children have no moral debt to their parents because they did not seek to be born from their parents.

Two Chinese scholars, Wang Qingjie 王慶節 and Li Chenyang 李晨阳, rebuked English's argument. They primarily criticize her example for being limited. For example, if person B is not at home when their house catches fire and person A saves person B's house and rescues a child, then can you say that person B has no moral debt to person A to the point that when person A's home has trouble then person B should not have a duty to try all they can to help solve person A's problem? The answer should be in the affirmative. Wang also points out that it is a dubious argument to argue from the fact that children do not choose to be born by their parents because if we want to make this argument tenable, then the case needs to be that children originally have this choice and that it was taken away from them by the external force of their parents or other factors. However, because children are yet to exist before birth, they cannot have such a choice. Thus, to pull out a series of conclusions based on the fact that before children were born they did not choose to be born is meaningless.[5]

I agree with this rebuttal. From this we can see that no matter what perspective one takes, no matter if we refine and deepen coarse and shallow arguments such as that of Lu Xun which rejects the moral nature of parent–child relationships, none of them can hold their own ground.

Are Husband–Wife Relationships and Parent–Child Relationships Founded in Human Nature?

If we go even deeper, does Lewis H. Morgan's (1818–1881) argument, which Marxism is based on, that there was a stage early in humanity's development that did not have marriage or families or the so-called "communal husbands and wives" period, hold its ground? Many anthropologists from the twentieth century have shown it to be false. It appears that Morgan provided an explanation of tribal Indian kin relationships that did not fit with reality and thought up that period of humanity's history without families. What can be seen from modern anthropology text books, specialized books, and related essays is that modern anthropology has already reached a consensus on this: although families and parent–child relationships can take all kinds of forms, humanity has always had some kind of family, and there was never a time entirely without families where mothers and fathers did not mingle even if the role of the biological father can be taken over by an uncle. To use the words of Levi-Strauss and the French scholars who wrote *The History of the Family*: the family exists in the long course of human society and is the same as language, one of the markers of human existence.

The contemporary anthropologist Conrad Kottak, in his *Anthropology: The Exploration of Human Diversity and Cultural Anthropology*,[6] writes: "Humans choose mates from outside the natal group, and usually at least one spouse moves. However, *humans maintain lifelong ties with sons and daughters*. The systems of kinship and marriage that preserve these links provide a major contrast between humans and other primates" (84). Taking a mate—a wife—from outside of one's own social group, such as the family or the clan, implies there is an incest taboo, that there is a restriction on marriages with people from one's own family or lineage. And having an incest taboo implies that there is some system to establishing a family, that there is a family system, a lineage, and a clear parent–child relationship. *Liji–Jiaotesheng* 禮記・郊特牲 says: "As for the marriage ceremony, it is the beginning of the ten thousand generations. Because wives are taken from different families, in this way bloodlines are strictly demarcated in marriages with clans from far away. As long as men and women have their differences, then father and son can be affectionate. As long as father and son are affectionate, then appropriateness can be generated. As long as appropriateness is generated, then the rituals can be performed. As long as the rituals can be performed, then the ten thousand things can be settled. If there is no differentiation and no appropriateness, then that is the way of beasts and birds." Incest or the non-differentiation of the sexes talked about here will disorder family relationships and will lead to the relationships of father and mother, especially that between the father and children, to become clouded or replaced. And the differentiation between men's and women's families will lead to the prominence of the relationships between husbands and wives and parents and children (for a discussion of this point, see chapter 5.)

Can incest taboos only appear at a certain stage in human history or can they cover all of human history? This has already been answered above. Mainstream twentieth-century anthropologists such as Levi-Strauss have affirmed the second conclusion, and the first conclusion held by people like Johann Bachofen, John McLennan, Morgan, Marx, and English cannot hold its ground.[7] The next question is: are incest taboos related to acquired culture or are they related to humanity's innate nature? The former conclusion was more popular in the international academic world in the past half century or so. Westermarck[8] represents the latter judgment that incest taboos are related to humanity's innate nature or their natural method of survival while still occupying an inferior place. However, several investigations within the past half century—regarding the physiological dangers of reproduction between relatives, the lack of inter-relative reproduction in animals, child brides in Taiwan, the relatively low sexual attraction between men and woman who grow up together in Israeli kibbutzim—have altered this state of affairs.[9] Now, the view of Westermarck has at least received the level of respect it should have. In sum, modern research has reached a relatively trustworthy conclusion: although the expression of incest taboos is related to culture, it nevertheless has a universal existence and is not constructed by culture. Instead, it has a foundation in human physiology and psychology or in human nature. The famous "Westermarck effect," that is, men and women who grow up together will usually not be sexually interested in each other, can be seen as the common structure of human nature and culture. This common structure is founded in the natural mechanism of the family.

It is precisely the family that turns those rules against incest among animals that already exist into a systematic thing that has been thought to be the origin of humanity's system by some scholars like Levi-Strauss. Therefore, the family has a physiological and psychological foundation, like how the differentiation between men and women or incest taboos have physiological and psychological foundations but at the same time experiences the shaping forces of culture and current trends. This is one of the special characteristics of humanity: it finds its existential base in a naturalized culture and technology. There are many contained within the one, and the one is fused with the many. It is not an absolutely transcendent One, so it cannot be without exceptions. The large brains and profound temporal consciousness of humanity thinks according to a dynamic probability.[10] There can be exceptions on almost all levels, however, the guiding and transhistorical tendency or the so-called "essential nature"—"What Heaven endows people with is called human nature" (*Zhongyong* 中庸)—also continuously emerges in a process of construction. Therefore, the guiding incest taboos and Westermarck effect within human social groups will have their exceptions, for example, if two relatives do not grow up together and then meet after reaching sexual maturity, it is possible they will have incestual impulses. Within some cultures and certain time periods, there is an erosion of the tendency to care for the old. In a time like today when de-familialization is rampant, these kinds of exceptions will increase greatly. However, as long as we are wise moderns, these exceptions will not fundamentally destroy the special human characteristic of the family.

The second half of that passage from Kottak quoted above says that "humans maintain lifelong ties with sons and daughters. The systems of kinship and marriage that preserve these links provide a major contrast between humans and other primates" (*Anthropology*, 84). This expresses another important fact: it is only humans who will recognize relatives and maintain contact throughout their entire lives, and chimpanzees, who are closest to humans genetically, do not do this. From this we see again the uniqueness and originality of the family to humanity. Therefore, humans are not like other primates in that there is a familial division of labor between men and women and care of the elderly within the family.

This also means that the family is an entirely meaningful organism. Every individual therein must realize their own roles. No one is self-sufficient and entirely independent. In this way, the differentiation of men and women and the parental compassion and filial reverence that the Confucians talk about obtains an even more abundant internal meaning. Other than chimpanzees sharing small amounts of meat, most of the time they seek food alone or a mother is carrying her child while seeking food. Humanity appears to have "retrograded" to be community animals where the mutual provisions of cooperation and transtemporality have become mainstream.

The human relationship between husbands and wives is also unique. Its main form is not that of polygyny (like gorillas), polyandry, monogamy (like some birds, penguins, for example), or one where there is no sexual regulation within the kin-group but nevertheless has some kind of mechanism to avoid incest (such as with chimpanzees, where young females leave the group). Instead, it is a relatively elastic monogamous system where there are, in general, more males than females. Why does the human family have the attributes described above? Other than the factors that went into shaping the structure of the family like the "theory of the hunting husband," the "theory of hunters competing for women," the "the bodyguard theory," and the "the theory of settling's one's young wife in a golden house,"[11] a key factor is that human children are not at all mature when they are born. Because humans evolved to stand upright and walk on two feet, the structure of the pelvis was limited to the opening of the birth canal; and the front limbs became the arms and hands, allowing for the greater use of tools, which in turn stimulated the growth of the head and the brain. This led to the dangers of human childbirth.

When human children are born, they are much less mature than other mammals, so there was an increase in the time required to rear a human child. Under these kinds of circumstances, if there is no "father," then mothers in hunter-gatherer societies would find great difficulty in raising infants, especially those after the first one. The division of labor between men and women would increase child-rearing capabilities, for example, the mother who takes gathering as her primary activity can reside near her work area and at the same time care for her child. And since meat is important for the nutrition of the group, effective hunting requires even greater strength and ability. Long before the breastfed child's brain has fully developed there is an *a priori* dimension to its relationship with its parents. The experiences of the child's early years fundamentally form the structure of its consciousness and behavior, so much so that there can form manifest or hidden long-term memories of these formative experiences. Therefore, the compassion in parents raising their children is something that their grown children can become aware of and who thereupon form the intent to repay them.

Looking at the whole picture, it was the special difficulty in giving birth to and raising children that forced humanity to develop a profound temporal consciousness so they could remember the knowledge and experiences of the past and effectively plan for the future and implement their ideas. With this refined balance, humans were able to make farther-reaching plans and obtain long-term rewards. Furthermore, through this balance they possess a sense of morality and ethics, and even aesthetic and the divine. A person will then become an even more complete and meaningful human being. Therefore, Confucius said, "Being consummate is being human, the grandest is treating family affectionately" (*Zhongyong*). The root of the entirety of Confucianism is within this "treating family affectionately" (*qinqin* 親親) and thus realizing the consummate being that makes humans human. From this it can be seen that the husband–wife and parent–child relationship that constitutes the family is not simply a result of sexual desire, nor is it constituted by culture alone. Instead, it is internally connected with the innate temporal consciousness of human nature. The trampling of the Chinese family and the human family by the New Culture Movement was the trampling of human nature.

Chapter 3

Anthropology and the Temporality of the Way of Filial Reverence

To investigate the philosophical foundation of the Way of Filial Reverence (*xiaodao* 孝道), its relations with human nature must first be known because the foremost philosophical problem of the Way of Filial Reverence is whether it is an expression of human nature or something formed through culture and education. Our understanding of human nature today, especially of the twentieth century, has changed greatly in comparison to that of two thousand years ago. Other than biology and genetics; psychology, especially Freud's theory of the subconscious; cultural sociology; and European continental philosophy (such as phenomenology and structuralism), among the major forces effecting this change are the new developments in anthropology and related sciences. For example, due to new developments in anthropology, we no longer see tool use, reflective consciousness, the use of symbolic language (nor the possession of vocal language), and other characteristics as uniquely human. We also are no longer limited by Lewis Henry Morgan's declaration that no relation exists between human nature and the family.

However, we also know that some topics on human nature are quite sensitive. For example, maintaining that human nature is influenced by genes for race, or that there is an internal connection between human nature and sex—be it heterosexuality, homosexuality, or other. These are positions that will probably be passionately criticized and even denounced from a position outside pure academia. Our closeness to anthropology can also be seen in Edward O. Wilson's 1975

Sociobiology, which caused great controversy.[1] This book incited protest and something close to a political movement not only because the last chapter of the book discusses human characteristics via the forms of social biology of other species—genes, gender relations, social structure, and others (*Sociobiology*, ch. 27)[2]—but also because this scientist revealed a dissatisfaction with the "past"-ness of this kind of thinking that human nature was "teetering on a jerrybuilt foundation of partly obsolete Ice-Age adaptations" and that the humanity of today should face the option of "press[ing] on toward still higher intelligence and creativity."[3] This dangerous position, which wants to alter humanity and human nature on a fundamental level to make humans "evolve" into "post-humans" becomes, to a certain extent, a kind of guiding goal for scientific research and practice.[4]

Obviously, anthropology and technology that can reform human nature do not stop at knowledge or techniques but are more and more related to our understanding and appraisal of human nature and the Way of Filial Reverence. Philosophers who have focused on human nature and the fate of humanity can less and less afford the costs of ignoring them. If modern humans existed three million years ago, then there would be four or more kinds of hominins of the genus Homo (*How Humans Evolved*, 253),[5] or just one hundred to four million years ago there would be three species—*Homo sapiens*, Neanderthals, and some species from Asia, such as *Homo floresiensis*—so when we discuss "human nature," would it not then be easy to say that "what comes first naturally does not betray its naturalness" or to make definitions that seem to be obvious? Once things are thus, it becomes much harder to form a "bill of human rights," and it becomes even harder to separate anthropology and philosophy. Along the same lines, advanced technology and the correlated culture, politics, and economy are right now creating a new human species. At that time, we will have entered the second stage of evolution. How is this not a more fundamental metaphysical question?

"Grass when seen from afar disappears when up close." Anthropology, primatology, sociobiology, and even biology are all internally linked to philosophy, and sometimes we see this only when we have reached the distance where we "feel remote," similar to how we can see ancient sites that are in a forest or wasteland only from high up. Up close, what we see is not the same and can even be conflicting.

Where Does the Distinction between Humans and Other Animals Lie?

First, Jane Goodall's discoveries in 1960, as well as other observations added later, show that chimpanzees and other primates are capable of using tools.[6] Moreover, chimpanzees and other primates are capable of hunting and sharing their catch with others of their own kind. A few primates (such as macaques and orangutans) are also capable of learning or forming "culture" that can be transmitted (*Anthropology*, 81).[7] Other than this, it has been shown that chimpanzees "can learn to use (if they cannot speak) language." Two chimpanzees, Washoe and Lucy, were taught American Sign Language from a very young age. They learned more than one hundred English vocabulary signs and were able to compose simple sentences to interact with humans, such as "you, me, go out, fast," "dirty monkey" (in the nearby monkey enclosure), "dirty cat," and other terms and phrases (*Anthropology*, 222–223).

Obviously, the capabilities of primates such as chimpanzees, bonobos, and gorillas are much more primitive and "incipient" in comparison to humanity, but they show that, in these regards, the difference between them and humans, as well as other advanced animals (e.g., dolphins), is one of degree and not of essence or essential nature.

Now, where is there a more real difference between humans and other animals? Kottak writes in his *Anthropology: The Exploration of Human Diversity* that

> humans appear to be the most cooperative of the primates—in the food quest and other social activities. Except for meat sharing by chimps, the ape tendency is to forage individually. Monkeys also fend for themselves in getting food. Among human foragers, men generally hunt and women gather. Men and women bring resources back to the camp and share them. Older people who did not engage in the food quest get food from younger adults. . . . Nourished and protected by younger band members, elders live past the reproductive age and are respected for their knowledge and experience. The amount of information stored in a human band is far greater than that in any other primate society. (*Anthropology*, 83)

Human pair bonds for mating tend to be more exclusive and more durable than are those of chimps or bonobos. Related to our more constant sexuality, all human societies have some form of marriage. (83)

Let us analyze these two passages. First of all, humans are the most able of the primates to cooperate with each other. However, other primates are also capable of some kind of cooperation, and thus the difference between humans and primates in terms of "cooperation" is one of degree. Nonetheless, there have certainly been structural changes in certain characteristics. Humans divide the labor of gathering food between men and women, which other primates do not do. Humans care for and respect their elderly, and other primates do not.[8] Humans have exclusive and enduring sexual relations, which is rarely seen in other animals. Unique to humans is the tradition of marriage, though other creatures have been observed to bond for life. Humans have incest taboos, which is seen in other primates. However, most important is what we have noted in the previous chapter: "humans maintain lifelong ties with sons and daughters" (*Anthropology*, 84). That is, the uniqueness of the parent–child relation in humans is that it lasts all one's life. In conclusion, it is the structure and style of human relations, that is, the temporal form of human existence that comes from the *yinyang* intercorrelations such as that between husbands and wives and between parents and children embodied as the lifelong acceptance of family bonds and bi-directional intergenerational care. This is not an isolated capability but one that truly differentiates humans from other primates in a meaningful way. This is insightful, and has become common knowledge after many years of anthropological investigations and research.

Obviously, clear differences exist between humans and other primates, such as the apes, in terms of anatomy and genetics. For example, humans stand upright and are bipedal, a fact that led to a series of important consequences for bodily structure (discussed further below). However, it is only through connecting these physiological characteristics with the structure of human relations and the basic behavioral forms created through these structures that an interesting difference will appear in terms of our understanding of human existence that is not simply of anatomical, taxonomic, or religious import.

Humans, or humans like us, are not only normal social animals. They differentiate between men and women, care for and respect elders, marry and maintain parent–child relations throughout life. If we do not adopt a philosophical anthropological perspective on human kin relations then we will fabricate some kind of theory of a non-abstract human nature or such a theory will be submerged in a general "sociality" and "cultural relativism." However, we certainly have "human nature." It is neither abstract or isolated, and therefore it cannot be fully encompassed by a single specialized skill such as vocal language. Instead, it is the original and structural expression of the time consciousness pouring out of the parent–child relation that entails "intelligence," "morality," and "politics."

We have always had ethics. And it is a fresh and lively ethics. It is not a nuanced moral regulation but something created by various cultural groups. Human ethics is absolutely less abstract than the "the sinful intelligence of Adam and Eve" or "reason," "language," and "sociality." Therefore, the "He who is benevolent is a human" (*renzhe renye* 仁者人也) and "treating others affectionately is grand" (*qinqin weidai* 親親為大) (*Liji–Zhongyong* 禮記・中庸) talked about by the Confucians was an exquisite anthropological insight reached from outside the context of Western anthropology.

Why Do Men and Women Want to Become Husbands and Wives?

Modern anthropology began in the West. Previous anthropologists have thus mostly taken the Western view on men and women and marriage as their basis when observing marriage relations in other cultural groups. As soon as they began, they believed that models resembling Western families and kin relations were universally applicable. Following this, they discovered that there were many ways for organizing the two sexes and the family among "primitive peoples" that differed from Christianity. This led them to a few over-the-top conclusions.

Some nineteenth-century anthropologists like Lewis Henry Morgan thought that early humans had a period of loose sexual relations without marriage or families. This is what is meant by his so-called period of "community of husbands and wives" (*Ancient Society*, 47),[9] and the shape of the family known to people was one of "the institutions of mankind [which] have sprung up in a progressive connected series, each of which represents the result of unconscious reformatory movements" (58). This view had a great intellectual influence evident in the theory of "communism." However, much stricter and more scientific anthropological research has shown that Morgan was wrong regarding this question: humans, from the very beginning, had marriage and families.[10] Moreover, there could exist many different kinds of family across different peoples at the same time. Marriage between one man and one woman and the resulting family does not have to be entirely a succession of private property. Neither is it necessarily based on emotions. Previous philosophical imagination has been too simple and has taken too much for granted. It was framed by a realism where one side must win out over the other (such as the dualisms of the subjective/objective, material/spiritual, utility/emotion) and by a view of linear evolution so that the convolutions of millions or even tens of millions of years of human evolution cannot be truly comprehended. Here, the few thousand years of "civilized history" recorded in writing explains nothing at all. Making use of fortunate archaeological discoveries and our imagination is unavoidable when the time scale is so large. Now, what reason do we have for saying that the relationship between men and women is primarily an elastic one between one man and one woman and not a monogamous relationship that is stricter than promiscuous relations between one man and many women, one woman and many men, or one where the social roles can be assumed by either sex?

The most common interpretation regarding the formation of the relationship between men and women is the theory that "rearing children requires a father" where the contribution of the "father" or "husband" in the long child-rearing process has a great impact on the child's survival. For example, Jared Diamond writes:

> Human babies continue to have all food brought to them by their parents even after weaning, whereas weaned apes gather their own food. Most human fathers as well as mothers, but only chimpanzee mothers, are closely involved in caring for their young. . . . That's because our elaborate, tool-dependent methods of obtaining food make weaned human infants incompetent to feed themselves. Our infants first require a long period of food provisioning, training, and protection—an investment much more taxing than that facing the ape mother. Hence human fathers who want their offspring to survive to maturity have generally assisted their mates with more than just sperm, the sole parental input of an orangutan father. (*The Third Chimpanzee*, 60)[11]

If this is the case, then sexual relationship must be long term and basically spousal. During the hunter-gatherer period—this is the longest evolutionary period for the formation of human nature—a single man was unable to care for multiple wives and their children. Conversely, it would be difficult to determine which child belonged to whom if a single woman had many husbands. Thus, the investment was not worth it for the husbands.

This hypothesis makes a lot of sense because it is based on an important anthropological phenomenon: the *special temporal characteristic of existence* that if a child is not "reared for a long time" then it will not survive. There is a series of reasons why this is the case, and perhaps the fact that humans are bipedal is the origin of it all,[12] causing changes like falling dominoes even if these changes formed very gradually. Bipedalism allowed primitive people to make better use of their arms and hands to manipulate tools more than chimpanzees can and this possibly stimulated the brain and skull to increase in surface area.[13] On the other hand, bipedalism also limited the width of the pelvic opening; otherwise it would not be able to support an upright body. In this way, childbirth in human females became dangerous: the unborn child's head was large, but the pelvic opening limited the birth canal. This caused women to be unable to have smooth births in the way that other mammals, including chimpanzees, can. Thus, childbirth can happen only when the child has yet to fully mature (*Anthropology*, 104–105). The result is that human child-rearing is both long and difficult, especially among people who have a mobile hunter-gatherer lifestyle. Thus, if there is no help from a father, it is not easy for a single human woman to raise one child, let alone many children.

However, how does the father help the mother? How does the husband help his wife? A popular theory from the end of the nineteenth century still influential today is that of the "hunting husband hypothesis." It hypothesizes that men since ancient times, such as the periods of *Homo habilis*, *Homo erectus*, and ancient *Homo sapiens*, were all hunters and that their prey—that is, meat—were essential to their wives and children (*Kinship*, 443). However, the research of the past decade has greatly weakened this hypothesis. According to the research on existing hunter-gatherer societies, the meat that a hunter acquires is not only shared among his own family but also with each family in the social group. This is to say that meat from hunting is "public welfare" that takes the social group and not the family as the basic social unit (*Kinship*, 457–458). Since this is the case, meat from hunting cannot directly help form husband–wife relations.

The hypothesis that wants to replace this is the theory of "male hunters competing for women." Some scholars have pointed out that male hunters or warriors took risks in order to win women because their success would bring a high level of food and safety to the social group and raise their value as a social member in the eyes of their peers. Therefore, women would be more willing to give themselves over to them, and thus the opportunity to mate with more women was even larger, as was the chance that the male's descendants would survive although he did not directly participate in rearing them (*Kinship*, 460–461, 463). It seems that this theory does not fully explain why men will maintain the husband–wife relationship and not try to sow their seeds wherever they can. Perhaps this hypothesis supposes that the chances for success between male hunters is relatively even. No matter what one says, both of these hypotheses say that the reason why men and women become husbands and wives is because of something other than sexual relations.

Since the 1960s, some scholars have said that within hunter-gatherer societies, it was the women's gathering and not the men's hunting that provided most of the food, even if some tribes gave more importance to hunting (*Kinship*, 444). This argument is helpful to the latter of the above two hypotheses.

Another interpretation is that the relationship between husbands and wives is one of "protection" or "guardianship." That is, the husband–wife relationship mainly came about through the man's providing for and protecting of his own spouse and children. Scholars have noticed that primates sometimes kill infants. When males become the new leader of a social group, they want to kill all infants that are not their own. Some scholars have paid particular attention to the function this has in forming male–female relationships among primates and even men–women relations among humans (*Kinship*, 452). According to this theory, the lifelong alliance or coupling between males and females and men and women is primarily an evolutionary adaptation to protect one's descendants. A Canadian investigation has verified that married women are less likely to be subject to sexual crimes and harassment (*Kinship*, 464).

There is also the "women concealed in a golden room" hypothesis. This says that humans differ from other primates in that ovulation is hidden, and thus it is impossible to determine when a woman can become pregnant. In order to guarantee that the children she gives birth to are one's own, the man must spend a lot of time with a woman in order to avoid being cheated on behind his back. This led to the formation of husband–wife relations. Moreover, women also lack a specific mark for their sexual receptiveness, which protects them from being assaulted by other men during certain periods of time (*The Third Chimpanzee*, 81).

In conclusion, almost all modern anthropologists accept the natural fact of the model of husband–wife relations—in societies where many people live together men and women live together their entire lives and even form lifelong partnerships; this includes a certain degree of polygyny[14] and extramarital affairs. Moreover, they think that in comparison to other animals, especially primates, this kind of relationship is unique. That is to say, the husband–wife relationship is an uncommon characteristic special to humans. It seems that the "way of the gentlemen" that "is initially formed among husbands and wives" (*Zhongyong* 中庸) maintained by the Confucians is very "human." When many anthropologists discuss the relationship of human pairs, they tend to attribute it to the perennial nature of human sexual activities and even physiological characteristics such as the reduction of body hair (*Sociobiology*, 554). Actually, this just explains that humans can continually have sex during their period of sexual maturation and, logically speaking, this includes promiscuous relationships. However, it is unable to explain the formation of husband–wife relationships. The reasons behind the formation of husband–wife relationships include both the physiological and extra-physiological ones and also the fact that it is not institutional.

This shows that humans are especially capable of reaching compromises or are beings who possess an internal time consciousness and that they are not like other advanced animals where males fight for females, are entirely exclusive, or are completely loose in their relationships. This internal time consciousness also allows for the possibility of "self-other consciousness" and the "deception capacity" in chimpanzees (*Primates in Perspective*, 671).[15] However, its depth in humans allows for the possibility of "husband–wife consciousness." Obviously, this can be turned around: from the perspective of the female, in responding to the physical superiority of a male, females evolved a unique measuring mechanism or "deceit" mechanism, such as so-called "hidden sexual receptivity." This made it so that not only do males have to be relatively focused, but it also reduced the intensity of competition between males in the social group. Therefore, humans *fundamentally have families*, including the basic monogamous family, because this is an expression of human nature. It is an expression of the wisdom of an internal time consciousness. It is where the evolutionary advantage of humans lies and is unrelated to private property.

However, until now a question has been ignored by all approaches, one that we deem of extreme importance: what significance does the lifelong maintenance of the parent–child relationship have for the formation of husband–wife relationships? Almost all scholars focus on the relationships between men and women of the same generation and at best focus on the one-way relationship of parents toward their child. However, the profound temporal intergenerational relationships, especially that of the relationship that children have for their parents, have fallen on deaf ears, as if they can be ignored entirely. As noted earlier, a human characteristic is the deepening and extending of time consciousness. So how can the basic structure of such beings be unrelated to intergenerational relationships? For example, we can imagine that the lifelong connection between parents and children was involved in the creation of the human social network, altering its structure, and promoting the formation and stability of the relationship between mothers and fathers or previous generations of elders. It is not hard to design an empirical model of this that can be tested.

Filial Reverence: An Ignored Characteristic of Human Nature

The human phenomenon of filial reverence has yet to become either an important anthropological or philosophical question. This situation should change because filial reverence is a concentrated display of human internal time consciousness that reveals the uniqueness of human nature. Without understanding filial reverence, anthropology will be greatly lacking and incomplete, and philosophers talking about human nature and the structure of human existence will be like a tree missing its root. However, the reflection on this problem by anthropology and modern phenomenology as well as existentialism has provided us with valuable perspectives and evidence.

Filial Reverence Is a Universal Uniquely Human Phenomenon

Just as the character for filial reverence (*xiao* 孝) shows, it implies the care, respect, cherishing, and succession of a child (*zi* 子) for their parents (*lao* 耂 or 老) of the previous generation. Does this exist in other animals? It appears it does not exist, even though Chinese books on

Anthropology and the Temporality of the Way of Filial Reverence | 37

filiality have such sayings as "kind crows feed their mothers" (*ciwu fanbu* 慈乌反哺),[16] despite a lack of definite evidence for such behavior. Nor is there evidence for its existence even among chimpanzees and bonobos. Those elements considered to be special characteristics of humans, such as tool use, self-awareness, symbolic language, and political authority, have all been found at least in their prototypical forms in animals, especially in related species like chimpanzees. However, the phenomenon of filial reverence, like bipedalism in primates, is found only in humans. Now, is it the case, as some people have said, that filial reverence is a phenomenon only of certain cultures and not universally human? It seems this is not the case. Anthropologists agree that filial behaviors—obviously, most anthropologists will not use this term—is a basic human phenomenon. For example, when *Anthropology: The Exploration of Human Diversity* describes human characteristics, there is this passage we have already seen: "Older people who did not engage in the food quest get food from younger adults. . . . Nourished and protected by younger band members, elders live past the reproductive age and are respected for their knowledge and experience" (*Anthropology*, 83).[17] It is clear that filial reverence is not just a phenomenon of certain cultures. This phenomenon has been noted by primatologists and anthropologists in their studies of the differences between humans, apes and even in their analyses of Neanderthals. For example, Neanderthal bones often have marks on them that possibly came from injuries while hunting (or perhaps from fights between individuals within the group), but most were wounds that had healed. This "has also been seen as evidence for social assistance in these hominins" (*Primate Evolution*,[18] 1729). This makes people suspect that families and filial behavior existed among Neanderthals. However, this kind of family and filial action is far surpassed by that of modern *Homo sapiens* because in comparison to modern *Homo sapiens*, the percentage of young and old Neanderthals was relatively low while those in their youth and prime were relatively high (*Primate Evolution*, 1728).

Animals—Including Chimpanzees—Have No Filial Reverence to Speak Of

The classical chimpanzee mother Flo observed for many years by Goodall and others was once the leader of the females in her chimpanzee troupe and reared a great number of children. When she became old, those children who were successful—Fabin, Figan, and Fifi—did not help her. Later, when she died on a riverbank, no chimps paid her any attention. Take a look at Goodall's description:

> By this time [Flo] was looking very ancient—she must have been close to fifty years old. Her teeth were worn to the gum, her once black hair was brown and sparse, and she was shrunken and frail-looking like a little old lady. She simply collapsed when Flint [Flo's son] tried to ride on her back. . . .
> Flo died in 1972. It was a very sad day for me—I had known her for so long, and she had taught me so much. She died crossing the clear, fast-flowing Kakombe Stream. She looked so peaceful—it was as if her heart had suddenly just stopped beating. (*My Life with the Chimpanzees*, 94–95)[19]

Another difference between humans and chimpanzees is that the latter does not have menopause, so when Flo died she was still fulfilling her duties as a mother. Three weeks after Flo's death, Flint also died. Flo's children all lived together in the same social group and they were all once fondly attached to her and helped her deal with other chimpanzees. Her daughter Fifi was also particularly interested in her younger brother Flint (perhaps she was unconsciously gaining child-rearing experience), so when Flo died she tried to help him. It can be seen that while chimpanzees have some degree of kinship recognition (*In the Shadow of Man*, ch. 10, 14, 17, 18),[20] they did not offer substantial assistance to their aging mother. Why was this the case? When Flo needed her adult children the most, they were not there. This does not mean that her children were bad but that they simply did not know that this was good or should be done. Chimpanzee consciousness has not yet reached the degree where "children should care for their aging parents" because their ability to sense time is not that profound. According to a general evolutionary explanation, the care given to Flo by her children is a result of there being no competition for survival. Flo had already grown old and was no longer useful (for example, the last son Flo gave birth to, Flint, was spoiled by her and hence there was no survival competition), so precious energy should be expended on caring for one's own offspring. "Twenty years after her death, Flo's descendants formed the most powerful family at Gombe and by far the largest" (*My Life with the Chimpanzees*, 104).

Why Did Filial Reverence Appear?—
A More Profound Internal Time Consciousness

However, filial behavior clearly appeared in humans—was it in *H. erectus*? Or ancient *H. sapiens*? Moreover, scholars of evolutionary theory can find evidence for the evolutionary adaptability of filial behavior, such as the assistance provided by the experience and knowledge of elders to the social group, especially during those times when abnormal situations occur, such as remembering where there is water in times of drought, where there is food in times of famine, and where medicinal herbs can be found during an epidemic. How did this transformation occur? How did old people turn from being useless to being useful? How did ancient people come to know this kind of usefulness? These are phenomena that this kind of interpretation cannot explain. It seems the situation is this: the emergence of filial behavior and the emergence of "usefulness" is actually a single process. Without a profound consciousness of time, old people will not be superior to younger people in terms of knowledge and experience.

The key is that, for humans, regardless of whether it was *Homo habilis* (brain volume of 600–700 cm^3), *Homo erectus* (brain volume of 900 cm^3), archaic *Homo sapiens* (brain volume of 1,135 cm^3), *Homo sapiens neanderthalensis* (brain volume of 1,430 cm^3), or the anatomically defined modern humans (that is, *Homo sapiens sapiens*, brain volume of 1,350 cm^3), at some time period, at some stage, there appeared a sufficiently profound time consciousness allowing them *to be able to remember and think of* the kindness that mothers and fathers had for them and that parents should therefore be repaid in their old age. If this reversed care is not given, then at some point the children will feel unease and shame. Someone who is able to have this kind of filial sense is certainly someone who will be able to think and imagine beyond physical time and space. They will be able to accumulate knowledge and experience. They will be able to cooperate in all kinds of ways, and will also be able to be seen as someone useful late in life by their descendants.

What Caused Profound Time Consciousness to Appear?— The Extreme Immaturity of Human Newborns and the Substantial Conjuncture between Parents and Children

In comparison to other mammals and primates, the immaturity of human newborns is not just a change in quantity. It profoundly altered the relationship between parents and children, be they biological or adoptive, and even altered the relationship between mother and father. It also altered the structure of kinship and social relationships. People are accustomed to seeing the relational, complementary, and novel relationships between men and women, husbands and wives as the clearest type of relationship between *yin* and *yang*.[21] However, regarding the history of the formation of humanity and the actual mode of human existence, it is only the new form of parent–children relations brought about by bipedalism that the generation of *yinyang* relationships could be possible. To just what degree are human newborns immature? Take a look at what anthropologist M.F. Small writes: "[T]he human infant is born neurologically unfinished and unable to coordinate muscle movement. Natural selection has compensated for this by favoring a close adult-infant tie that lasts years and goes beyond meeting the needs of food and shelter. In a sense, the human baby is not isolated but part of a physiologically and emotionally entwined dyad of infant and caregiver" ("Our Babies, Ourselves," 108).[22] This is not bad. The relationship between human newborns and their caregivers is not one between two individuals but is first of all one of *an entwined dyad*. Human infants must be birthed early, and although the umbilical cord between child and mother is severed, there remains a connective bond in the sense of Merleau-Ponty's phenomenology of body that vividly links the child to its mother and even its father. Therefore, the parent–child relationship can be better understood as a *yinyang* bond that may be taken as the process of generating existential meaning and time by two complementary opposites. It is this that led to the family. The human relationship of husband–wife, as noted before, also originates in this relationship to a large degree. From the perspective of the factual developmental process, there are only parents and children when there are husbands and wives. However, from the genetic perspective of anthropology, philosophy, or the history of the development of humanity, there are husbands and wives only when there are parents and children.

How did the immaturity of human newborns lead to the deepening and prolonging of internal time consciousness? The extreme immaturity of human newborns implies that their lives are very fragile and can easily lose life at any moment. Caring for this kind of life thus requires full investment from the mother, and even the father, profoundly altering their lifestyle. From having to carry the child, the parents lose "their own" life and enter into a life of an entwined dyad. The dependence of the child equals the dependence of the parent. This can be glimpsed in the way in which mothers and children sleep at night ("Our Babies, Ourselves," 110).

Other than this, because the brains of human infants are not fully developed at birth, the period of time after they are born sees rapid expansion, and in the end their skull finally fuses together. We can gather from this that the interaction between the infant and the mother, father, or caregiver during this period of formation or of the "being in progress" of the conscious body—primarily expressed in the head—has deep structural and lifelong consequences. In one sense, the internal connection between the child and its caring parents is built *by itself growing into its life* and not simply a general associative memory. This phenomenon can perhaps be called "the *a priori* connection of the *a posteriori*"[23] because what is *a posteriori* to the infant after birth is something *a priori* within the womb of the mother in other primates.

Psychologists separate memory into short term and long term.[24] The relationship of human infants and their parents at its core belongs to long-term memory, and moreover, it should be that kind of unforgettable instinctual memory or bodily memory in a phenomenological sense. Once we have learned a foreign language, even though we have established a long-term memory, due to infrequent use or because of old age, we lose some of that ability or perhaps forget a great amount of the foreign language. But once we have learned our first language, or how to ride a bike or how to swim, we will not forget what is essential to those abilities even if we do not make use of them. The relationship between infants and their caregivers is even earlier than the acquisition of the first language, and thus at the very least it belongs to long-term memory in essence. As people get older, and even in old age, this kind of memory becomes more powerful, even if the parents have died when the child was still young.

In addition to profound connection between parents and children, this kind of connection is also maintained for a long period of time. This is rarely seen in the animal world. The descendants of modern humans usually mature around the ages of fourteen or fifteen years old[25] and become independent even later.[26] From this we can imagine that the physiological development of the child during their period of maturation in the history of the formation of humanity is slower still because research into chimpanzees and gorillas has shown that life in the natural wild requires a longer period of development than life in captivity. The average age when a wild female chimpanzee gives birth to her first children is 14.5 years old, but that of a chimpanzee in captivity is 11.1 years old; the average age when a wild female gorilla gives birth to her first children is 8.9 years, but in captivity it is 6.8 years.[27] And modern humans, especially those who have a post–industrial revolution lifestyle, are like being raised in captivity.

Child-rearing in primates is more difficult than in other animals, including other mammals ("Our Babies, Ourselves," 107) and child-rearing in chimpanzees is more difficult than in gorillas. For example, chimpanzee mothers carry their children for as long as five years, but gorillas develop their own motive powers much quicker than chimpanzees. A six-month-old gorilla baby can ride on its mother's back without falling off, and by two years old it does not need to be carried by its mother at all. We know that chimpanzees are much closer to us than gorillas in terms of intelligence and physiology. It appears the situation is this: the more difficult child-rearing is, the more time it requires and, thus, this kind of "long-term investment" forces the development of an internal time consciousness.

These two kinds of situations can be combined, making it so that humans must have a long-term perspective of time so they can make all kinds of predictions and plans beforehand and also so they can reflect on and remember events after they happen. Otherwise, it would be difficult to raise children and pass on the family line.

The Difficulty of Child-Rearing and Time Consciousness

Compared to the extreme importance of the fondness for battle, polygyny, and fresh meat, and the like that E.O. Wilson constantly talks about (*On Human Nature*, ch. 4–6), the immaturity of human newborns is a constant and deeply influential fact that had a great influence on hunter-gatherer societies. Because of this, it was necessary for parents to have a long-term time consciousness in their constantly moving social group to know how to care for and protect their children. For example, women of that time "have to keep their children spaced at four-year intervals . . . since a mother must carry her toddler until it's old enough to keep up with the adults." (*The Third Chimpanzee*, 189–190) Because the productivity and mobility of the mother was limited by her having to support a child, we can imagine that she needed to acquire the cooperation of others in order to preserve the existence of the mother–child dyad. First of all, as noted above, she will pay close attention to the male's character in regard to protection when selecting a mate. Other than this, she will also pay attention to their reliability—faithfulness, sincerity, and generosity, all of which have an element of internal time consciousness. Moreover, the male cannot be too weak nor be quick to fight because, since there is no one who is undefeatable, then, in this kind of situation where "one bears the burdens of the family," the injury or death of the husband will lead to the end of the family. Therefore, the man has to be measured, cooperative, compromising, and be able to take hold of opportunities. Where can the best food be found? Who can be a good friend and not an enemy? Where can one hide in times of peril? What kind of survival plan is best able to ride out the turbulence of an unpredictable future? Such questions concern parents forever.

Again, the cooperation among mothers and the family, clan, and even neighboring women is of utmost importance. Grandmothers, aunts, sisters-in-law, and young girls are able to help her care for her children from time to time, so she has to coordinate with them as much as possible. At the child-bearing age of the twenties and thirties, whichever kind of consciousness can succeed will be that which is preserved in human nature after hundreds of thousands of generations. Because of this, or these "destined lovers," humanity cannot but be a temporal being.

Some anthropologists point out an internal connection between the opening up of an ecological niche and the use of new tools with the extended period of human maturation. However, have they turned cause and effect around here, or have they at least simplified what was originally a bidirectional process of interrelated causality into a single cause and single effect? Was it the increasing importance of complex tools and acquired capabilities that led to the extension of the maturation period, or should we say conversely, that the extension of the period of human maturation led to the necessity of acquired capabilities and tool use? Regarding the totality of the history of human evolution, this should be a bidirectional dialectic feedback "auto-impetus" process of interrelated causes and effects. However, regarding the early evolution of *Hominins* and the genus *Homo*, this is also related to the original impetus of the origin of humanity. The extreme immaturity of human nature and the correlated length of the human maturation period appear to be even more fundamental or more instinctual. The reason is as follows: first, the average volume of chimpanzee brains is 390 cm^3, and *Australopithecus*—the species considered to be the beginning of humanity and the earliest known bipedal hominid—has average brain volumes ranging from 430 cm^3 (*A. afarensis*) and 490 cm^3 (*A. africanus*) to 540 cm^3 (*A. robustus*) (*Anthropology*, 110, table 8.2). Their skulls are certainly larger than chimpanzee skulls, and the difference in value of 100–150 cm^3 is not insignificant. Moreover, the birth canal of *Australopithecus* is narrower than later humans (108). Therefore, even though the size of their skull is smaller than that of modern humans, infant immaturity and a long period of maturation was probably a phenomenon already present even if we cannot quantitatively compare the two (*How Humans Evolved*, 263). Kottak writes: "Young australopithecines must have depended on their parents and kin for nurturance and protection. Those years of childhood dependency would have provided time for observation, teaching, and learning. This may provide indirect evidence for a rudimentary cultural life" (*Anthropology*, 109–111). Therefore, it should be the case that the maturation or selection pressures formed by the lengthening of the period of youth of *Australopithecus* encouraged but did not force their parents to seek out and value new foods and tools because bipedalism necessarily leads to extended periods of infancy and maturation but does not necessarily lead to a search for new foods and tools. Regardless, the lengthening of the maturation period cannot be later than nor should be reduced to the search and implementation of new tools. It is possible that the biggest difference between *Australopithecus* and chimpanzees is not the manufacturing of tools but instead the presence and absence of the extended period of maturation brought about by bipedalism.

Bipedalism began about 4 to 4.4 million years ago in "Ardi," the original *Australopithecus*. The earliest manufactured stone tools discovered today date to about 2.5 million years ago (*Anthropology*, 114; *How Humans Evolved*, 284) and are said to have been used by the *Australopethicus* species "*garhi*." Obviously, there have not been any discoveries that disprove that stone tools could not have appeared earlier, but it seems that the situation is that bipedalism appeared the earliest in the history of the formation of humanity and that the extended period of maturation and tool use followed afterward. If the extended period of maturation brought about by early childbirth is even with the tools and foodstuffs of that time, and if climate and environmental changes were not so great, then human evolution might have had a long period of stagnation, such as how the tools of *Homo erectus* did not change for more than a million years (*How Humans Evolved*, 312). If evolutionary impetus is found only in hunting and related tools, there would be no

Anthropology and the Temporality of the Way of Filial Reverence | 45

way to explain this long period of evolutionary stagnation because it should have been constantly in effect. However, if the original evolutionary impetus was primarily the extended period of maturation, then this lengthened period of maturation could have found a balance with a certain kind of environment or other factors.[28] Tools will constantly change through their being used, and the human body can maintain its original form in the presence of appropriate conditions. This difference can be known if we just think of how no great change in the human body has occurred since the "great leap forward" (*The Third Chimpanzee*, ch. 2, Epilogue; *The Emergence of Humans*,[29] 239) of human evolution that happened forty thousand years ago and the appearance of agriculture ten thousand years ago. In contrast to this, there was a great transformation in the terms of tools within this same period.

The Opportunity for the Appearance of Filial Reverence

As was shown above, filial reverence refers to the care, respect, cherishing, and succession of children for their elderly parents, and even other older family members. The Way of Filial Reverence (*xiaodao* 孝道) thus refers to the making of filial behavior into something self-conscious, profound, and faithful. Philosophically speaking, filial reverence implies that the lifetimes of children and their (elderly) parents and ancestors all converge together on a conscious level. Its appearance and subsequent retreat cannot be explained by the answer some anthropologists have offered that "elders preserve and transmit knowledge" because the appearance of filial reverence and the preservation of knowledge are not two processes but one. Therefore, pragmatic considerations on filial reverence already presuppose it. Regarding other nonhuman animals, including our relatives the chimpanzees, filial reverence is useless. It is not beneficial to the survival of these groups to expend resources in vain taking care of elders rather than spending the energy on one's self and one's descendants.

It is possible that one of the turning points in the appearance of filial reverence is when human children go to care for their own children. Caring for one's own children is isomorphic with the experience of being cared for. This situation that is continually being repeated calls for and gives rise to a kind of instinctual memory in the extended time consciousness of humanity. It is a long-term and perhaps hidden memory in which the past and present care given by one's parents and one as a parent, are interwoven and correlate. The present instinctual love for one's children communicates with the memory of the past instinctual love received from one's parents. Thus, when one's parents have become old and helpless, there occurs a reversal where the child feels uneasy, sad, and even fearful. Thereupon, the sense of filial reverence appears. Children begin to care for their useless parents without appealing to rational considerations of survival. Neither will they seek any kind of causal explanations for why they begin to care for their parents. The existential position of the children and that of the parents begin to link up even if we cannot say they are equal. At the beginning, children will not know the "use" of their parents, or even if they do know, it will not affect their daily lifestyle. As old people become older and weaker, they move closer to death; there are also no disasters that reveal their wisdom because before the appearance of filial reverence people could not live to be very old so they could not accumulate much knowledge that exceeded what a middle-aged person could know. However, relying on the interweaving of the past, the present, and the future in internal time consciousness, more and more "past" experiences are preserved in the hidden stream of time. As long as there is a sufficient stimulus, it is possible for intergenerational memory to rush forth. This is the realization of the instinctual time of human consciousness and is unrelated to considerations of profit. The old Chinese saying that "when raising one's child, the compassion of one's own parents is known" is about the timeliness of the formation of filial reverence.

The appearance of the sense of filial reverence shows that human time consciousness has already reached a great depth and extension and hence is able to achieve a great measure of internal inversion. Moreover, because filial reverence forces past children–present parents to carry the burden of caring for the future (their own children) and the past (their own parents) on their shoulders, they bear a great pressure for survival and consequently humanity becomes weaker and less likely to mature. Thereupon, internal time consciousness was forced to extend and deepen even more so that new tools and ecological niches became survival aspirations and creations. Based on this mode of thought, the "great leap forward" in human evolution forty thousand years ago is perhaps the latest period at which filial reverence could have appeared. After this, there were a great many inventions—exquisite new tools such as bone tools, complex tools, fishing hooks and nets, bows and arrows, and brilliant art such as cave paintings, sculptures, rituals, and even the languages that we speak—as well as the mind–body characteristics that embody the basis for the existence of modern humans.

Conclusion: He Who Is Benevolent Is Human

The above philosophical and anthropological research has used a method that "turns towards things—the formation of human nature—themselves," that is, the method where "the way is not far from humanity" and "he who is benevolent is human" (*Zhongyong*).

Sociobiological anthropological research excessively emphasizes the universal determination of genes. And liberalism, extreme feminism, and so on excessively emphasize human culture, as if human nature is a blank piece of paper that dresses up as any particular culture. Human beings have their own bodies, a *temporal body that is not individualized or entirely corporeal*. And prior to the dualism of the material and spiritual, to genes and culture, the human body has already formed, evolved, and reformed within the long river of evolution. The "distinction between men and women" talked about by the Confucians seems to certainly be a human phenomenon and principle with a long history and abundant connotations, such as physiology, division of labor, and exogamy. Not only does it not entail a discrimination against one or the other, but conversely, it implies that differences between men and women are complementary. Obviously, it is different from an ideology of external "equality of the sexes" that comes from the modern West.

However, all of the ways of existence that originate in humans—including Hominids, Hominins, the genus *Homo*, and *Homo sapiens*—that primarily rear children to maturity enables humans to rear their own children. The most important consequence of bipedalism is the extreme immaturity of human newborns that leads to their being difficult to raise as well as a series of other consequences. Through these the structure of the formation of humanity itself was formed.

Because of this immaturity, difficult child-rearing, and subsequent extended period of maturation, the descendants of the caregivers must have a father within the social group with many other men and they cannot be like other primates, those "single-parent caregivers" (mothers), polygyny, or isolated couples. Aristotle's saying that man is "a being meant for political association" is very insightful, but his determination that "man is by nature an animal intended to live in a *polis*"[30] is problematic because, regarding human nature, humans are animals that must first of all live in the household of their parents or relatives/in-laws and are not animals that must live in a state. The "Liyun 禮運" chapter of the *Liji* 禮記 writes: "What is the meaning of being human? It is these ten things: the kindness of fathers, the filial reverence of sons, the goodness of older brothers, the deference of younger brothers, the duty of husbands, the obedience of wives, the wisdom of elders, the compliance of the young, the benevolence of the ruler, and the dedication of the minister. This is the meaning of being human." This "human meaning" or the items listed in the "meaning of being a human" can be seen as the sequence of the occurrence of human politics, that is parents and their children are the origin which leads to husbands and wives, clans, and even the state. The state is an extension of the family and is referred to as "*guojia* 國家" (i.e., "state-family") in modern Mandarin. Yet *Mengzi* 4A has already stated that "People have a constant saying: they all say 'all under heaven,' 'the state,' and 'the family.' The foundation of all under heaven is the state, the foundation of the state is in the family, and the foundation of the family is in the person." This shows that the most real meaning of the family must be obtained through "self-cultivation" in the six arts, but this "self" is not at all an individual self. Instead, it is the self-body of an intertwined parent–child unity or family unit. Therefore, *The Classic of Filial Reverence* or *Xiaojing* 孝經 states that "the hair and skin of the body are received from the parents, do not destroy or harm it."

All of this will bring about the deepening of human internal time consciousness, that is the so-called "exhaustion"—"change"—"penetration"—"endurance."[31] "Exhaustion" (*qiong* 窮) here refers to the complete passivity of infants and the difficulty of raising them; they must be raised through "change" (*bian* 變). They must be raised by mothers, fathers, and other relatives; they must be planned for and have implements made for them, and they must be responded to appropriately as things change. This creates a new ecological niche: "Improve daily, and improve daily again, then once more improve daily" (*Daxue* 大學, quoting the *Panming* 盤銘 inscription). Therefore, there is "penetration" (*tong* 通), that is, discerning what is hidden in the past and seeing what is incipient in the future. In this timely middle way there will be "endurance" (*jiu* 久), the deepening and cycling of internal time consciousness allowing people to be able to go through innumerable hardships and changes and to arrive here today after several millions of years without cessation while those brothers and sisters of other hominid species who have come before or alongside us have gone extinct. Because the Chinese ethnicity and culture obtained this proper way of humanity, they have been able to endure the longest of all the ancient ethnicities and civilizations.

When human internal time consciousness is able to turn toward the intergenerational bodily self, that is, when one is caring for one's own children, when consciousness arrives at the same affection that one's parents gave in raising them, then the consciousness of filial reverence will begin to appear. It is possible that this is the marker of *Homo sapiens sapiens*. Afterward, humans became human in the fullest sense or in the sense we are familiar with, no matter if it is a hunter-gatherer manufacturing bows and arrows, painting on cave walls, sowing and plowing in a field, making clay or metal utensils, creating writing or establishing a systems of ritual and music, laws and nations, or even humans with advanced technology and world wars.

Filial reverence is the beginning of the "sense of being unable to bear the suffering of others" (*buren ren zhi xin* 不忍人之心) that the *Mengzi* talks about. Unlike chimpanzees and other primates, humans are unable to bear the declining health of their parents as they grow old. The phrase "He who does not have the sense of compassion is not a human" (*wuceyin zhi xin fei ren ye* 無惻隱之心非人也) (*Mengzi* 2A) indicates the mark of being human. This sense of compassion or of being unable to bear the suffering of others is the fountainhead of filial reverence. Animal parents, especially birds and mammals, also have a sense of not being able to bear the suffering of others for their children, but animal children lack the same sense in regard to their parents. Humans can be considered to have a different life world from animals only if they begin with filial reverence. "Filial reverence and fraternal deference are the root of humanity!" (*Analects* 1.2). "Now, filial reverence is the root of virtue and the source of learning" (*Classic of Filial Reverence*). Humans did not become humans because they can use tools, engage in politics, or because they have self-consciousness or an external consciousness of others. Instead, humans became human because they were able to filially treat their mothers, fathers, and other elders and were thus especially able to be taught—note the connection between the origin of the characters for "filial reverence" (*xiao* 孝) and "education" or "teaching" (*jiao* 教).

All of this points to a key dimension: the deepening and prolonging of human internal time consciousness. Therefore, the *Mengzi* said that Confucius is the "sage of the timeliness" (*sheng zhi shizhe ye* 聖之時者也). We think, therefore, that this Confucian studying of "always reaching the timely middle" (*shizhong* 時中; *Zhongyong*) is far from empty talk.

Chapter 4

Imagination and Historical Memory
The Stratification of Internal Time Consciousness

Edmund Husserl and Martin Heidegger were both interested in the "*a priori* deduction" and "schematism" in Immanuel Kant's *Critique of Pure Reason*. Heidegger even wrote *Kant and the Problem of Metaphysics*. According to him, this book, especially the first edition, is important because Kant brought up "*a priori* imagination" regarding the interaction between sensation and reason in order to make possible their connection and even the existence thereof. This kind of imagination can take the form of an "image" (*Bild*) situated between the sensible manifold and conceptual affirmation, and the big image or "pure image" of these categories of images is primordial time. The schema that comes out of this original time allows concepts to be able to connect with sensation so that the phenomenal world can reveal its epistemological objectivity.

Below we will first detail some related ideas of Kant and then we will discuss the relationship between temporal consciousness and temporality in the imagination of Husserl and Heidegger. Lastly, we will try to differentiate two kinds of temporal consciousness and temporality through distinguishing the multiple operations of this kind of imagination—maintaining connection and maintaining cyclicality: one kind is that which is shared by humanity and other highly developed animals, while the other is that especially developed in humanity and that only a few animals show signs of initial development. This chapter further draws on a differentiation made by cognitive science between two kinds of memory: semantic memory and historical memory.

The *a priori* Imagination Revealed by Kant

In the *Critique of Pure Reason*, Kant writes: "Synthesis in general is, as we shall subsequently see, the mere effect of the imagination, of a blind though indispensable function of the soul, without which we would have no cognition at all, but of which we are seldom even conscious" (*Critique of Pure Reason*, A78, B103).[1] Imagination creates a "synthesis in general" (*Synthesis überhaupt*). This means that all synthesis—no matter if it's *a posteriori* or *a priori*, sensory or rational—is provided by the imagination although we often use other names to refer to it. For example, Kant immediately says that we "use concepts to express" it; he thus sees this kind of synthesis as a function of reason. One reason there is this replacement or usurpation is because of imagination's "blindness," and this blindness belongs to intuition: "intuitions without concepts are blind" (*Critique*, A51, B75). However, imagination does not stop with intuition. Instead, according to the view of Kant's passage quoted above, it is the source of all synthesis and knowledge. Thus, in the first edition of the *Critique*, Kant maintained:

> The principle of the necessary unity of the pure (productive) synthesis of the imagination prior to apperception is thus the ground of the possibility of all cognition, especially that of experience. (*Critique*, A118)

> We therefore have a pure imagination, as a fundamental faculty of the human soul, that grounds all cognition *a priori*. (*Critique*, A124)

According to Kant, *a priori* or pure imagination is generative or spontaneous, and the imagination of experience is reproductive or submits to rules of association (*Critique*, B152). If imagination is *a priori* or prior to objects, then it will be "prior to apperception" thus becoming the source of all knowledge. According to this way of thinking, *a priori* imagination should also be that original synthesis or original structure which *makes apperception possible*. Even if Kant, a subjective idealist, was unable to accept this last conclusion, in the first edition of his *Critique* he repeatedly emphasized that "the ground of the possibility of all cognitions, the transcendental unity of the synthesis of the imagination is the pure form of all possible cognitions" (*Critique*, A118). This created a tension with the way of thinking that "transcendental imagination is first," and because of this, in the second edition there was a reactionary adjustment, a "recoil" (*Kant and the Problem of Metaphysics*, 166–176).[2] However, this book which profoundly influenced modern Western philosophy flashed into existence an imagination with an original position that was hard for people to forget, allowing Heidegger and other philosophers to grasp it and write a great deal about it. And what they wrote, more often than not, was of great philosophical importance.

Now what is imagination (*Einbildungskraft*)? Kant writes: "*Imagination is the faculty for representing an object even without its presence in intuition*" (*Critique*, B151). We can rely on imagination to express, in our consciousness, some things and objects that have already gone by, such as an unforgettable trip three years past. This capability is usually called recollection. We can also rely on imagination to predict those things which have yet to occur, for example, predicting that in a few days we will see a friend we have not seen in a long time. This is usually called planning. We can also use imagination to have fanciful journeys through the heavens, daydreams or fantasies, or free imaginations to help improve the creativity of our writing, music, art, science, and techniques. Even more fundamental is that *spontaneous imagination* which allows for the possibility of all of these kinds of imagination, intentional action, and behavior, causing them to be constructed and to appear within consciousness. They no longer rely on the association and division that moves from A to B and from B to C. Instead, it relies on something deeper, a completely non-objectified original power of construction in order to make initial associations and synthesis possible. Without this last kind of imagination, people would be unable to have the kind of structure to conscious action and method of objectification they do have; Kant thus called it "productive" (*produktiv*) or "pure." It is the occurrence of that most original construction that "makes them possible." This is why it is called "*a priori*," that is, it is that which makes experience possible. And those previous forms of imagination, be they recollection, planning, free association, or analogy, are all not so pure and have some kind of ready-made object that they are dependent on and are thus called "reproductive imagination."

This pure imagination cannot itself be objectified, and what it produces first of all is not an object but instead is the "pure image" (*reines Bild*) that makes objects possible. Its rough draft is thus the "schema" (*Critique*, A140–142, B180–182), like how the schema of a pure triangle is the connection between the concept of a triangle and the image of a particular triangle (an acute angle, an obtuse angle, or a right-angle triangle). Therefore, the realization of all sense objects and rational concepts must first be guided by the pure image and the schema, and the *most original image of all the pure images is time* (*Critique*, A142, B182). Kant found the temporal schema for the twelve basic categories of reason and through this made the "gathering up" of apperception tie together all cognitive capacities.

Regarding common-sense thinking and even the conceptualized thought of traditional Western philosophy, the association of reproductive imagination that moves from A to B is easy to understand, but *a priori* imagination is not so easily understood. Empiricism maintains that reproductive imagination or association is our highest internal cognitive capacity, and idealism thinks there is an even more important *a priori* epistemological capability, one that can be used to know ideal forms and *a priori* categories. This is not only the method with which the *a priori* regulates the emergence of the objects of experience, but it is also able to directly understand and comprehend *a priori* concepts and obtain *a priori* knowledge. The way of thinking of *a priori* imagination is very different from all of these. According to the traditional way of thinking, imagination is only experiential or reproductive; it "belongs to sensibility" (*Critique*, B151) and that kind of pure imagination not dependent on ready-made objects and yet produces images as if out of nothing cannot find its own position within the traditional framework. Its "blind productivity" or "spontaneity"—expressed as the "hidden art" of pure images or schemas—appears to be mystical. Therefore, Kant wrote: "This schematism of our understanding with regard to appearances and their mere form is a hidden art in the depths of the human soul, whose true operations we can divine from nature and lay unveiled before our eyes only with difficulty" (*Critique*, A141, B181).

Moreover, Kant did give us a clue to help us understand this kind of human mental technique, that is, that the most important thing which this imagination produces is the pure image of time. By exploring the phenomenon of this kind of original time and the association of cognitive objects, it is possible to know what kind of thing this *a priori* imagination is and why it can be prior to apperception and be the foundation for all human cognition. It is just that the time schema described by Kant—based on linear succession and permissible synchronicity—is excessively stiff so that people (and Kant himself) were unable to understand the spontaneous productivity of imagination; we can thus only turn our attention to a phenomenological description of time.

How Did Primordial Imagination Create Husserl's and Heidegger's View on Time?

In *Phenomenology of Internal Time-Consciousness*, Husserl's description of some methods by which temporal objects are revealed or "produced"—such as a portion of a melody—reveals a thread for understanding internal time-consciousness.[3] Simply speaking, temporal objects such as the perception of sound originate in the stimulus of a "primordial impression" and the spontaneous "retention" thereof and this impression even brings with it a "protention" (*PITC*, 410, appendix 6). That is to say, any impression must be like a comet in that it possesses its past in its tail and predicts its future in its coma. Husserl focused his discussion on retention, however, the meaning therein should be able to be turned toward or turned around back to protention (*PITC*, 413).

Retention is maintaining the primordial impressions received at every moment. That is to say, when a primordial impression has already gone by in terms of the abstract object and is already "not on the scene" in this abstract sense, then the internal perception will keep this impression in place and preserve it. Regarding this, retention is the operation of imagination. However, it is too primordial, and is in no way reproductive imagination. This kind of retention has these special characteristics: first, it is completely spontaneous; it is human consciousness and the living instinct of the human body, especially the physiological nervous system. We can imagine that other animals, especially mammals, possess retention in a broad sense; it is just that they are not as developed as human beings in terms of consciousness. Second, due to its complete spontaneity, it simply "has no time" to distinguish what it preserves and is instead pure retention. Or it can be said that it is the spontaneous variation of irreell primordial impressions. It still cannot be said that it is the manifestation of some object or the "primordial association" talked about by Brentano (*PITC*, 377–382).

Again, due to the above-mentioned two special characteristics, there is no difference in principle between retention and the impression that retention preserves in terms of phenomenological time. The so-called "previous point" of physical time does not become a phenomenological "before" in retention but is still a projection, adumbration, or the halo of a "present." That temporal object that we are listening to right now—for example, a part of a melody—is not a primordial impression or a retention, but rather an ambiguous totality interconnected in an instant that has been grasped through protention and given meaning that is either pulled forward by or catches up to other sounds. That is to say, the sound that we hear is already a product continuously constructed out of a primordial image. In consciousness, there has never been that passive and independent reception of sensations talked about by the empiricists. To make this more clear in terms of our example, we do not first hear single physical impressions one after another every instant with our ears and then connect these all together to turn them into a connected and complete sound that can be heard. If this were really the case, then what we hear is really just noise, because this kind of after-the-fact connection cannot keep up with the demands of immediate perception.

Again, this spontaneous retention does not only operate once or a limited number of times; instead, it is operating all of the time to the fullest of its capabilities. Sounds obviously have their beginnings and their ends; however, the impulses of the organic retention-protention of consciousness flow unceasingly like the waters of a river as long as the physiological and neurological life of that consciousness exists. Finally, the retention allows for the possibility of the reemergence or reproduction of imagination.

Husserl did not do enough regarding the continuous totality of this internal power of continuity, so much so that he still relied on the "double intentionality" of retention (*PITC*, section 39)—one side creates the temporal object, and the other creates the flow of time through the retention of retention. Actually, the pure spontaneity of retention's previous object guarantees that it is not bidirectional but instead multidirectional. This is where the adorableness and clumsiness of Husserl's genius lies. He, more often than not, cannot see the hidden potential of the children that he births but gives the possibility of substantially expanding them over to later people. A spontaneous retention like this is prior to objects and is also the possibility of objects being formed. Thus, it must be an *a priori synthesis* and is even the origin of synthesis; it is necessarily "horizontal" and also "vertical." It can not only construct temporal objects but can also merge with the flow of time to bring the operation of the retention of retention to completion in many dimensions. Regarding this, where is there any "primordial" impression of retention?

All sensible stimuli are already within the deep temporal flow that is the interweaving of the retention of retention and the protection of protention. Husserl calls retention "primary memory" (*PITC*, 391). It is that which participates in the depth and flow of time (*PITC*, section 10), making secondary memory or re-collection possible (*PITC*, 409). And the "phantasy" (*Phantasie*) that he talks about, other than marking out "primal phantasy" (*Ur-Phantasie*), usually points to reproduced or immediate behavior (*PITC*, 451). In conclusion, the source of the internal flow of time should be in retention and protention and is not an antenna of a primordial impression outside the flow of time. It is also not that "absolute beginning" that Husserl thought it was (*PITC*, 451). Retention and protention can be compared to the *a priori* imagination talked about by Kant. However, there remains a phenomenal structure that can better understand them from within so that we can begin to understand the structure and characteristics of our imagination and the spontaneity of pure time. They produce the flow of time and are not the schematism of time.

For Heidegger, the original state of time "*is the primordial 'out-side-of-itself' in and for itself*" (*Being and Time*, 329, 377). That is, the three dimensions of time (past, present, and future), in order to win themselves and be situated in time itself, must spontaneously go beyond themselves where they are not or are no longer themselves. In other words, they have no kind of ready-made existence. They and their temporality emerge only out of the mutual interweaving that overflows beyond them, just as how any instant with turbulence does not have its own ready-made existence but instead can only win for itself existence and its flow through the passing over of its instances. This is precisely the special characteristic of the internal time structure talked about by Husserl. That is, in order for retention to complete present temporal perception, it must be "outside" of the primordial impressions these perceptions rely on. Therefore, the "temporal halo" (*Zeithof*) itself situated in the present becomes itself an impression also (*PITC*, 396). This is also the special characteristic that the *a priori* imagination of Kant should have. Of course, the temporality (*Zeitlichkeit*) talked about by Heidegger makes the internal time structure of Husserl that still has psychological characteristics become existential. That is to say, he turns to the Dasein; however, he stills preserves the pre-objectified structure of spontaneous retention and protention. Thus, he states that the three dimensions of time—future, past, and present—are ecstatic (*Ekstasen*) (*Being and Time*, 329). This state of ecstasy has been

58 | Family and Filiality

entirely "prepositionalized"—the "towards" (*zu*), the "to" (*auf* . . .), and the "alongside" (*bei* . . .)—it is also a pure convergence and formal guide awaiting completion, just like how retention and protention neither has its own essence. However, they are within their "being outside themselves" and "being beyond themselves." These will necessarily interweave into and *a priori* synthesize into one unity obtaining their own "spirit," that is, their own temporality or temporalization (*Zeitigung*). Through this, a vague understanding of meaning and existence is obtained. Therefore, the essence of time "is a process of temporalizing in the unity of the ecstasies" (329) This spontaneous time does not allow for the special position of primordial impressions and *a priori* subjects, its origin is the future and not the present. This temporality is how humanity acquires a non-dualistic source of existential meaning, experience, and understanding.

Of all the important positive terms that Heidegger discusses, no matter if it is Dasein and the world, *Zusein* or *Jemeinigkeit*, the state of being-in-the-world or the state of present-to-hand, understanding or *mit-sein*, fear, terror, worry, care, being-towards-death, decision, and so on, there is no single one that does not the carry the eventful tension of retention and protention. There is no ready-made objectivity. They are all always situated within the productive existential structure. Therefore, *Being and Time* reveals that the essence of Dasein is care (*Sorge*) and then reveals the pure time essence of this care as "a future which makes present in the process of having been" (*Being and Time*, 326) or as has just been quoted above, "*the primordial 'out-side-of-itself' in and for itself*." This thus takes Kant's *a priori* imagination and Husserl's internal time-consciousness and binds them so tightly that they become a pure mechanism of occurrence that does not allow for the interference of any external things.

The Temporal Differences between Humans and Other Animals: Two Kinds of Memory

The flashing of Kant's phenomenology in his *Critique* and the research into time of twentieth-century phenomenologists opened a perspective from which to understand the essence of human beings and the world. Prior to subjectivity and pure sensible experience, meaning and existence have already happened, the world has already appeared. The root of their completion is primordial temporality and the experience of time.

The revolutionary nature of this thinking has even surpassed the field of understanding of those who brought it up and its full digestion is still a challenge today. An important problem here is this: if the experience of time is first, then what difference is there between the experiences of human beings and animals regarding time? Even Heidegger was not aware of the pointedness of this question and just habitually thought that only humans are Dasein, that only humans have a world, are able to reveal the truth, and possess temporality and that animals are not like this. Actually, if subjectivity and rationality that have been traditionally defined as belonging to humanity do not have the privilege of temporality and only rely on *some kind of general experience of time*, then there is no means to differentiate human beings from other animals. For example, if animals should be able to also perceive temporal objects such as sound and even melodies, they have to do so by means of the internal time structure described by Husserl. Since they have this internal time structure, there must be within their consciousness internal streams of both consciousness and time. For example, do animals such as gorillas not have the existential mode of "being-in-the-world" (*In-der-Welt-sein*) talked about by Heidegger? If they can use tools that are "at hand," are able to "be with" others of their kind, are able to have a "rumbling" style of conversation, are able to enjoy dancing in the rain, and have a "gorilla government," then can they be without their own worlds?

This is not to deny that there are meaningful differences between humans and other animals. It is to doubt Husserl's and Heidegger's perspective and even the standard that Aristotle used to distinguish human beings from animals and to doubt whether or not we can even compare the two. If all of this remains a muddled ambiguity, then the real uniqueness of human beings will be smothered. Thus, for some very serious thinkers, it is not only subjectivity that is lost—the human being is lost too. What I am concerned with here is precisely the search for the special characteristics of human beings by discovering their different kinds of temporality from within this new mode of thought, even if the value of internal existential value no longer has a special place that allows us to think less of other animals or to be as proud of ourselves as we once were.

Cognitive science appears to have provided us with a useful clue, and if the naturalization of phenomenology's appropriateness is reasonable, or is unavoidable, then following this clue should not be seen as non-phenomenological. After all, Husserl, the founder of phenomenology, and Merleau-Ponty, who showed the phenomenology of the body, both substantially absorbed things from psychology and neuropathology. What raises my interest is what psychologists, anthropologists, and primatologists like Endel Tulving and Charles Menzel—they have their differences—have discovered: normal human beings have two kinds of memory, their possibility relies on experiential capacities for internal time (Menzel). But one of the two still relies on a more special, more evolutionarily late capacity for internal time; this can thus be used to differentiate human beings from other animals (Tulving). This kind of memory has been called "episodic memory," and the other kind that both human beings and other animals share is called "semantic memory."[4]

Simply speaking, episodic memory is a kind of "time travel" (*The Missing Link*, 9). Humans vividly and self-consciously revive events they have experienced before; and semantic memory does away with all activities and capabilities of memory outside of episodic memory. Tulving compares them in a chart (*The Missing Link*, 11). He acknowledges that semantic memory is a kind of cognition that can differentiate, store, and utilize shareable knowledge about the world. It is a noetic conscious awareness that is representational, capable of being propositionalized or can speak of truth or falsehood, can be used to make inferences, be symbolized, and is rational, but it has no requests of or anything to do with temporal awareness. It can be imagined that this is already a kind of strong rational capacity from which emerges a plethora of conscious phenomena, for example, those possessed by advanced mammals and human children. Moreover, it makes us think of the characteristics of early contemporary analytic philosophy. Episodic memory is based in semantic memory. That is to say, it has all of the capacities that semantic memory does; however, it has an extra "subjective" ability or dimension that travels through time and that accompanies autonoetic conscious awareness. Further, the capacity to remember one's own experiences can be turned into predictions of and plans for the future (*The Missing Link*, 20). It makes me think of Husserl's phenomenology.

The key here is the distinction between recognition and remembering. A dog can remember where it has buried a bone to come back later and enjoy it. According to Tulving and other cognitive scientists, this is not only incapable of proving that this dog has the capacity for remembering but also cannot prove it has a capacity for recollection. The dog mostly relies on visual and olfactory representational characteristics of the environment to remember where it buried the bone and then follows the semantic memory of physiological signals like hunger impulses to recognize the place in order to find the bone. Phenomena like squirrels finding the nuts they have stored away and migratory birds flying back to previous mating grounds can also both be seen as examples of this kind of recognizing cognition that is without time traveling memory. That is to say, squirrels and birds cannot return to that moment when they stored away the nut or how they arrived at the mating grounds the year before, how they spent good days there, and what kinds of experiences they had. Tulving says that "semantic memory allows the individual to *know*, at Time 2, something about what happened at an earlier time, Time 1, but it does not allow the individual to remember what happened" (*The Missing Link*, 18) because this kind of memory does not carry a "time marker." Taking this basic kind of memory a step further, individuals are still able to vividly remember all of the previous experiences they have personally had. This is episodic memory. It has been seen as the last to appear in evolution that relies on the prefrontal cortex of the brain (*The Missing Link*, 11).

Tulving also brings up the example of human beings to explain two more differences. Four- to five-year-old children begin to have episodic memory that is expressed in the ability to remember their own experiences. However, children under three years old generally do not have this ability. Three- to four-year-old children can easily be taught the names of colors, but if they are asked when they learned the color names, most children will claim they always knew them. Children five or more years old will acknowledge that they learned it on that day (*The Missing Link*, 32).

Another famous example is K.C., a Canadian who in 1981 suffered brain damage in a traffic accident. What is important is that this injury did not affect the knowledge he had previously learned, and did not injure his semantic memory. Rather, what he lost was the ability to remember his previous personal experiences; that is to say, he lost his episodic memory. Therefore, his intellectual capacities were normal and his thought clear, his speech was no different from that of other people, when he closed his eyes he could accurately describe the CN Tower, he could read and write, distinguish objects, and even name them. His abilities in mathematics, history, geography, and other fields of study all accorded with the education he had received. He was able to play chess, cards, and the piano, and even had a sense of humor. His general memory was normal as well; he was able to remember semantic information from his past life, such as his birthday, what school he attended, and the color of a car he had previously owned. In conclusion, he preserved the information that could be known about him from the perspective of an observer. His short-term memory was also normal. However, he had lost the ability to remember all of his personal experiences, those before and after the accident, including those of the sudden death of his own brother. He remembered nothing that had happened to him. He could remember the address of the house he lived in nine years prior, and standing in front of the house he could recognize it, but he could not remember the things that happened to him there (*The Missing Link*, 24). That is to say, he lost the ability that four- to five-year-old children have to recount their own experiences but preserved the high level of cultural awareness possessed by five- to ten-year-old children (*The Missing Link*, 26). In short, he could know time, but he could not experience time. Tulving thinks this explains that these two kinds of memories—semantic memory and episodic memory—belong to separate neurological mechanisms (*The Missing Link*, 24). To discuss this in terms of what we said about Kant, K.C.'s unifying function of apperception remained operational, but there was a problem with the apperception's function of *self-awareness*—that is, the structure in the pure functioning of *a priori* imagination—rendering him unable to reproduce memories about his past experiences.

The Human Method of Traveling through Time

Based on the above facts, Tulving distinguished two kinds of time—physical time and subjective time. He writes: "The time in which episodic memory operates is the same in which all physical and biological events occur, physical time. But the time in which remembered events occur is different. We can call it subjective time. It is related to but not identical with physical time" (*The Missing Link*, 16). It is only within "subjective time" that there will be that "warmth and intimacy" talked about by William James (*The Missing Link*, 15). This is basically parallel to the distinction between physical time and phenomenological time that Husserl made.

Moreover, Tulving denies that there is a relationship between semantic memory and internal subjective time, or that is to say, he denies that animals can have episodic memory. This viewpoint does have some similarities with that of Husserl and Heidegger, and was even doubted by the authors of *The Missing Link*. According to this, since semantic memory is memory, it should have some relationship to internal time consciousness, especially retention; otherwise, how could it *pick up* past information on the spot? If there is no multi-level internal retention, how is it possible that K.C. was able to remember the address and appearance of the house he had lived in many years ago? How is it possible that there is no internal retention when the dog goes to dig up his buried bone? Tulving explained this through appeal to a recognition that has no time markers. However, no matter what environment the dog remembers, if it is a spatial layout or behavior for finding the bone, it is relying on its own knowledge of an affair that goes across time. Therefore, regardless of whether it has a time marker, this behavior has some kind of retention as a premise. In brief, the "re-" of "re-cognition" necessarily has a "re-tentional" function.

Moreover, some new experiments have shown that even animal behaviors have time markers. For example, Clayton and Dickinson have observed that because some of the food that scrub jays store can rot (such as worms and crickets) they have to eat it within a few days. Therefore, since they must eat it within a few days, there is a difference in remembering the time when these kinds of food are stored and when other kinds such as nuts and non-degradable foods are stored. That scrub jays are certainly capable of this shows that they are able to recall experiential time markers (*The Missing Link*, 37). Tulving acknowledges that if this observational experiment was done in 1972, it would only prove that scrub jays have episodic memory (*The Missing Link*, 47) because due to the advancement of science, the standard for determining whether this episodic memory is present or not has also changed and the threshold has risen. Therefore, today, this experiment can only explain that such intelligent animals "know, on some other basis, how to act at the time of the recovery of the food" (*The Missing Link*, 38).

However, Menzel raises even stronger and more difficult to rebuke experimental evidence showing that, at least for a chimpanzee named Panzee, there exists real recall and not just recognition (*The Missing Link*, 212, 214).[5] Indeed, his experimental design was rigorous and it repeatedly appeared on different levels, with different variables, and he set up many measures to exclude the possibility of other explanations. Of course, due to the ambiguity and malleability of "recollection," especially "episodic memory" itself, not even this experiment can finally determine that animals also have episodic memory. However, they have at least strengthened the believability of this conclusion, that is, that animals have an internal time consciousness, especially retention. Regarding this, the anthropocentrism within the views on *a priori* imagination and primordial time of Kant, Husserl, and Heidegger should be seen as untenable.

However, this does not absolutely deny that there is large difference between the time consciousness of humanity and animals (even our spiritual brothers the chimpanzees), it just thinks that this difference should not be expressed as whether they have it or not, or whether this is a hierarchical difference between internal values and rights to exist, but that the styles of internal time-consciousness differ, or that there is a sequential difference in evolution or functional capabilities. Even if the animals like chimpanzees have the episodic memory that accompanies self-awareness talked about by Tulving by which they can travel through time, its maturity and development cannot be talked about in the same breath as that which humans possess because the giant difference between them can be seen in the basic behaviors and self-organizing methods of human beings and chimpanzees.

Now, where does this difference originate? Perhaps we should search in the method of retention. According to Tulving's explanation, what semantic memory preserves is the cognitive information connection between Time 1 and Time 2, such as the address of the house that K.C. lived in or the name of school he attended. But episodic memory preserves the cognitive information connection between Time 1 and Time 2 in addition to the path through which this information was obtained (how the address of that old residence is known) and that path is situated in the knowledge of the past phases of one's own experiences (self-knowledge). Therefore, if semantic memory can be compared to the method of communication by mail where there are letters of the past and the present, then episodic memory can be compared to the method of communication situated between video communications of the past and the present, as well as the self-awareness of this kind of communication's changing with the times, that is, precisely to become aware of this present I-am-recollecting while recollecting. Therefore, the information channels and data required by episodic memory are much greater than that of semantic memory, which is to say that the dimensions of retention have a greater depth, width, and density. The transformation of the quality of this kind of retention should have something to do with the evolution of neurological psychology, such as that of the brain. And the cause of this kind of change can be found in the guidance of early humanity's environment, genetic mutations, and environmental selection. After all, ever since humans began walking upright, the direction of the environmental pressures on them were different from other mammals and other advanced primates.

Regarding consciousness phenomena of reconstruction and making present, Husserl made a very fine differentiation. For example, he differentiated between memory and image consciousness (the reconstruction according to an object) (*PITC*, section 28). He also differentiated between unset pure imagination and set reconstruction. The reconstruction of a pure image naturally does not include this kind of "arrangement," but a true memory certainly does. It appears that Husserl has made the same differentiation between semantic and episodic memory of the cognitive scientists talked about above, but his differentiation obviously is from the perspective of a phenomenological analysis of internal time consciousness. He writes:

> Now recollection can occur in different forms of accomplishment. Either we execute it in a simple grasping, as when a memory "rises to the surface" and we look at what is remembered in a flash. In this case what is remembered is vague; perhaps the memory brings forward, intuitively, a privileged momentary phase, but it does not repeat its object. Or we execute a memory that actually does reproduce and repeat, a memory in which the temporal object is completely built up afresh in a continuum of re-presentations and in which we perceive it again, as it were—but only "as it were" . . . but everything has the index of reproductive modification. (*PITC*, section 15)

The memory prior to the "or" Husserl is talking about is semantic consciousness. It is a remembering but primarily the execution of a "simple grasping." Although it is making past information reappear, it does not carry a marker that crosses time (information arranged into a temporal order) and related self-awareness. Therefore, it is not a repetitive memory; it simply *preserves a kind of connection*. After the "or," Husserl is talking about episodic memory. It is a "a memory that actually does reproduce and repeat." Therefore, we seemingly perceive it again, to once again vividly experience our own past experiences, and at the same time are aware of this this seemingly "as it were." That is, we clearly know that it is something that has happened to us previously and not something that is currently happening. Therefore, it preserves even more things, that is, *it preserves the melody of memory or the possibility of vividly reliving it.*

Husserl has even more discussions regarding the differentiation of these two kinds of memory. For example, the "memory of the present" discussed in section 29 of *Phenomenology of Time-Consciousness* is similar to semantic memory. It can be possessed in according a present knowledge of things past. "This 'memory image' does serve me, but I do not posit what is remembered as remembered; I do not posit the object of the internal memory in the duration belonging to it . . . but we do not posit it *as* 'past'" (*PITC*, 417, 62). Regarding episodic memory, there are even more discussions and examples, such as the example of "memory of the illuminated theater" (*PITC*, section 27). The deep structure of this kind of memory is like the memory of the care received from one's parents that the Confucians encourage; this should be the memory that is unique to humanity. However, just as Husserl has pointed out, the so-called "looking-back" is possible because of retention and the internal stream of consciousness created thereby (*PITC*, appendix 9). This is a place where Husserl is more clear and profound than Tulving.

For Heidegger, human beings are entirely temporalized beings; therefore they are "always" a "being-towards" or are "becomings" situated between retention and protention. Existentialism's protention is the future, that is "the letting itself come towards itself" (*Being and Time*, 325); and the retention of existentialism is what is already there (the being that is already), that is the "coming-towards-oneself." Moreover, temporality is the present interweaving of these two. That is to say, the present is released from their interweaving and authentic presents or pasts are expressed as retrievals. It should be they that allow for the possibility of episodic memory. And authentic *"having beens"* or pasts are things forgotten; however, forgetting is not the same as "not being able to retrieve or remember." It is just that the "coming-towards-oneself" that one has purposefully forgotten or that has slipped the mind let's this "coming-towards-oneself" be expressed as an everyday memory.

Therefore, the authentic *"having been"* that Heidegger talks about, or the retrieval, is similar to the episodic memory talked about in *The Missing Link*, although it is more original because this "coming-towards-oneself" is neither objectified nor ready-made. However, regarding the authenticity, there are two places of similarity. The inauthentic *"having been"* he talks about, the memory within forgetting, is somewhat comparable to the semantic meaning talked about in *The Missing Link* even though it is missing a deeply transparent self-awareness. However, there is an important distinction between these two kinds of views. That is, Heidegger thinks that the inauthentic *having-been* relies on the shape of the authentic Dasein to be possible (*Being and Time*, 326). More particularly, everyday memory relies on retrieval to be possible. And regardless of whether or not it is the structure of the brain or the expressions of functions discovered by cognitive science, semantic memory is still more fundamental and independent than episodic memory. K.C.'s episodic memory disappeared, but the functioning of his semantic memory more or less remained intact. Other nonhuman animals can have a highly developed semantic memory even if their episodic memory is not developed or is nowhere to be seen. Therefore, Tulving, conversely, says that semantic memory is the premise of episodic memory. However, just like what was said above, this semantic memory or all memory in general needs to have the retention within time-consciousness and even the interweaving of retention and protention as its premise. This is precisely what the scientists often call "forgetting." If we take the phenomenological premise of retrieval, then there is no valuable "categorical" difference between semantic and episodic memory. Instead, there is only the difference in the "degree" of the quantity of information retained. This is what some modern scientists and very many philosophers are unwilling to accept.

Conclusion: The Style of the Moment When One's Parents' Compassion Is Known

"In raising one's own children, the compassion of one's own parents is known." Most human beings are only able to "come back to itself futurally" (*Zukünftig auf sich zurückkommend*) (*Being and Time*, 326). That is to say, parents go from the care that they have for their own children's "mode of being" and remember the compassion given them by their own parents. However, this kind of memory that allows us to know compassion itself is our special human characteristic. Drawing on the efforts of Kant, Husserl, Heidegger, other philosophers, and Tulving, along with other scientists, we have found that the source of the special human characteristic of "rationality" is *a priori* imagination and the sense of primordial time. It is not in the unity of a non-*a priori* subjectivity;

it is in episodic memory and not semantic memory. Previously it has been thought that the most classical expressions of reason, such as logical deduction, a cold objective mode of thought, originally had more to do with semantic memory and that the more profound reason and human nature began from the ability to describe events in one's own life, that they are within primordial and vivid memory itself (they can be particulars, but most of all they should transcend particulars), and the furthest reach of the future that is arrived at through transcending particulars. Therefore, the Zhouyi 周易 (Book of Changes) has already told us: "in the fu (i.e., returning) hexagram can be seen the heart-mind of the heavenly and earthly" and "it manifests what has gone and observes what will come, it reveals the insipient and illuminates the obscure."

Chapter 5

Incest Taboos and the Way of Filial Reverence

Incest taboos and the exogamy that it leads to have been seen by some scholars as the origin of human systems; and the Way of Filial Reverence was seen by Confucians to be the "Root of virtue, and the origin of education" (*Xiaojing* 孝經) What kind of relationship is there between these two?

The Meaning of Incest Taboos

Incest refers to sexual behavior between relatives—especially fathers and daughters, mothers and sons, brothers and sisters—and the reproductive and cultural consequences. Incest taboos are thus the restriction and rejection thereof by individuals and groups alike.

Incest and the sexual differentiation of reproduction are internally connected. Life at the very earliest reproduced asexually, such as reproducing through splitting and forming germs, or reproduction via stolons. In comparison to later sexualized reproduction, these forms are much more self-sufficient, convenient, and stable. For example, some phasmids have a million-year long history of asexual reproduction, and some jellyfish rely on asexual reproduction to live forever. But following sexualized reproduction, a living thing naturally has a fundamental lack. In order to reproduce, the chromosomes of two individuals of different sexes must combine; this can be frustrating, dangerous, and painful. Once there are sexes, then there is the greatest system in the world and the self-sufficient circle is split into two parts whose combination requires the right opportunity and rules. "Split into *yin* and *yang*, suppleness and strength repeatedly activate" (*Zhouyi* "Shuogua" 周易 • 說卦). Thus, there are the all kinds of "images" (i.e., trigrams or hexagrams) of *yin* and *yang* combining, not combining, and mixing together. Males and females need to be different and even opposite one another, but they need to be mutually attractive and mutually selective. If sexual desires are not satisfied, there is suffering; if there is no chance to find a mate, there is frustration, suffering, and danger; males choose females, females choose males, males fight amongst themselves, and females struggle amongst themselves. The process is not economical or efficient, and there appear all kinds of single "men" and resentful and leftover "women" until finally the "grave of love" is entered. Because of chromosomic splits, switches, and inappropriate matches during the period of reproduction, there is a high rate of abnormal, deformed, and disabled births.

However, goddess Gaia of the living world—see the hypothesis of Earth's Gaia—did not differentiate the sexes because of sadism, but instead because she wanted to obtain the abundancy that could adapt to the unpredictability of the future, even if it is painful and dangerous. Every time there is sexual reproduction there is a combination of the two sexes to produce new forms, which will necessarily bring with it a great many new possibilities. No matter how much waste there is, during a long period of environmental change, this kind of chaos is possibly more beneficial regarding complex biological beings.

Incest is a reaction against the methods of selection and reproduction brought about by sexualization: it is a "reminiscing" about asexual reproduction. Even today, asexual reproduction, metagenetic reproduction, and hermaphroditic reproduction still exist in some animals and plants (*Phänomen Sexualität*, 22–32).[1] Incest uses the structure of sexualization, but betrays its open reorganization to seek out more directions, bringing this "reorganization" back into the small circle of family relatives. Therefore, incest also possesses a kind of naturalness and sense. The members of a family or a lineage are sexualized, and sexualization was originally for sexual reproduction. The length of human life is also sufficient to allow for the occurrence of these kinds of relationships to obtain between close relatives, and it is even more convenient for those who live in the same household. Incest can even be meaningful in order to preserve the family or its resources (land, houses, etc.) or some kind of tradition (such as a special technique). Therefore, we can imagine that in the history of life, animals, and the human species, incest's counterattack against sexualization has been partially successful. Humans have fully interbred and crossbred the histories of other animals.

However, time stands on the side of sexualization. Incest in the end loses out to the principle of sexualization unless the tide commanding this world becomes less sporadic and turbulent. There is not a single species, including humans, that clearly knows what kind of bodily structure and way of living can best adapt to the shape of the future, therefore the extinction of whole species and populations is unavoidable. After sexualized reproduction pays out a great cost and sheds off those abnormal forms, it will still be able to produce families and populations that can better meet the environmental challenges in key times than those produced by asexual reproduction or incest (*Phänomen Sexualität*, 19–22, 36). Therefore, it is possible that taboos against incest were contained in the very beginning of sexual reproduction, and when it came to mammals, primates, and especially humans, it became more and more evident. It is not the case as some sociologists, such as Émile Durkheim, have thought that incest simply came from some culture like totem worship. Even if parts of their theories are somewhat reasonable, because living populations, including humans, do not all recognize the principle of sexualization, the reality of asexual reproduction has not become entirely extinct.

Regarding this, even Freud's theory of the "Oedipus complex" is not completely nonsense. But nonetheless, sexualization early on became a guiding principle and instinct for relatively complex forms of life. For human beings it was systematized into incest taboos and exogamy. We can say that we carry on our shoulders the entire history and instincts of life.

Incest Taboos and the Family

Incest taboos and the family are internally connected. Regarding humanity, incest and incest taboos are not only biological but have penetrated into influences and interpretations of social and cultural systems. For example, in some ethnic groups, marriage between cousins on the father's side is incest, but not on the mother's side. Clearly, this taboo has a cultural and systematic interpretive space.

However, the core of incest taboos is a recognition and rule accepted by a great number of groups; that is, there should be no direct sexual relations and reproduction between fathers and daughters, mothers and sons, or brothers and sisters. Incest between parents and children is the most unacceptable because it flips the temporal nature of the existence of the family on its head (the reason will be discussed in the next section).

Even if an incestuous family is still a family in appearances, and moreover appears to be even more "affectionate," that is the so-called "affection upon affection" such as that expressed in Gabriel Garcia Marquez's *One Hundred Years of Solitude*—it nonetheless destroys the root of the family.

Morgan's discovery of the extensive use of the titles "mother," "father," "brother," and "sister" in various Pacific islands still in the "primitive state" is an unrelated fact; it is just that he *inferred* from this that earlier there was no incest between family members of the same generation and that there was no real family, but only what he considered a "kin group" where husbands and wives were communal (*Ancient Society*, part 3 ch. 2).[2] The theory arrived at by Marx and Engels that followed this maintains that a primitive communism lacked families before undergoing social transformation to having a state (correlate with the single-parent family and private property) and then dialectically developed to a communist society without families. However, twentieth-century anthropology rejected Morgan's once influential yet sloppy inference (this inference can be known just by looking at the sloppiness of how he explained the nine clans of China—but this is not one of his important accomplishments) to confirm that incest taboos and the family are internally connected.

Levi-Strauss wrote: "They [observers of the family and ethicists] all together abandoned that old theory that there existed in the history of humanity a stage of 'primitive promiscuity' prior to the emergence of the family;" "It is only when the family, in terms of duty and prohibition, is seen in its place as a knot within the web of human work that society can follow to allow its continued existence;" and "In reality, marriage taboos [incest taboos that create limitations in marriage] are present everywhere, therefore, every family comes from the combining of two other families . . . [and] from the breaking of two other families" (Preface to *Historie de la Famile*).[3]

According to this point of view, incest taboos were social restrictions added onto human physiological needs by culture, and their mutual coordination created the family. And this book's viewpoint is this: humans and even natural sexual differences in the biological world contain "systematic" limits and reproductive structures and in humans; these have been promoted into incest taboos and exogamy while at the same time creating the family. Yet the same ancient forms of asexual reproduction have not gone extinct and still exist in the world alongside sexualized reproduction and even exist on the fringes of human love and the family. For example, incestuous impulses are irregular, but they can be seen as a peripheral atavistic instinct; thus, there is a need to turn it into a "taboo." Otherwise, what would be the point of it all?

In other words, human instincts have not been unified, but there is a distinction between primary and secondary ones, and thus a "system" regulates the relation between the two. The family is a human embodiment of this system, and healthy and real parent–child relations and relations among relatives are natural realizations of this system.

Incest Taboos and Parent–Child (Father–Son) Relationships

More specifically, why are incest taboos universally present throughout all of humanity? Western thinkers have provided some explanations, such as Durkheim in his *Incest Taboos and Their Origins* (*La prohibition de l'inceste et ses origines*) saying that Plato, in designing his republic, in order to continuously produce acceptable members of the ruling class, maintained that exceptional men and women of the right age need to be paired, wherein he touched upon avoiding incest to produce the best offspring (book 5). However, as seen in the next chapter of this book (*Incest and the Republic*), Plato clearly does not discourage incest between the gods, and even directly approves of physical incest between people of the same generation (book 5, 461D–E). Other reasons provided for incest taboos include Aristotle's and Augustine's theory of "preventing narrowness of the passions," Luther's theory of "preventing marriage for the sake of a family without love," and Montesquieu's theory that "incest leads to racial degeneration." The Confucians provided a separate reason: that incest destroys the parent–child relationship, especially that between father and son.

Against this background, we can understand the profundity of this passage from the "Jiaotesheng 郊特牲" chapter in the *Liji* 禮記:

> As for marriage rituals, they are the beginning of the ten thousand ages. Take a wife from a family with a different name by marrying those far away and taking seriously sexual

differences (*fuyuan houbie* 附遠厚別) . . . If men and women are differentiated, then fathers and sons will be affectionate. If fathers and sons are affectionate, then rightness will be produced. If rightness is produced, then rituals will rise. If rituals rise, then the ten thousand things will settle. If there is no differentiation and no rightness, then that is the way of birds and beasts.

That "men and women are differentiated" (*nannü youbie* 男女有別) here extends the principle of sexualization to all of humanity to prevent incest within the household or the family and strictly separates the affectionate love (*qinai* 親愛) from sexual love (*xingai* 性愛). Therefore it is necessary to "Take a wife from a family with a different name by marrying those far away and taking seriously sexual differences (*fuyuan houbie* 附遠厚別)." "*Fuyuan* 附遠" means to marry someone from a family on the periphery or from a far-away place; "*houbie* 厚別" means to take seriously the principle of the differentiation between the sexes or the principle of the other. Only by beginning from this "differentiation," "distinction," or "differentiation between men and women" will "fathers and sons be affectionate." Why? Because affectionate sexual love or love not based on marriage to someone from a different place will devour affection.

Regarding this, we can imagine that a specific cause is the prediction that marriage between direct or close relatives will lead to the "possibility of sexual relations" between family members and that originally there is a possibility for affection within the family. As soon as there is this kind of thought, desire and the locked-away evil of sexuality are called forth, and then this desire is relatively easily satisfied and relations within the family are thrown into chaos. Incest between people of the same generation might extend to incest between different generations, where the relationship between parents and children becomes ambiguous or is even destroyed. Other than this, if brothers and sisters marry and the wife is from one's own home, then it is easy for her to work with other women in the family to care for her descendants, and the role of the "father" or the "husband" will become bland or replaced, leading to distance between parents and children, especially between fathers and sons. Therefore, we can say that if "men and women are not differentiated, then fathers and sons will not be affectionate" (*Guodian Chujian* "Liude" 郭店楚簡・六德).[4]

Conversely, if incest taboos lead to exogamy and if the wife comes from a different family, then her relationship with her husband is unique and singular within the family and her relationship with the other women in the family will be established through her husband. In this way, the most difficult task in the animal world, raising children, will not be easily accomplished without the presence of a husband. Thus, the relationship between parents—especially the father—and the children will be essentially improved and strengthened. Therefore, "If men and women are differentiated, then fathers and sons will be affectionate."

The Way of Filial Reverence and the Parent–Child Relationship

Incest taboos clearly show the experience of mothers and fathers in raising children. This experience has a determinative significance for the appearance of filial behavior because filial reverence is a kind of life between parent and child (the first meaning of "treating family affectionately") and is what follows the kindness of parents. The temporal existence between parents and children—the interweaving of past and future—is its lifeline.

Above we talked about "if fathers and son are affectionate, then rightness will be produced." "Rightness" (yi 義) is first of all "ceremony" (yi 儀; the ancient Chinese lexicon, the Shuowen defines "rightness" as "one's dignified ceremonial posture"), and this "ceremony" also refers to ritual ceremonies and rites, as well as implies the appearance, poise, standard, and measure of their participants. Thus, "rightness" has the meanings of "appropriate," "proper," "good," "just," "significant," and other positive characteristics. The rightness "being produced" here includes filial behavior. The kindness of parents is a spontaneous selfless love that is grand and extensive, being the prerequisite behind rightness, but it is not itself rightness because, even though it is good, it does not include self- or ceremonial consciousness. Therefore, children can be unworthy of their parents' kindness. And the appearance of filial consciousness, especially for those past their youth, seems to require self-consciousness and a ceremonial consciousness of respect, and thus there is rightness within it.

Filial reverence is the primed nature of human beings and is even the respectful and inherited consciousness that returns to its roots. Therefore, there must be a profound ability to retain and historically remember the meaning of travels in time. That is, in the deepest layers of the child's consciousness, they remember the kindness of being raised by one's parents or ancestors. No matter if it is an objectifiable or incidental kindness, it remains an unobjectifiable and non-incidental kindness. The stream of consciousness is formed through this.

Incest taboos cause the kindness of parents in raising their children to show itself in the life experiences of the children, and then goes through their own experiences of child-rearing created through exogamous marriage of the children to return to its source, and through this "going upstream" of respectful consciousness the possibility for the existential structure of filial consciousness is formed. "If rightness is produced, then rituals will rise. If rituals rise, then the ten thousand things (the existential structure of the people) will settle."

In conclusion, "affection" or "affectionate love" is the temporal stream of human existence. It is both the stream of kindness that follows the flow of physical time and also the flow of filial love that goes against the flow of physical time. And "sexual affection" is incest, that is, it is the disordering of sexual love and affection that stirs up the affectionate flow of time because this sexual love that should not have an existential temporal identity also has a kind of temporality. Incest between parents and children causes cancer in the temporality of sexual transgenerational love—that is the temporality of filial love; and incest between siblings causes cancer in the temporality of sexual intergenerational love—that is deferential love.[5] Incest taboos want to strip away the existential temporality of sexual love to make something entirely of space and exogamous relations so that it appears only within the existential space of the communication between families.

This kind of family formed through the temporalization of affection and spatialization of spouses is a healthy family that possesses a survival capability. And other than its function to establish human nature, the Way of Filial Reverence can also be seen as a kind of supplement to the bifurcation of life contained within the principle of sexualization, allowing the state of affairs described in Levi-Strauss's saying that "every family comes from . . . the breaking of two other families" to obtain existential repair and renewal.

Chapter 6

Incest and Plato's *Republic*

Incest is a profoundly meaningful phenomenon, and our treatment of it and other related problems influences our methods for organizing human nature and humanity, and of course, most of all, the family. This phenomenon, especially in Western culture, has caused people concern, fear, and confusion. It has clearly influenced the self-expression of Western civilization. Marc Shell remarks on the "spiritual incest" of Christianity, saying that various theologians "emphasize[d] that Jesus is at once Parent, Spouse, Sibling, and Child of Mary and that, even when he denies his earthly family, he retains his position as Father, or Son, of himself (and, by analogy, Father of all humankind)" (*End of Kinship*, 12).[1] Although we can use "spiritual incest" to explain this kind of "divine familial" relationship, however, Christianity's theological explanation of "incarnation" still causes it to be universally inapplicable. Moreover, spiritual incest is still, in the end, incest. This chapter focuses on this kind of incest as understood in the culture and philosophy of ancient Greece. The main theme of the argument is that at the height of Greek and even Western philosophy, the core thought of Plato's *Republic* is related to the phenomenon of incest.

The Origin and Meaning of Incest

Incest refers to sexual relationships between close relatives and the consequences this leads to. The question is this: is incest a derivation from or sickness of normal and appropriate ethical relationships or is it

78 | Family and Filiality

an important human phenomenon that human nature relies on? Many Western thinkers such as Bachofen, Morgan, McLennan, Marx, Freud, Levi-Strauss, and others have either explicitly or implicitly maintained or approved an explanation of incest in terms of human nature or biology. Westermarck (1882–1939) and contemporary anthropologists (*Inbreeding*)[2] maintain the former interpretation, that is, that incest is not natural to human nature but is brought about by some kind of irregular environment or physiological divergence. A very influential theory of the "Westermarck effect" discussed earlier in chapters 2 and 3 claims that people who grow up together have no interest in each other as adults—those who are close in young age rarely have sexual interests in one another. In addition to this theory, there are the theories that offspring produced through incest will be weaker and prone to sickness. Thus, this school of thought maintains that incest taboos are an expression of natural passions and instincts and are an adaption to natural selection.

Both of these theories make sense, yet neither presents the whole picture. The human societies that anthropologists have seen have nearly all been societies with the same kind of form of incest taboos—explicit or implicit—where sexual relations between close family members are not allowed and even punished and where spouses must be found outside of the family, or even outside the clan. The two sides have separate explanations of this single phenomenon. The second school of thought thinks that incest is a systematic expression of a main part of human nature and is inculpable. But the first school of thought (represented by Freud) maintains that even though it is "prohibited," it must be the prohibition of a powerful impulse in the other direction—otherwise, it would be something that daily behaviors paid no attention to, such as how the behavior of not eating poisonous foods is not due to a prohibition. Therefore, humans must have a bio-psychological incestual impulse that is prohibited in order to maintain family and social order. Because of this, some thinkers, such as Levi-Strauss, view incest taboos as the origin of all human systems, considering incest to be a human creation on the levels of culture and systems. Notwithstanding, views in this school differ on whether there was a time in the history of humanity where there existed a form of "promiscuity" without any families. Bachofen, McLennan, and Spencer confirmed the existence of this in their own theories, Morgan inferred its existence from the kin names of primitive peoples, and Marx accepted and developed it into his theory of communism. But Levi-Strauss and others rejected it, thinking that humans have always had incest taboos and that their appearance could be no later than the appearance of language.[3] Given the depth of these theories and the conflicts between them, incest taboos are certainly a key to understanding human nature and the rationality of human systems.

Incest taboos do not seem to have come randomly lacking a physiological or psychological basis. Biology tells us that the origin of life was asexual reproduction, such as fission and budding; sexual reproduction came later. Moreover, there is also hermaphroditic sexual reproduction, which is an ancient form of sexual reproduction (*Phänomen Sexualität*, 31). Sexual reproduction is much more complicated and dangerous than asexual reproduction. Males and females are each an individual and must come together at the right time with the right method to produce offspring. If a problem arises at any stage, it could lead to reproductive failure. But asexual reproduction avoids all of these troubles through self-replication, which is much simpler, safer, and more stable. We can say that, in terms of the means of reproduction, asexual reproduction is internalized and unified, tending toward the unchanging (there are asexual reproducers, such as some species of *Hydractinia*, that do not get old and, recently, a 9,500-year-old asexually reproducing Norway Spruce was found in Sweden), while sexual reproduction is external, heterogenous and tends toward the changing. The advantage of sexual reproduction is the genetic diversity or species alteration won through all of the necessary hard work, and it is this point that enables sexual reproduction to adapt to the environment and gain the evolutionary advantage it maintains today.

Incest taboos came about due to sexual reproduction because it is this kind of reproduction which has sex at all. However, asexual reproduction is still a kind of hidden "primordial" incest; the offspring produced through "sexual intercourse" with oneself are much stranger than those produced between parent–child incest. However, the behavior appears to be blameless and innocent because it is asexual.[4] Nonetheless, the move toward asexuality after sexuality has arisen, to attempt to "take a shortcut" in reproduction, is clearly incest. It is obvious that incest has its origins in life, that is, the possibility before it is possible, or that it was asexuality and hermaphroditism that allowed for the possibility of sexuality.

There will of course be a need and method for resisting incest once there is sexual reproduction. In biological terms, incestuous sexual reproduction will lead to a certain increase in inherited disorders[5] and reduce the possibility of offspring survival (*Inbreeding*, preface, chs. 2, 9). A common method for avoiding incest is for one of the sexes among the mature members of the new generation to leave their original group in the manner similar to that of male wolves and female chimpanzees. Moreover, in a broad sense, there is a kind of natural mechanism of suppression, such as the emotions between mothers and sons, fathers and daughters, and brothers and sisters. Yet when it comes to humanity, lifelong recognition of relatives and the appearance of the nuclear family lead to a period of time where mature members of the new generation do not leave their parents' home, or they return home, thereby increasing the possibility of incest. The "Westermarck effect" is not enough to resist this "sexual-emotional" impulse. Thus, there was a need for the formation of incest taboos.[6] This is a third explanation that renders a compromise between the two schools described above.

From the perspective of anthropological philosophy, we are beings invested in "sexuality" and cannot imagine completely asexual reproduction. However, it seems that there is a method that has been attracted by the mode of asexual reproduction. In Western culture, no matter if it is religion, philosophy, or science, each world civilization has vividly expressed this kind of fascination. In religion, it is expressed as monotheism; in philosophy, as asexual idealism and empiricism; and in science, as senior derivatives analysis as well as research into clones and stem cells. They all want to find the most intimate, convenient, internal, unified, and final method with which to sexually reproduce; that is, they also want to find immortality. "[T]hat moral nature seeks as far as it can to exist for ever and to be immortal. But the only way it can achieve this is by continual generation" (Plato, *The Symposium*, 207D).[7]

Greek Religion and Early Philosophy on Incest

Nearly all ethnicities touch upon incest in their explanations of the origins of the world and humanity. We are already sexually differentiated and when we want to find the origin of all of life, we are only able to use a sexualized method to enter into the asexual; that is, the differentiation of the sexes is necessary. This is possibly why China, with its philosophical principle of *yinyang*, has no origin myth. Beginning with the myths of Sumer, creation myths around the world all involve mother–son, father–daughter, and brother–sister incest. In the beginning there was but one or just a few gods—if you tell them to reproduce without incest, what can they do?

According to the *Theogony*,[8] the Goddess of Earth, Gaia, was one of the first gods to appear, and she gave birth to the gods Uranus and Pontus. However, she copulated with her son Uranus, giving birth to a series of third-generation gods, including the goddesses Rhea and Cronus. Gaia also gave birth to another series of gods with her other son Pontus. "If men and women [husband and wife] are differentiated, then fathers and sons will not be affectionate" (*Guodian Chujian*, 132).[9] Gaia discovered that her son Uranus was cruel to some of her sons, that he had locked up the three one-eyed Cyclopes and the three hundred–armed fifty-headed sons deep underground; thereupon, grieving, she thought up a scheme to overthrow her husband. Under her encouragement, the smallest of her children, that is the "scheming and mischievous Cronus" went out bravely, with the serrated sickle that Gaia had prepared for him, and hid in a dark place. Later, when his mother and father met to have sex, Cronus castrated his father, casting his penis into the sea, and usurping the position of the king of the gods. One of the metaphors here is that the process and order of time represented by Cronus controls the world. This is the time when humanity entered the golden era (*Theogony*, line 111).

Next, Gaia and Uranus told Cronus that he was going to be overthrown by one of his own sons. At this time, Cronus had already married his sister Rhea, and in order to prevent usurpation by a son, he consumed each son he had sired with Rhea. In her grief, Rhea received instruction from Gaia and Uranus, and when she gave birth to Zeus she hid him on the island of Crete, while at the same time giving to Cronus a stone wrapped in cloth to replace the newborn he would consume. After Zeus grew up, he defeated his father and took his throne, liberating all of his brothers, sisters, and uncles that had been consumed and locked up; he then married his third cousin, Hera. However, according to the logic of Greek theogony, he also feared being overthrown by his own son. Regardless, in the *Theogony* and the Greek world, Zeus maintained his position on the throne. He represented a higher, extra-temporal order. Yet it was during the thunderous and calculating period of Zeus that humanity went through the silver, bronze, and heroic centuries to finally enter the age of dark iron where being "ignorant of the punishments the gods mete, as they are / They'll not be likely to repay their parents for their care" (*Works and Days*, lines 187–188), a century that made Hesiod claim, "I wish that I were not among this last, fifth race of men, But either dead already or had afterwards been born" (*Works and Days*, lines 174–175).

Although the gods could have incestuous relations, humans nonetheless could not. Yet the gods were nevertheless the objects of human worship and yearning. This is where tragedy lies. In Greek tragedy, there is none more tragic than Oedipus who killed his father and married his mother. "Oh fates, where are you rushing?" (*Oedipus the King*).[10] The thing people fear the most is where they must be most careful. As soon as the intimacy that gives people their lives turns in the reverse direction, it becomes a "dreadful thing," calling forth "anguish and despair, madness, dishonor, and death" and where "every evil assailed them; no curse forgotten" (*Oedipus the King*). From the perspective of Oedipus, he killed the person who gave him life and also made a new life with she who birthed him; from the perspective of his mother, Jocasta, "Weeping, she cursed her evil double fate: to bear a husband from a husband, and children from her own son" (*Oedipus the King*). That king who was loved by all thus became a criminal and beggar spurned by all.

Philosophy seems to exist between people and the gods, seeking the unchanging with a changing body and mind. From the very beginning, ancient Greek philosophy sought the origin (*arche*) of all being and discovered that undifferentiated foundation for life that is either before or after all distinctions. "Most of the first philosophers thought that principles in the form of matter were the only principles of all things . . . the substance persisting but changing in its qualities, this they declare is the element and first principle of existing things . . . but Thales, the founder of this type of philosophy, says that it is water, perhaps taking this supposition from seeing the nurture of all things to be moist" (KRS 87).[11] This is what is meant by the so-called "immovable" or "aither." However, some philosophical theories contain a mode of thought that appeals to sexual reproduction, such as the theories of Heraclitus, Empedocles, and others. Heraclitus said: "For there would be no musical scale unless high and low existed, nor living creatures without female and male, which are opposites" (KRS 216) and "They do not apprehend how being at variance it agrees with itself: there is a back-stretched connexion, as in the bow and the lyre" (KRS 212). Empedocles said: "And these things never cease from continual shifting, at one time all coming together, through Love, into one, at another each born apart from the others through Strife" (KRS 418). For Protagoras, awareness of asexual and sexual philosophical theories was achieved, giving rise to a transition. He thought that "numbers" were the origin, and that "one" was the most original and real, while "two" came next because of its indetermination. This embodied an asexual mode of thought. However, he also thought that number elements were odd and even, where the internal "opposites" of "male and female" were also the source, seeming to also embody a sexed mode of thought. Regardless, the first line leads the way, therefore, even though there was an oppositional origin, it was a truth had by the left side's "one," "odd," "limited," "male," "light," and "good," oppressing the right side's "plurality," "even," "unlimited," "female," "darkness," and "bad." From this was produced Parmenides's completely unsexed "ontology," which thought that all that is real is in existence, one, spherical, at rest, and present (KR 347–352). It can be said that Plato is a synthesis of the thought of Protagoras and Parmenides, writing the intellectual theogony of Olympus for all of Western philosophy.

The Incestual Spirit of Plato's *Republic*

Plato was also not willing to live with the indeterminacy of sexed "duality:" "Once upon a time, our anatomy was quite different from what it is now. In the first place there were not merely two sexes as there are now, male and female, but three, and the third was a combination of the other two . . . [this is what is referred to as "*yinyang* people"] . . . Secondly, the form of every person was completely round . . . two sets of genitals and everything else as you might guess from these particulars . . . they tried to make an ascent to heaven in order to attack the gods" (*Symposium*, 189D–190B). Obviously, the gods could not accept this kind of androgynous person. Thus, Zeus split this original person into two halves, made some alterations, and created male and female "half people" like us. This greatly decreased our powers and made it so we think about "finding our other half" all day, and when we do find them, we just want to embrace them without ever separating again (*Symposium*, 191A–E). There is a defense of incest hidden in this. Because people were originally of one body with their spouses, dating and marriage that came later were a return to this unity. And out of the whole world, it is only close relatives who are of one body with oneself, and thus inbreeding between relatives makes sense.

A more philosophical defense differentiates two kinds of love, "Common Love" and "Heavenly Love (*Symposium*, 180E). This differentiation can be said to distinguish spiritual love from fleshly love. Common Love is happenstance, either passionate or the physical possession of an object; it is unrelated to morality. Yet Heavenly Love is rational, can be emotional without desires, and is lofty (*Symposium*, 181). Earthly love can be heterosexual and also homosexual, but Heavenly Love appears to tend toward homosexual love or love between two men (*Symposium*, 181C–D). Eastern authoritarian countries could not tolerate such lofty love, including love of philosophy and physical education, but Athens' democracy encouraged it (*Symposium*, 181B–E). If Heavenly Love can transcend passion for objects, then can it transcend the differentiation between affection and emotions of sexuality, between relatives and intimates? Since these distinctions are established on the blood relationship between two individual subjects, then on the level of Heavenly Love, which transcends the body, are incest taboos still rational? Moreover, since incest between gods is acceptable, and even praised, then in the spirit, where gods and humans are most alike, why is incest not acceptable? There is sexuality there because burning love persists, as well as spiritual intercourse and child birth. Therefore, we can still speak of a distinction between those who are close relatives and those who are not. There is also a quest for asexuality there (it can be expressed as either heterosexual or homosexual); moreover, since it is a quest for asexual sex, there can also be incest taboos.

Plato's *Politeia* imagines an "ideal state" or the perfect "model for a state" (*Republic*, 592B). It can not only embody complete justice but can also be imagined in accordance to the most good and truest form (*Republic*, 505A). This state thus requires a philosopher be king because it is only the philosopher who is "able to grasp what is always the same in all respects" (*Republic*, 484B). Other than this, it also requires protection by those guards that it educates and molds, constituting a ruling class alongside the philosopher-king. The remaining merchants, craftsmen, slaves, and others all belong to the class of the ruled because they are controlled by their passions and everything they seek is changing, uncertain, and mortal, while the ruling class seeks the forms of the Good, the Beautiful, the Just, and even that of the State, which are the most good, the most beautiful, the most true, the most just, and also unchanging and eternal. The eternality of forms is both an ontology and an epistemology, and thus it has been said to be "eternal, it does not come into being or perish, nor does it grow or waste away . . . [it is not] beautiful in one place and ugly in another because it is beautiful to some people but ugly to others . . . It exists on its own, single in substance and everlasting" (*Symposium*, 211A). We can see from this that the love of wisdom of the philosophers and the gods is Heavenly Love that seeks a kind of "asexual reproduction." That is, it takes an eternal, undifferentiated, and even asexual form where "sameness" is the final object of its love, reproducing wisdom in one's own soul. Yet there are sexual differences within the process of this search, no matter if it is in terms of the form of the ideal state or in terms of the means through which the evidence for the constitution of this state was obtained. According to the above analysis of the origin of incest taboos, this kind of sexed method seeking an asexual method necessarily leads to incest.

Since this is a state designed in accordance with an ideal form, its people, especially between the members of the ruling class, must have a relationship where they are fundamentally "the same." Thus, Plato, drawing on a legend, maintained that people all "were under the earth within, being fashioned and reared themselves, and their arms and other tools being crafted. When the job had been completely finished, then the earth, which is their mother, sent them up. And now, as though the land they are in were a mother and nurse, they must plan for and defend it, if anyone attacks, and they must think of the other citizens as brothers and born of the earth" (*Republic*, 414D–E). This legend was not quoted out of a passing interest and it resulted in a series of consequences. One of its connotations is that the people in this state all cut their ties with the secular families "on the earth" and enter into a completely new group. Another connotation is that the men in this new group all see each other has "blood brothers." Thus, the outer shell of familial and sexual differences is preserved at this higher level. According to this ideal and universal logic, Plato believed that women and children must be communal possessions (among the ruling class). "All these women are to belong to all these men in common, and no women is to live privately with any man. And the children, in their turn, will be in common, and neither will a parent know his own offspring, nor a child his parent" (*Republic*, 457D). In this way the state is able to educate and raise descendants according to the ideal; that is, it selects the most superior offspring of the most superior people and eliminates those of others. Moreover, it educates these parentless children according to an ideal standard and method of the state. Much of the *Republic* discusses this kind of education and the basic philosophical problems it gives rise to.

However, these children are not completely without parents or siblings. Instead, in the great family of this ideal state, they have many parents and siblings: "With everyone he happens to meet, he'll hold that he's meeting a brother, or a sister, or a father, or a mother, or a son, or a daughter or their descendants or ancestors" (*Republic*, 463C). Although this is beneficial to their social binding (*Republic*, 464A–B) (note that what appears to be lacking a family still draws on secular family relations), sexual reproduction here cannot avoid incest: "The law will grant that brothers and sisters live together if the lot falls out that way and the Pythia concurs" (*Republic*, 461E). This is the original model of the promiscuous state of affairs that Morgan and others inferred. This kind of "universal fraternity" that eliminates the distinction between kin and non-kin or "universal siblinghood" was seen by Marc Shell as "inform[ing] the major religious and philosophical traditions of the West" (*End of Kinship*, 4). Indeed, we can not only see it in the religious groups, political parties, and all kinds of social entities that have been called forth by a transcendent ideal, but it is also growing fast within science and philosophy.

Even purely formal spiritual incest is necessary in order to recognize the philosophical foundation of the ideal state: "when a man tries by discussion—by means of argument without the use of any of the sense—to attain to each thing itself that *is* and doesn't give up before he grasps by intellection itself that which is good itself, he comes to the very end of the intelligible realm just as that other man was then at the end of the visible" (*Republic*, 532A–B). The senses are the diverse, coincidental, and external method with which humans interact with the world and can be seen as the premise for spiritual exogamy. Plato believed that the senses cannot bring us to truth but they instead disorder our understanding. Therefore, although the senses must be used at the beginning to bring out a memory of the forms, as soon as the world of forms is entered into, one "only needs to use reason" to gain knowledge of each thing, its corresponding form, and even through it recognize the Good itself. This is "dialectics"; it is also the method for tracing back the source of spiritual and intellectual ascension within the kin group.

Plato highly praised the value of pure mathematics in recognizing truth (*Republic*, 525B–526B) and even wrote above the entrance to his academy "Let no one ignorant of geometry enter." However, he thought the mathematical method was not internal enough, that it still required "hypotheses," that is, it supposes the existence of geometrical shapes expressed in images such as triangles and circles, and that it actually supposed the definitions, axioms, and postulates later established by Euclid's *Elements*. Yet images cannot leave behind the senses; we must still use our sense of sight and vision, and as such, it is just a "model" or "shadow" of mathematical forms (*Republic*, 510C–E). In seeking higher forms and "first principles" (*Republic*, 533D) these kinds of "merchants, craftsmen, and slaves" cannot be relied on, but instead, only the "ruling class" or the best of the best, that is, the "purest thought," can be relied on (*Republic*, 532B), and the dialectics is the method of self-differentiation, opposition, and unification performed by pure thought. Plato writes:

> Well, then, go on to understand that by the other segment of the intelligible I mean that which argument itself grasps with the power of dialectic, making the hypotheses not beginnings but really hypotheses—that is, steppingstones and springboards—in order to reach what is free from hypothesis at the beginning of the whole. When it has grasped this, argument now depends on that which depends on this beginning and in such fashion goes back down again to an end; making no use of anything sensed in any way, but using forms themselves, going through forms to forms, it ends in forms, too (*Republic*, 511B–C)

From this quote we can see that the dialectics is the method of reason itself; it acknowledges no shadows of the senses at all, nor does it any longer take mathematical hypotheses as the source of truth. Instead, it utilizes these as a springboard from which ascension to absolute truth begins; it is the form of the Good. Afterward, beginning again from this starting point, all kinds of conclusions are drawn out. When doing this, things of the senses are no longer employed, "making no use of anything sensed in any way, but using forms themselves, going through forms to forms, it ends in forms, too."

This is an extreme internal method where all deductions are performed with "forms" or "ideas" (*eidos*), yet still, therein is generation: "When an expert dialectician takes hold of a suitable soul and uses his knowledge to plant and sow the kinds of words which are capable of defending both themselves and the one who planted them. So far from being barren, these words bear a seed from which other words grow in other environments. This makes them capable of giving everlasting life

88 | Family and Filiality

to the original seed, and of making the man who has them as happy as it is possible for a mortal man to be" (*Phaedrus*, 276E–277A). Indeed, even though dialectics has many meanings in Plato's philosophy, they all involve two oppositional or fundamentally different aspects. For example, it is the refined form of argumentation that develops the initiating powers of the "contradicting art" (*Republic*, 454A) to their fullest. It is not the pursuit "of contradiction in the mere name of what's spoken about." Instead, as Socrates said, it allows people's thoughts or ideas to produce self-contradictions by "separating it out into forms" (*Republic*, 454A) or to "divide and collect" the "natural unity and plurality" of things (*Phaedrus* 266B) and then give rise to more fundamental forms closer to the form of the Good: "They use the conversation to collect those beliefs together and put them side by side, thereby revealing them as contradicting one another not just on the same subjects but in relation to the same things and in the same respects . . . and it is in this way that they are liberated from those great, obstinate beliefs about themselves" (*Sophist*, 230).

"Division and collection" imply that "everything must mix, or nothing can, or some things will mix and some won't" (*Theaetetus*, 252D). This is similar to a kind of taboo against spiritual incest. Plato's quest for an asexual single form of the Good makes this a taboo in name only and functions only at the lowest level, but it is, in the end, forced into reproduction between close relatives, "going through forms to forms, it ends in forms, too" (*Republic*, 511C). That person who has climbed out of the cave of the senses "then finally I suppose he would be able to make out the sun—not its appearances in water or some alien place, but the sun itself by itself in its own region—and see what it's like" (*Republic*, 516B). People not only rely on the light emitted by the sun to see things but also to see the sun itself. If things are as the above described and this is a spiritual or intellectual reproductive process, then this dialectic method that relies on that which is produced (light) to see or know the producer (the sun) cannot escape intellectual incest between spiritual parents and children. And although Plato claims that the philosopher who "has an expertise in dialectics" has a "pure and justified love of wisdom" (*Sophist*, 253E), it yet makes us think of Oedipus's love and wisdom. Oedipus's life was bitter and difficult, yet he died wise and divine. Prior to his death, he said to his two daughters: "But one simple word, I hope, will recompense all your pain and toil. Never will you be loved more than I have loved you" (*Oedipus at Colonus*, 129–130).[12] This not only moves us but also causes us to fear. This love has already gone beyond the love of fleshly incest and has entered a higher level possessing an ability to predict the future. However, it cannot fully free itself from spiritual incest because it is both the love of a father and the love of a brother. Is there nothing more intimate than this within Plato's description of the ideal state and world of forms and his quest for them?

> Anyone who has been guided to this point in the study of love and has been contemplating beautiful things in the correct way and in the right sequence, will suddenly perceive, as he now approaches the end of his study, a beauty that is marvelous in its nature—the very thing, Socrates, for the sake of which all their earlier labors were undertaken. What he sees is, in the first place, eternal; it does not come into being or perish, nor does it grow or waste away. Second, it is not beautiful in one respect and ugly in another, or beautiful at one time and not at another, or beautiful by one standard and ugly by another, or beautiful in one place and ugly in another because it is beautiful to some people but ugly to others . . . All other beautiful things partake of it, but in such a way that when they come into being or die the beautiful itself does not become greater or less in any respect, or undergo any change." (*Symposium*, 210E–211A)

Facing this kind of ultimate love that is essentially different from the love that exists between parents and children and also the ultimate beauty that it reveals, people are either completely attracted by it to the point of fanaticism or they are shocked by it and attempt to escape the complete enclosure of internal intimacy.

The Origin of Spiritual Incest: The Ontology of Pure Mathematics and Ontological Knowledge

Why did the ancient Greeks and Plato produce this thought with a characteristic of spiritual incest? There are two reasons in particular that we can point to now. One is the mathematics that molded the mainstream of Greek philosophical thought and the other is the view on the relation between knowledge and existence among mainstream philosophers. Below is a brief discussion of this.

As noted at the end of this chapter's second section, Plato was the successor of Protagoras's and Parmenides's mathematical ontology, and thus he was greatly influenced by mathematics, especially the methods of geometry. Other than the *Meno*, the *Republic*, and the *Theaetetus*, let's reconsider the *Timaeus*. We can say that Plato's theory of "forms" or "ideas" is a philosophical and ethical embodiment of geometry and arithmetic and that his "dialectics" is the formal operation of mathematical reasoning. In his "four-line segment allegory," although mathematical forms are situated below philosophical forms, they already belong to the world of knowledge and are the basis for knowing the whole world of forms. "Then it would be fitting . . . to set this study down in law and to persuade those who are going to participate in the greatest things in the city to go to calculation and take it up not after the fashion of private men, but to stay with it until they come to the contemplation of the nature of numbers with intellection itself, not practicing it for the sake of buying and selling like merchants or tradesmen, but for war and for ease of turning the soul itself around from becoming to truth and being" (*Republic*, 525C).

According to Protagoras, numbers are the origin of everything, and to use Parmenides's words, numbers are the being of things themselves—being and numbers are interchangeable. Parmenides writes: "On this way are full many signs that what *is* is uncreated and imperishable, for it is entire, immovable and without end. It *was* not in the past, nor *shall* it be, since it *is* now, all at once, one continuous" (KR 347). This "one" is consistent with Protagoras's saying that "the One is substance" (KR 295). Regarding these three philosophers who founded Western rationalism, Protagoras expresses the true appearance of the world in this way: "Reason (which was the name they gave to soul) and substance they identified with the One. Because it was unchanging, alike everywhere, and a ruling principle they called reason a unit, or one; but they also applied these names to substance, because it is primary."[13] Even though Parmenides was excessively passionate toward the "one" and excludes all "variety" from truth and being, Plato certainly rescued the varieties of forms, that is, the variety of Protagoras's numbers, because without them there is no true mathematics, regardless of it being in a formal or an ideal sense.

Regarding these three philosophers, the truth of pure mathematics does not rely on the relation between thought and the external world of experience. Instead, it relies on the forms within the internal structure of mathematics. Plato writes: "It [The study of calculation] leads the soul powerfully upward and compels it to discuss numbers themselves. It won't at all permit anyone to propose for discussion numbers that are attached to visible or tangible bodies . . . Do you see, then, my friend . . . that it's likely that this study is really compulsory for us, since it evidently compels the soul to use the intellect itself on the truth itself?" (*Republic*, 525D–526B). This forces philosophy to remove the world of senses from its very core and enter a world that can be known only through the use of pure thought. This is not different from the later *Elements*' deduction and proofs of his theorems through the mutual interaction and generation of the forms and ideas thereby arriving at inner reproduction or incestual reproduction of the spirit. This is both where it is most profound and pure as well as where it is sick and where a danger lies.

Second, under the guidance of this philosophical method, these philosophers equated being with what can be known leading to a formalized theory of ultimate knowledge. This tendency is clearly visible already in Parmenides: "The only thing that exists for thinking is the thought that it is. For you will not find thought without what is" (KR 352). This kind of theory on the unity of thought and being continued up to Hegel two thousand years later where the dialectical method was maintained. This intellectual tendency is expressed most clearly in Plato: "To that which *is not*, we were compelled to assign ignorance, and to that which *is*, knowledge" (*Republic*, 478C). In this way, knowledge and being or beings are equal. The most ignorant or the most unknowable has the least being, but what is most knowable has the most being. And those things that are "both to be and not to be" (*Republic*, 477A) are sensible, changing things; that is, they are phenomena. Their expression in the mind is not fully knowable and yet not fully unknowable. They are "opinions" that exist between ignorance and knowledge (*Republic*, 478D). Plato preserves the half-rationality of opinions in terms of his ontology, and this is one of the places where he differs from Parmenides. The phenomenal world that opinions involve possesses the ability to allow thought to avoid the diversity and otherness of incest. Plato and many later Western philosophers are not willing to consider the rationality of the phenomenal world and always want to begin there with the process of recognizing the truth from their "memory."[14] This gives their philosophy a few hidden special characteristics. However, they cannot find truth and being itself from within the "exogamy" of the phenomenal world. Thus, under the ineffable influence of Parmenides's theories on unity and the unity of thought and being, the love of wisdom turned toward the "One Form of Goodness," the "Immovable Mover," "freedom, equality, and universal love," "concept of the absolute," and "communism *sans* the family," therefore leading to an intellectual and spiritual endogamy.

Regarding this, Eastern philosophers have a much more sensitive consciousness of "incest taboos." They also wanted to find the source and origin of meaning, but they clearly understood that as soon as this source and origin is made into an ontology and something completely knowable, then intellectual incest necessarily appears. And the appearance of intellectual incest leads to chaos at the foundations, as well as odd methods for sensing meaning and for human ways of life. Although it is possible for thought to obtain a more pure, unified, and creative ability, at the same time this calls forth an instability and inherited sicknesses.

For example, the hexagrams and basic reasoning of the *Zhouyi* 周易 (*Book of Changes*, including the commentaries) is established on the notion of *yinyang* and clearly possesses a character of sexual differences. "The way of *qian* becomes male, the way of *kun* becomes female" (*Zhouyi* "Xicishang" 周易・係辭上), "*Qian* and *kun*, are they the gate of change? *Qian* is a thing of *yang* (i.e., the masculine) and *kun* is a thing of *yin* (i.e., the feminine). *Yin* and *yang* combine their virtues and the rigid and supple are embodied, thus embodying the patterns of change of the heavenly and earthly and connecting the virtue of the numinous and luminous" (*Zhouyi*, "Xicixia" 周易・繫辭下). It seems that seeking ultimate reality with this kind of consciousness of sexual differences must lead to a path toward spiritual incest. For example, the eight trigrams were given connotations of sexual differences within the family: "*Qian* is the heavenly, thus it is called father. *Kun* is earthly, thus it is called mother. *Zhen* is one line thus obtaining the male, thus it is called son. *Xun* is one line thus obtaining the female, thus is called daughter. *Kan* . . . is called middle son. *Li* . . . is called middle daughter. *Liang* . . . is called youngest son. *Dui* . . . is called youngest daughter" (*Zhouyi*, "Shuogua" 周易・說掛). It seems that incest is unavoidable when these base eight trigrams are used to produce the sixty-four hexagrams. However, this is just how things appear on the surface. The *Zhouyi* has all kinds of imagistic mechanisms and explanations to avoid it. Simply speaking, there are these few methods. The first is that the basic element of an image is not the trigram, but the "one *yin* one *yang*" *yao* lines, these constitute the "two modes" of the *taiji* 太極 ("ultimate polarity") and also all of the trigrams and hexagrams. And while the *yinyang* lines can be expressed via sexual differences, they are not limited to a single family. Second, the images of the *Zhouyi* are the sixty-four hexagrams composed of six *yinyang* lines (or it can be said to be three two-*yao* lines or two three-*yao* lines); in other words, they are composed of two trigrams (which are composed of three *yinyang yao* lines each). Regarding the two trigrams that compose a hexagram, "Take the three materials (i.e., heavenly, earthly, and humanity) and double them to get the six lines that compose the hexagrams and then again divide each of the *yao* lines into either *yin* or *yang* and set them in positions corresponding to suppleness and rigidity. In this way the various patterns of the hexagrams in the *Changes* will be formed" ("Shuogua"). The levels of the three *yao* lines *first of all* imply that the images of the natural phenomena are composed of members from *different* families and not members of the same family. That the bottom trigram in a hexagram is called the "inner trigram" and the top one is called the "outer trigram" implies that they have a relationship of inner and outer. "The changes in position of the *yao* lines have their own standard and changes in position of the trigrams also have their own standard" ("Xicixia"). Third, the trigrams or hexagrams composed of three *yao* lines can also be seen as involving all family structures and not just *a single* objectified family. The reason these eight trigrams are considered "trigrams of the warp" (*jing* 經卦) is that, just like the classical texts, different interpretations can be woven in many ways.[15]

Related explanations in the *Yizhuan* 易傳 (commentaries to the *Changes*) also explain that there is a taboo here. For example, the above quote from the "Xicixia" that says "*Yin* and *yang* combine their virtues and the rigid and supple are embodied, thus embodying the patterns of change of the heavenly and earthly and connecting the virtue of the numinous and luminous" is saying that *yin* and *yang* mutually match to form virtue and that the relation between *yin* and *yang* or "rigidity and suppleness" has a disposition or organization through which the creative structure of the world of the heavenly and earthly is embodied and that connects to numinous luminosity. Incestuous matches between *yin* and *yang* are without virtue or "nature" (the meaning of nature, i.e., "*xing* 性*,*" here has some modern connotations but still has an original basis) and do not fit any already existing dispositions or organizations. It turns toward or seeks asexuality through sexuality, which is itself a betrayal of *qiankun* and *yinyang* by seeking a simple principle of the unchanging within the interchange between them and is thus unable to embody the creativity of the heavenly and earthly. Therefore, immediately following this passage, the "Xicixia" says: "The names it uses to refer to the various things are many yet its patterns are not dispersed." That is to say, although the names provided by the *Zhouyi* that take *qiankun* and *yinyang* as its gate (as represented by the heavenly and earthly, the father and mother, elder and younger brothers, elder and younger sisters) are many, they are absolutely not allowed to disorder or go beyond the proper degree of the principle of sexual generation. Therefore, "The *dao* of these three are constantly in flux therefore the name given to the six lines which emulation their changes is *yao*. The six *yao* lines and the ten thousand things they refer to both have differences therefore they are also called things. The lines of the trigrams interact in all kinds of ways therefore they are called *yao* lines. Whether the positions obtained by the *yao* lines are appropriate or not determines whether there will be auspiciousness or inauspiciousness" ("Xicixia"). The *yao* images of the *Zhouyi* are used to express fluctuation, and thus the *yao* lines must have differences such as *yinyang*, *qiankun*, and *yang* things or *yin* things. The method for the interactions between *yin* and *yang* things is the pattern for the life of the world. This pattern is differentiated into what is and what is not appropriate, and through these images of auspiciousness and inauspiciousness are produced.

The "auspiciousness" and "inauspiciousness" that the *Zhouyi* talks about is whether or not something accords with the principle of generation of mutual differentiation and interaction of *yin* and *yang*: "The great virtue of the heavenly and earthly is to generate" ("Xicixia"); "Generation upon generation is called to change" ("Xicixia"). It is not the capability to generate that is change but rather the ability to generate continuously without exhaustion. To use modern language would be so say it is "sustainable." This is auspicious. Continuous generation that does not hinder incest thereby destroying the family, clan, and species is thus inauspicious. "The key in understanding auspiciousness and inauspiciousness is in comprehending whether or not *yinyang* can be controlled. The key in understanding the way of the heavenly is in observing the changes appropriate to the times. The key to understanding the sun and the moon is in becoming aware to their coming and going and their filling up and emptying out. The key in understanding the phenomena of the world is in comprehending the regularity between rest and motion." Regardless of whether or not the "key" (*zhen* 貞) here is understood in terms of the traditional commentary as "right" (*zheng* 正), that it represents continuous process of generation embodied by the phrase "*yuan heng li zhen* 元亨利貞,"[16] or if it is understood in terms of its original meaning of "to divine," both have a sense of incest taboo. "*Zheng* 正" (later extended to be the root meaning of "*zheng* 政" i.e., "government" or "to govern" by Confucius in *Analects* 12.17) implies the proper way for the generation of the two sexes and fundamentally cannot allow any reduction in differences or intense incestuous intercourse. "*Zhan* 占" ("to divine") implies a turn toward the temporal way of the future. It also cannot allow any incest that goes against time. The past of the parents and the future of the children come together to create the present. This is a non-objectified differentiation and interaction. Yet incestuous interactions, primarily parent–child incest, appear to be unified therewith but are actually not. Instead, they are objectified and do harm to the interaction between differences. It is thus an act that disorders *yin* and *yang* that goes against the temporality of intergenerational life. It might be somewhat effective within a short period of time, but if it extends over a long time it will give rise to disasters. The *Yizhuan* repeatedly emphasizes "temporality"; for example, it says that "the *yin* and the *yang yao* lines set the foundation for the trigrams and the penetrating transformations between these *yao* lines reflects the appropriateness of timely changes" ("Xicixia"). These "penetrating transformations" are of great importance but will not be discussed here.

Eastern people also have another strategy for dealing with the threat of incest, which often appears in quests for ultimate reality. That is, they use the non-objectified method of "nothingness" (*wu* 無) or "emptiness" (*kong* 空) to contain or to harbor diversity and otherness and prevent spiritual incest. The phrase that "Nothing and something mutually produce each other" (*youwu xiangsheng* 有無相生; *Laozi* 2) implies that in any occurrence or reproduction, there is "nothing" or a dimension of nonconceptualization or ideal knowledge. The Neo-Confucians of the Song and Ming dynasties thought that this "emptiness" and "nothingness" would threaten the morality based on filiality and deference, so they forcibly removed it. They were unable to understand that, at its base, it protected the intellectual function of *yinyang* transformations. Even though they left their families in order to cultivate themselves at the level of objectified reality, this did not have the effect of absolutely destroying the family, much less of spiritual incest. Contrarily, it had the result of strengthening the natural and intellectual ecology that morality relied on. This is another big topic to be discussed at another time.

Chapter 7

Who Should Care for the Elderly?

A married couple of PKU professors caused controversy by moving into an assisted living center. These two elderly people did not have children and required people to care for them in their old age. At the time, it was not easy to hire someone to manage their household affairs, and community services for the old were probably not up to par. And because their other relatives were not available to help, they chose to move to the assisted living center. In modern society, this is entirely normal. Yet some people felt a sense of alienation, thinking it was not right for famous university professors to move into an assisted living center. But if we adopt the perspective of an elderly person in the modern age, this choice seems completely reasonable. Moreover, even elderly people who have children still choose to move into assisted living centers to spend the rest of their years. What is unreasonable in this? Children are busy with their own work and families, and moreover, they do not often live with their parents, so to have them care for their parents is like rushing a duck onto the barbecue rack. In the end, both sides might run into difficulties. Is someone who visits their mother-in-law or daughters-in-law like a natural enemy? It is already enough to be able to provide funds for elderly care by using what one has earned through one's own labor in exchange for someone else's service.

Yet, theorists will argue that a sign of social progress is the taking up of responsibilities for the traditional family by society—that is, to move away from sons and daughters caring for their parents to society caring for the elderly. This is similar to the transition from rural life to urban life. It is not only a momentous trend but also internally rational. Have not the United States and Europe already been this way for a long time? What is more important than individual independence? A hundred years ago, Kang Youwei 康為为 (1958–1927) said in his *Datongshu* 大同書 (*Book of Great Unity*) that human progress must move from a Chinese-style family to a Euro-American style family and then from a small family to no family, where the care of descendants and the elderly is entirely taken up by society. In this view, the traditional way of children caring for their elderly parents is already backward (China has at least entered the era of small families) and in the process of disappearing. No matter how you look at, caring for the elderly in assisted living homes is rational. However, in China, some people, including the author, cannot keep up with the spirit of this age; they have opinions on children sending their parents to live in assisted living centers, and even on the choice of university professors to move to such a center.

Is what those theorists say correct? As an affirmative defense of reality, it is correct. Humanity is progressing along the Western road and has the final goal of society where there are no families—at least not having what we recognize today as families. In recent years, a certain progress has been made in this regard. Some countries in Europe and many states in the United States have legalized gay marriage. However, in terms of human reason, this progress toward not needing to care for the elderly is also a step backward, a return to a state preceding humanity. Twentieth-century anthropologists, primatologists, and other scientific researchers have shown that humans are the only species among all of the known animals who clearly care for their elderly. Chimpanzees, who are genetically quite close to us, are able to use primitive tools (this discovery of Jane Goodall's once shook the academic world), can learn language, can recognize themselves in mirrors, and are able to play "Chimpanzee politics"—but they cannot care for the elderly. Goodall observed the wild chimpanzee Flo over a long period of time. This chimpanzee successfully raised many children, yet when she was old and in need of assistance, her children were too preoccupied to care. In the end, Flo died on a riverbank, being paid no heed by other chimpanzees. This kind of unfilial behavior is rational from an evolutionary perspective. If a child currently raising their own children expends precious resources and energy to care for their parents, who are already losing their health, this will have unbeneficial consequences for the whole species. However, for humans, the situation appears opposite to this. Ancient humans did not concern themselves with the uselessness of the elderly and cared for them so that those who were no longer able to reproduce lived long lives, nevertheless. Thus, humans discovered that old people had the function of storing useful information. However, in this fast-paced information age of ours, it seems that memories of elderly people are useful again.

Let us begin the discussion with a principle that people can directly understand. Should children care for their parents or not? According to reason, caring for those people who once cared for you is reasonable, and not caring for them is cause to feel uneasy. It seems it is not just Chinese culture that thinks this way, as the intuitions of other cultures and ethnicities are also like this. Even the classics of Greece, the origin of Western thinking, and the Hebrews, such as Hesiod's *Works and Days* and the *Old Testament,* believed it is wicked to disrespect one's parents. Therefore, from this perspective, caring for the elderly is not just important for the elderly but also essential for children to become healthy human beings, too. What elderly people cannot get from assisted living centers is, first and foremost, the special care that revolves around affection and shared memories. And what do children get from not caring for their parents? Perhaps it is the waning of human life.

In modern times, Western individualism—which was also influenced by Christianity—is the mainstream, and in addition, socialization and flourishing of high technology has made Western culture the first to walk down the path of children not taking care of their parents. Philosophers and ethicists (with Kant at the head) still want to defend not caring for one's parents. They say that parents did not obtain the permission of their children before giving birth to them, and thus they have a duty to raise their children until adulthood, at which time no one owes anything to anyone. Following this kind of thinking, Lu Xun 鲁迅 (1881–1936) said that parents have children as a result of sexual impulses, and not only are they responsible for raising them to adulthood, but they also must understand that this is repaying a debt, so there is no kindness for the children at all, nor should any reimbursement be requested. Is this keeping the books correct? If so, then other than for altruists, it seems no one would give birth to children without first obtaining their agreement. Indeed, among those who think that this book-keeping is reasonable, fewer and fewer children are born, even while sexual desires are being satisfied. However, if in a situation where a person is not able to win your agreement and in your absence saves your children from a house fire, will you say you owe nothing to this person, that you have no moral duty to do whatever you can to repay them? Is not the feeling of kindness one has in raising one's children similar to this? Could it possibly be even larger?

Are there any forms of elderly care in this modern society where individualism and institutionalism—they are mutually necessary—are popular? Of course, that is certainly an unmanageable situation. Frequently returning home is caring for the elderly; calling one's parents on holidays and the weekends, and communicating with them via video over the internet also counts as eldercare. When it comes to hiring someone to manage household affairs, making purchases for one's parents online, and paying the fees for an assisted living center are even more substantial forms of eldercare. Even success in your career is a kind of spiritual eldercare for one's parents. "There are no unfilial sons in front of the sickbed." Is it not excessive to have a modern person attend everything personally, to year in and year out cook, do laundry, and prepare medication for their parents? There are certainly sons and daughters who are filial in this way, but today, in this contemporary China where "ruling all under heaven with filial behavior" has been criticized by the New Culture movement and where funerary rites have been globalized, this kind of personal attendance to eldercare is just one kind of choice—moreover, it is a rare choice.

We can even see a new method of eldercare that is less personal because commercialized high technology always goes hand in hand with social progress. What do wheelchairs, elevators, smart cooking implements, electric blood pressure measurement tools amount to? It seems that care robots that can replace the role of the children are nearer and nearer. We can imagine that the future robots will be more reliable, more accurate, more effective, more subservient than hired humans; even the children's voices, personalities, and memories—obviously, those that make the parents happy—will be programmed into the robots. At that time, if children can prepare a robot to take care of their parents and grandparents in their stead, this is an even more creative model for eldercare. However, such robots will certainly be expensive, and we're talking complex high technology, so maintenance will also be a hassle and thus from a long-term perspective perhaps fragile. That is to say, the more carefree one is about it, the more dangerous it will be once a problem arises. The intellectual capacity of this robot replacing a person is too low; it can only repeat those few memories, tell those few stories. It will likely cause parents to become weary of it. But if it is intelligent enough that it can learn autonomously, it will always be able to create new things, which will make one's parents happy, and it is uncertain that this attitude regarding one's parents will not change. What if, through dialectical means, the robot becomes the master instead of the slave? More important, this kind of eldercare allows for a closer distance between parents and children but also creates a greater distance in actual significance. However, who can deny its reasonableness in this modern society? Is it not the "higher, faster, stronger" technological improvement of assisted living?

But the problem is still this: if this kind of eldercare is acceptable, then is raising children in this way also acceptable? Using the logic of Kang Youwei and other progressives, society should entirely free itself from this kind of troublesome parent–child relationship so that "raising children" becomes entirely social and entirely technological. Children are sent to infant centers as soon as they are born, not knowing their parents at all, and the "parents" need not worry about who their children are. Men and women simply satisfy their sexual desires, and individuals are even selected to participate in planned pregnancies. Their spare time is used entirely for creative innovations and the development of personal potential in the search for personal happiness. Technology is going to be more advanced; perhaps even the difficult affair and problems of inheritance and of raising children will be avoidable. That is to say, not only is the optimization of childbirth brought about by new research institutes and factories able to produce more beautiful new people, but these are also able to make alterations at the genetic level to modern humans—which was formed during the Neolithic period, this is backwards according to some scientists—to improve and create a "post-humanity" that has a much higher level of intelligence than we do. At that time, this super-human species will not have a problem of eldercare because they will have been designed and altered to not get old, thereby freeing us from this series of modern problems. You readers who are fond of reflection, are you jubilant in the face of the elimination of humans or the descent to the position of chimpanzees? If you answer in the affirmative, then continue to advance along this boundless, ever-innovating modern path of technology. If, on the other hand, you do not like what is before you, then where do you think we should draw back? What are the limits of where we should go?

Previous people were cared for in their homes or by their children; they grew old and left this world surrounded by their relatives. When modern people get old, they more and more turn toward assisted living centers and make their final trip in palliative care. Old people of the future might be cared for and die under the care of more and more technological services or intelligent robots. After that, "people" will not die; and after that, there will be no "people" at all—there will just be. . . .

Chapter 8

Parents, Children, and the Confucian Classics

The relationship between parents and children is the most fundamental of all human relationships. There are but minor points of difference between humans and chimpanzees, but their parent–child relationship is basically limited to the nursing period, yet human parent–child relationships and kin recognition last entire lifetimes. There is only mother's love among chimpanzees, no filial love, while humans have both parental love as well as the filial love of sons and daughters.

The reason why complete love between parents and children and the family appears in humans is, first of all, because the structure of the pelvis brought about by bipedalism limits the width of the birth canal, and tool manipulation with the hands also promoted the growth of the brain and skull, causing human infants to be born in a much less mature state than other mammals. The subsequent difficulties in child-rearing caused humanity to rely on a complete family, parent–child and kin relations, and a more profound time-consciousness in order to survive.

In human history several million years ago, or at least in the history of the *Homo sapiens* of twenty thousand years ago (humans like us), the human nature that has the parent time-consciousness child relation at its core was formed. Our most profound sense of love, human meaning, and moral consciousness can form only with the family, and the whole structure of society is the expansion of the structure of the family. After the appearance of agriculture, civilization, and the state, the uniqueness of the family began to falter and heterogenous structures established outside the family established greater authority. But the previous seven or eight thousand years of the history of civilization and the culture of a limited family (such as American culture) is not enough to alter our family essence.

Confucianism is the only one among the world's great philosophies and religions that consciously sources itself to the nature of our parent–child relations or the family. It found a method of "cultivating oneself, organizing one's family, ordering the state, and pacifying all under heaven" by adapting the human family nature formed in the pre-civilization period so that it was appropriately expressed during the period of agricultural civilization. This is its greatest accomplishment. Its classical texts clearly embody this characteristic. The "four books" all see familial affection (affection among family members) and filial deference as the root of benevolent virtue, of states, and of the world. "Filial reverence and fraternal deference are the root of benevolence!" (*Analects* 1:2); "Being affectionate to family members is benevolence" (*Mengzi* 6B/7A); "The gentleman completes education in the state without leaving his family" (*Daxue* 大學); "The way of the ruler begins between husbands and wives . . . King Wu and the Duke of Zhou had achieved filiality! . . . Benevolence is being human, and affection for family is the grandest" (*Zhongyong* 中庸).

The "five classics" are also like this. For example, the *Documents* "Canon of Yao" (*Shangshu* "Yaodian" 尚書・堯典) records that because Shun was abnormally filial and good to his parents and younger brother, Yao went among the lowest level of society to personally select him, put him to the test, and transferred the highest political power to him. The *Classic of Poetry* (*Shijing* 詩經) discusses ambitions; that is, it expresses people's deepest emotional aspirations, within which most of the poems are about the aspiration natural to humans of initiating, loving, passing on, and bringing prosperity to the family. Just how beautiful and flawless this aspiration is can be seen in the opening lines of the *Zhounan* 周南 and *Zhaonan* 召南 sections of the *Guofeng* 國風 division. The *Guanju* 關雎 poem praises the love between a man and woman and their becoming husband and wife. Confucius approves of this, saying "its music is not licentious and its grief not hurtful" (*Analects* 3.20). The *Taoyao* 桃夭 poem eulogizes the household of a married couple: "A peach tree in full bloom is adorned in brilliant red. When daughters go to get married, they find a suitable place in their husbands' home." These are just a few examples. The *Liji* 禮記 (*Book of Rites*) records Confucius as saying, "The serving of one's parents by a benevolent person is like serving the heavenly and serving the heavenly is like serving one's parents" (*Liji* "Aigongwen" 禮記・哀公問). It equates serving one's parents with serving the Way of the Heavenly, and serving the Way of the Heavenly must begin with serving one's parents. The *Zhouyi* 周易 (*Book of Changes*) sees *qian* 乾 and *kun* 坤 as a doorway, where *qian* is masculine and *kun* feminine: "*Qian* is the heavenly, thus it is called father. *Kun* is the earthly, thus it is called mother. *Zhen* is one line thus obtaining the male, thus it is called son. *Xun* is one line thus obtaining the female, thus it is called daughter" (*Zhouyi* "Shuogua" 周易・說卦). The *Zhouyi* interlinks the heavenly and the earthly and *yin* and *yang* with parents and children in this way, and thus says that "*Yin* and *yang* combine their virtues and the rigid and supple are embodied, thus embodying the patterns of change of the heavenly and earthly and connecting the virtue of the numinous and luminous" (*Zhouyi* "Xicixia" 周易・繋辭下). The *Spring and Autumn Annals* (*Chunqiu* 春秋) says much in few words, manifesting the interconnection and unity of the ways of kings and of the heavenly, which has the essential feature of "respecting elders, being affectionate to relatives, and respecting the respectable" (*Chunqiu Fanlu* "Wangdao" 春秋繁露・王道). Those who wickedly do harm to this way of filial reverence of being affectionate to relatives and the loyalty of loving the state must be retaliated against to recover justice: "As for the meaning of the *Spring and Autumn Annals*, ministers are not ministers if they do not punish brigands [who assassinate their rule]; sons are not sons if they did not retaliate [against those who kill their fathers]" (*Chunqiu Fanlu* "Wangdao" 春秋繁露・王道). Therefore, it is only the Confucians who will have a *Classic of Filial Reverence* (*Xiaojing* 孝經) and throughout the various dynasties "rule all under heaven with filial reverence" (*yi xiao zhi tianxia* 以孝治天下).

The Confucian classics clearly confirmed the position of the family as the origin of love and laid special interest on the function of filial love to realize human nature, educate morally, and establish governments. Regarding this, Confucianism differs from other religions, especially Western religions, because the place of faith is not the transcendent family of a divine son and divine father or strict church. Instead virtue, ritual and music, organization, and faith come out of familial affection and ethical relationships among kin. The ancestors are divine and can be sacrificed to as deities, and the family is a whole that includes the forbearers, descendants, and kinship clan. The family possesses a historical perspective oriented toward both the past and the future. Humans poetically and sincerely exist within this spontaneous and fully divine temporality of life and household space, fully realizing themselves, establishing their own destinies, and achieving immortality. "To plow—to read—to transmit—to family" succinctly expresses the Confucian way of life. In order to pass on this family in the long river of changing and unpredictable history, there is a need for an economic method that is beneficial to the stability and glory of this kind of agricultural family; and in order to realize the affectionate essence and ethical order of the family, there must be a reading of the classics and moral education by sagely individuals.

From this perspective, parents teaching their children to read the classics or parents reading the classics together with their children is the most reasonable thing in the world. It is also the most harmonious process for bringing about affection. The main point of reading the classics is not to learn external models of history, literature, or knowledge; instead, it is to deepen and enlighten the essence of the family natural to humans. Mengzi 孟子 called this "*liangzhi* 良知" and "*liangneng* 良能" (often translated as "pure" or "innate" knowledge or ability respectively): "There are no children who do not know to love their relatives and elders, there are no children who do not know to respect their elder brothers. Being affectionate to relatives is benevolence; respecting elders is appropriateness. There is no other way [than to follow this *liangneng* and *liangzhi* to cause them] to achieve success in all under heaven" (*Mengzi* 7A). If the Confucian classics depart from the affection of the parent–child relationship, they will lose their root and wither to become merely an object of academic research and a resource for gaining fame. Among classical texts of the world, it is only the Confucian classics that are so intimately linked with familial affection. The *New Testament, Gospel of Matthew* says: "Then one said unto him, Behold, thy mother and they brethren stand without, desiring to speak with thee. But he answered and said unto him that told him, Who is my mother? And who are my brethren? And he stretched forth his hand toward his disciples, and said, Behold my mother and my brethren!" In reading this kind of classical text, or in maintaining that there is a higher, more "brilliant" book than love among relatives, then the more one reads, the weaker the parent–child relationship becomes.

In conclusion, the relationship between parents and children is a source, and the classical texts are also a source. The Confucian classics consider love between parents and children as their source, and the relationships between parents and children also take the Confucian classics as the source for their healthy realization. If parents and children read the classics together, then the classics will obtain their affectionate root and will more and more affect people; and if parents and children are nourished and inspired by the classics, they will be more and more affectionate and benevolent. If reading did not begin with affection, these kinds of classical texts would not become classical texts. And if the Confucian classics are not chosen to be read, there will be no more affection in the stormy sea of human life.

When parents and children read the classics together, it is actually parents reading the classics themselves, and thus children reading the classics at the same time becomes parents reading the classics. The deeper they read, the more parents become like parents and children like children. This is what is meant by parents and children reading the classics. In being affectionate to relatives, the classics are easy to understand, and in treating the classics as classical texts, being affectionate to relatives is achieved; thus, there is affection upon affection and classical texts upon classical texts.

In a society like today's, relatives are becoming less affectionate and classical texts less classical. The family sways in the wind and has fallen to become a custom in the process of destruction to no longer be the cradle that opens a complete human nature. The classics have lost what makes them morally worthwhile to degenerate into literary, historical, and philosophical texts to never again be texts that weave together human lives and the world. And parents and children reading these texts together is but a small boat upon a wild sea, carrying an intellectual species of the past toward a difficult-to-reverse future that yet still holds something precious.

Chapter 9

Toward a Confucian Special Zone by Way of an Intercultural Dialogue with the Amish

The most challenging question facing Confucians today is how the Confucian philosophy or the Confucian religion can obtain for itself an actual living form within mainstream contemporary society and the future. The pragmatics and thought of the continuity of the three traditions of the Confucians produced during the pre-Qin era gives us inspiration. The vision of a Confucian special area can be seen as a contemporary embodiment of the continuity of these three traditions, and the shape of the real lives of the Amish people can hint at, provide evidence for, and support this vision.

A Brief Introduction to the History of the "Three Traditions"[1]

The "continuity of the three traditions" (*tongsantong* 通三统) is the political and cultural idea of ancient China, especially the pre-Qin era; it is also related to the reality created through this kind of ideal. Regarding its political connotations, the "three traditions" point to the leading political authority in effect at the time and two other previous political authorities that had once existed. For example, after the Zhou dynasty was established by King Wu, it became a part of the "three traditions," along with the Xia and the Shang. In today's world, the People's Republic of China, the Republic of China, and the Confucian political culture representative of the Qing dynasty also form three traditions. Culturally speaking, "three traditions" point to the cultural and political forms represented by these three political authorities, as well as many forms from the past, such as the "five emperors" (*wudi* 五帝) or the "nine august emperors" (*jiuhuang* 九皇) that were outside of these three traditions or prior to them (Dong Zhongshu: *Chunqiu Fanlu* "Sandai Gaizhi Zhiwen").[2] "Continuity" (*tong* 通), then, points primarily to the mutual respect between the main tradition and the peripheral traditions that exist alongside each other and that together create a political form or the "Way of the Heavenly" (*tiandao* 天道) whose meaning goes beyond climate connotations, human morality (the way of benevolence), and historical justice. The historical embodiment of the so-called "method of center and the periphery" has mainly been that of the leading political authority enfeoffing descendants of the previous dynasty's royal family with a state of one hundred *li* (Ban Gu: *Baihutong* "Sanzheng"): "Allow them to don their attire, practice their rituals and music, consider them guests and have them pay tribute" ("Sandai Gaizhi Zhiwen"). Regarding the current situation that China is already in, there is the method of the central government and special zones existing at the same time. First there were the special zones of Hong Kong and Macau, and in the future there will be the special zones of Taiwan and Confucianism.

The historical facticity of the continuity of the three traditions is proved by much ancient textual evidence and has obtained the acknowledgment of the academic world. For example, *Yizhoushu* "Zuoluo" records: "King Wen conquered the Yin and then established the prince while providing an official salary for his father, enabling them to maintain the rituals of the Shang." The *Lüshi Chunqiu* "Shenda" says: "King Wu triumphed over the Yin and when he got to Yin he did not disembark his carriage but ordered the descendants of the Yellow Emperor enfeoffed in Zhu, those of Yao enfeoffed in Li, and those of Shun enfeoffed in Chen; disembarking his carriage, he ordered the descendants of the Xia enfeoffed in Qi, established the descendants of the Tang in Song and gifted them mulberry trees." The *Shiji* "Zhoubenji" records: "King Wen thought after the first sage kings, thereupon he enfeoffed the descendant of Shen Nong in Jiao, those of the Yellow Emperor in Song, and gifted them mulberry trees." And contemporary scholar Zhang Guangzhi 張廣志, after describing and analyzing the viewpoints of modern academic research regarding the opening up and feudalizing of the Western Zhou, concludes that "The feudal state of the Western Zhou had the six kinds of categories of the descendants of the royal Zhou state of Ji, families through marriage, ministers, the royal descendants of ancient emperors, the descendants of the Yin, and important peripheral states (like Chu)."[3] The "royal descendants of ancient emperors, the descendants of the Yin" talked about here is the fact of the continuity of the three traditions and the five emperors realized during the Zhou dynasty.

The main point of this theory is that the cultural, political, and lifestyle forms that are no longer prominent or that belong to the past are still given an opportunity to exist and, moreover, their values are respected. In addition to this, according to a more detailed expression of the three traditions, that is, the endless cycle where the beginning month of each of the three traditions is January, December and, November as well as the cyclicality of the ancient Chinese Way of the Heavenly, the particular forms of these three traditions repeat themselves in a cyclical fashion. That is to say, the most distant form will reappear in the future. This mutually supplementing and dynamic interweaving of the past and the future constructs a present with profound historical perspective.

Another chief point of this theory is that it thinks that the rationality of the political authority's Way of the Heavenly is determined by the actual creation of the three traditions. If a new or current political authority does not go to enfeoff "the descendants of the two kings," or if the descendants of the previous dynasty are not willing to accept this enfeoffment, then the new political authority has no means to prove that it has received the mandate of heaven and thus be able to obtain the recognition of the largest number of scholar-officials and the people. Therefore, historically speaking, there has not been a new political authority in China that did not wish to first of all realize the continuity of the three traditions: "To raise a destroyed state, to take up an ended genealogy, to elevate a people lost, this is what all of the people under heaven want" (*Analects* 20.1). This pursuit never ended, although the feudal system existed in name only after the Qin dynasty. For example, the last Chinese emperor of the Qing dynasty that honored the political authority of the Confucians still wanted to embody the continuity of the three dynasties by sacrificing to graves of the Ming dynasty and providing the descendants of the Ming and Yuan dynasties with appropriate official positions (see Su Yu's comment in *Chunqiu Fanlu Yizheng* "Sandai Gaizhi Zhiwen"). Finally, the continuity of the three traditions expresses a universal opinion of the ancient Chinese; that is, there is not one political body, authority, or culture that surpasses all others. The most beautiful can be realized only through the mutual supplementation of and synchronistic existence with the heterogeneous. Do not forget that Confucius was from after the Yin, that his family was the second tradition of that time; that is, he represented the political tradition and culture of the Yin preserved in the state of Song. He moved to the state of Lu only later, for some reason. Confucius, who said "I follow the Zhou" (*Analects* 3.14) and "I was originally of the Yin" (*Shiji* "Kongzi Shijia"), became a sage within the tension between these two.

In conclusion, the political and cultural expression of the temporalization of this human community or ethnic group goes beyond the closed perspective of a single culture and its corresponding political entity; it possesses a profound consciousness of the other and historical wisdom. Deng Xiaoping and the Chinese government employed the saying of "one state two systems" when dealing with the identities of Hong Kong and Macau after their return to China. It appears as if he was also under the influence of this tradition even if it was hidden from view. It does thus seem to be the case that the continuity of the three traditions has not completely died out in the process of Chinese history. Instead, if it is again reignited, it can be beneficial to the reappearance of the living Confucian community.

A Preliminary Outline for a Confucian Special Zone

In comparison to other world religions, the special characteristics of Confucianism are entirely rooted in human living, the family, and the parent–child relationship. In other words, it is through these that the sacred realm where "the above and the below flow together with the heavenly and the earthly" (*Mengzi* 7A13) is realized and a substance that transcends the world is not sought after where an essential higher eternal existence can be entered into. As the *Zhongyong* says, "He who is benevolent is he who is humane. It is treating family affectionately which is grand," thus, if one wants to realize the important Confucian virtue of "benevolence" (*ren* 仁), one cannot rely on what transcends human limitations but instead must rely on the profound parent–child relationship to fully realize the latent potential that makes human beings human beings. Therefore, in comparison with other world religions and ideologies, the advantages of Confucianism are mainly in that they construct a beautiful, stable, and enduring human world by making the family the root of everything. Because of this, the Confucians have historically not had an interest in proselytizing or holy wars, nor have they tried to expand empires beyond the boundaries of China (Mongolian culture does not belong to Confucian civilization). This special characteristic was even noticed by the missionary to China, Matteo Ricci.[4]

Today, humanity is situated in a globalizing environment where the family is in decline. Faced with an unfortunate situation like this, Confucians want a living community where they do not simply stay within the limits of an awareness of the heart-mind/nature, the transmission of cultural education and thought; nor can they stop at the same place religions do with the establishment of their own religious organizations; nor do they even want to make famous a "state religion" in these very anti-Confucian times. Instead, they must take their own family living as a basis through which they can form a new existential experience in this new era so that they can reveal to mainstream society and other civilizations the advantages of Confucianism and as such await the emergence of a state of affairs that is beneficial to them. This existential strategy is precisely what the continuity of the three traditions reveals and allows for. As a mode of living that has already gone into the past, Confucian political authority and culture has not lost its communal existential right in the perspective of the continuity of the three traditions. It still exists in the mode of a peripheral "fiefdom" in which they preserve the special characteristics of their own culture and livelihoods. As noted above, the modern expression of this "fiefdom" is the "special zone," and thus a Confucian Culture Special Zone can be seen as the third tradition in a modern continuity of the three traditions.

The political change most favored by the Confucians is also related to this. The *Shiji* "Kongzi Shijia" records that Confucius said, "Now, Wen and Wu of Zhou rose up from the twin cities of Feng and Hao and ruled as kings." The meaning of this is that kings Wu and Wen of the Zhou ethnic group began in the small cities of Feng and Hao, and because they did good work, they embodied the charisma of filiality and dedication in their lifestyles to the extent that a great number of people and feudal states throughout the world acknowledged and were drawn to them, thereby creating an aura of kingliness and realizing the historical continuity of the three traditions. This saying also has another meaning. That is, broadly speaking, Confucians reveal that their most prosperous method is not ideological propaganda, nor is it conquest through military force; instead, it is a vivid and good lifestyle through which they can win the hearts of the people and establish the foundation of a political governance. Thus, if the third tradition within the three traditions wishes for a future form to be realized as an actual form, it must do as kings Wu and Wen of the Zhou did. They must not only preserve an "old state" that is struggling at death's door but also realize a new beautiful life for it—that is the so-called "new mandate"[5] of an existential rejuvenation.

Seen in this way, a Confucian Culture Special Zone bears the new fate of the old state; its design and establishment are for the revival of Confucian communal living, and it is also so that there is a more diverse and even more beautiful and secure choice for the future of humanity.

Now, how should a Confucian Culture Special Zone be established? I have previously done some thinking on this,[6] and here I will just provide a few essential points.

First, the family and parents–children relations are the foundation and core of the establishment of this special zone. The "family" talked about here is not limited to the "nuclear family" of modern society or that composed of two generations or even those small families of one generation. Instead, it is the even more robust and larger human family household or genealogy that includes these smaller families and that also is natural to humanity. It is a family composed of the members of three or more generations; it has its own family traditions (e.g., clan rules, family education, and family pedigrees), ancestral obligations (e.g., clan halls, ancestral temples, and ritual ceremonies), and a consciousness of others (the acknowledgment of the rights to exist of other families with which there is cooperation and not opposition). This special zone is thus not only not established according to a treaty of freedom, but nor is it established according to a theory of centralized state power; instead, it relies on the principles of family ideology of Confucian ritual and musical education—including the series of designs which will be discussed below—that they promote for self-governance. This family ideology does not have any natural tendencies to discriminate against or oppress women or any member of the family, it only acknowledges that there are different family roles, and moreover, that these roles must be adjusted with the changing times.

Second, this special zone makes use of the clean technologies and knowledge of human families, human nature, and natural friendship. This also implies that it forgoes all technologies that threaten the human ecology and endurance of the natural ecology and only adopt those traditional (like Chinese medicine and traditional farming techniques) and green technologies. In principle, they do not utilize machines that operate through chemical combustion, nor do they obtain electricity through methods that do harm or pollute the ecology (such as nuclear or large-scale dams), they do not pollute the environment with pesticides or manufactured fertilizer and neither do they use electronic products in their normal day to day lives, and so on. At the same time, they expend great effort to research and develop novel, traditional, green, or appropriate technologies in order to satisfy the needs of a harmonious and colorful life.

Third, their political structure is a system rooted in the family that plans for the measured and balanced flourishing of the Confucian common people. The so-called "measured and balanced" points to the balance created through the mutual supplementation of the opposites of the Confucians and the common people, the family and the individual, the social group and the family, benefit and righteousness, the present, the past and future. The "common people" points to the residents of the special zone, but they are zone residents or people who have been familial or clan relationships through a consciousness of "family names" (*xing* 姓). The administrative authority of the special zone can thus be split into two sides that can be called the "House of the Common People (*baixing yuan* 百姓院)" and the "House of Confucians (*ruzhe yuan* 儒者院)." The former is generated through voting by the common people—family votes take precedence for individual votes—and the former is formed through mature Confucians who have obtained their status through testing, prestige won through long years of practice, and who have the approval of the House of Confucians (this requirement does not exist prior to the establishment of the House). Both Houses can bring up important affairs, but they must have the approval of many sides, and cases that would alter the basic laws of the special zone require at least a two-thirds majority. The core guiding principle of the special zone has two articles that cannot be altered, but only actual practice can be adjusted in accordance with circumstances. The Zone Chief is nominated by the common people and approved by the Confucians. If the chief is rejected then they can nominate another person, however, the Confucians must select one of three nominees. The primary members of the zone government are nominated by the Zone Chief and approved by the common people.

Fourth, the economy must be beneficial for both familial and natural ecologies. Therefore, agriculture must be its basis while husbandry, commercialism, and other such things are simultaneously attended to.

It is neither egalitarianism nor extremism; nor is it privatization—the land is not private and cannot be bought or sold, and in most important situations the special zone can distribute property according to the law—and nor is it publicization; instead it encourages things to be done at the level of the family. The base is relied on without oppressing those above, and when people are promoted they should give back to the community that reared them so that every family, person, and lifestyle can have that which it deserves and has something to strive for, and so every person has dignity and basic guarantees.

Fifth, education needs to return to the foundations of Confucian teachings in aestheticized virtue ethics, which also needs to be improved. There are, first of all, two kinds of the six Confucian arts: the *Poetry*, the *Documents*, the *Changes*, the *Rituals*, the *Music*, and the *Spring and Autumn Annals* as well as ritual, music, archery, charioteering, history, and numbers. Next, there are the Four Books, and there are also some things that need to be appropriately included such as the arts of agriculture, military, and crafts. "Virtue ethics" has its root in filial reverence for one's elders and deference for one's elder brothers. Their aestheticization and achievement includes benevolence, appropriateness, dedication, reliability, and other traits. The "improvement" thus requires an assimilation of beneficial knowledge, technologies, arts, and virtue ethics, especially those pure and lifelike natural knowledges, technologies, institutions, and methods of sacralization that can be taken over from the West and other ethnic groups. The special zone should not be a conservative place stuck to tradition but instead a place where young people can fully explore their passions and develop in ever-new ways.

The exams for officials are to be revived to test the virtues, beliefs, understanding of world affairs, and even the technologies and knowledge produced in relation to life within the special zone so that Confucians can be produced therein and future officials and technologies of the special zone can be selected.

Six, the basic character of their beliefs is Confucian (philosophical or religious) in nature and is preserved through the multidimensional existential structure described above. However, due to the source of religious Confucianism being the family and not doctrine, and because this special zone is morally educated, it has self-confidence in and tolerance for its existential structure. It does not fear existing alongside others and different religions, and thus it does not prohibit other beliefs.

Toward the Confucian Special Zone by Way of the Amish

Can what is created out of the principles described above be a living community of the third Confucian tradition? Of course it can. Because it has as its root in the family, filial reverence and deference, takes *yinyang* as its mechanisms, is embodied in benevolence and reliability, and has wings made of the six arts. There, the heavenly (or nature) and humanity respond to each other in step and balance is kept throughout the times, appropriateness is at the head and so both appropriateness and benefit are present. The people living there are cultivated, families are organized, states (zones) are governed, and all under the skies is pacified. Therefore, obviously, it is Confucian and not any other belief or ideology. Now, is this a refreshed and revitalized renaissance or is it simply the lifeless replication of an ancient way of living? From the considerations rehearsed above, it can be seen that if it is to be realized at all, it should be an old state with a new fate; it should have a specific energy and creativity specific to its era that is conservative and withdraws into itself. In today's world where new fashions appear all the time to an excessive degree, being able to take a few steps back is an expression of a greater choice and the spirit of freedom.

Now, can this kind of communal living continue to exist in this world of high technology that seeks the novel and the different and has the atmosphere of individualism? Can it live of itself under the premise that it has no protections or involvement from the outside? These are some of the greatest doubts raised concerning consideration of a Confucian special zone or a conservation zone. Regarding this, other than answering with the cornerstone of the family that is humanity's most ancient and renewable principle, we can also answer through an examination of the experiences of the community of the North American Amish.

The Amish are Protestant Baptists who originated in Europe during the seventeenth century. Because they were oppressed, during the eighteenth and nineteenth centuries they immigrated in many waves to North America. Now, Amish communities are found only in the United States and Canada, and most are located in the former.[7] What leaves the biggest impression on people is that they do not seek and even limit as much as possible advanced technologies and the culture of individualism. That is to say, they use no technologies from the twentieth century onward except when doing so becomes unavoidable, and then they only use them after making some positive alterations. The highest value is not the realization of an individual, but the harmony and robustness of the church, the family, and the community. For example, the Amish present today still use horse carriages for transportation and cannot possess their own vehicles. They basically do not use electricity, and when they need a little bit of light for their work spaces, they do not connect to the electric grid but instead produce their own electricity. They promote agriculture and related handicrafts, but within the past half century they have suffered environmental oppression and have also adopted some other low-level technological professions, such as milk production. They primarily educate their children in faith, virtues, and life skills. Their education goes only as far as graduation from primary school. Their belief is pure and simple: they have not established a theological church that transcends this world; instead they select church officials through an election where all members of the committee participate. They do not have a formal church; religious activities are held in individual homes on a rotating basis. The family and the household are the foundation and center of the entire community. They cherish their children but do not spoil them; they support their parents and ancestors, and care for the disabled and all those in need of assistance.

From this it can be seen that the basic lifestyle of the Amish is extremely different from the leading lifestyle of the United States and Canada and shares important similarities with the form of the Confucian culture special zone described above. Comparing this social community that has lived for centuries in an environment that is inconducive to their survival with the Confucian special zone being considered here perhaps allows us to imagine a greater sense of historical reality and a clearer awareness of the troubles and opportunities it will encounter. It might also provide us with a more plausible method and determined belief for establishing this kind of special zone.

Let us first summarize two related points. First, the Amish community and the Confucian special zone both face very different and even opposite environments in their search for their own survival. They have both been forced to feel a need to physically separate themselves from mainstream society and not just have differences in ways of thinking. They even need to be separate in their lifestyles and the places where they live; otherwise, there will be no way for them to realize their own ideals. In order to do this, the Amish had to buy a plot of land as a community of twenty or more families to turn into an agriculture zone, and even make every effort to demand autonomy to reduce outside interference as much as possible. For example, Levi, an Amish individual living in the state of Pennsylvania, was arrested and jailed five times during the four months prior to January in 1954 because he refused to allow his daughter to attend a middle school in regular society. Similar cases have happened to more than a hundred Amish people. They maintain that child education is the concern of their community, and their community thinks that it is sufficient for children to attend school only until the eighth grade and that to continue to attend high school in regular society will destroy the tradition and vitality of their society.

Actually, due to various elements of religious oppression, the separation (Absonderung) from mainstream society is the special characteristic of the entire history of the Amish people. Ever since the twentieth century, this separation has brought a resistance to advanced technologies (because previously everybody's technology was roughly the same). For this reason, the Amish struggled tooth and nail for their "right to not be modernized," and they also had to painstakingly maintain "regulations" (Orderung) for all aspects of life, that is that divine order and other regulations that have been proven throughout history. They are very clear on the fact that this struggle to not be modernized directly determines the fate of their community. "Within two generations, the progress-seeking churches would surrender their distinctive Amish identity and merge with neighboring Mennonites" (*The Amish*, 43).

In the history of ancient China, especially during the pre-Qin period, the tradition of the continuity of the three traditions allows for and even encourages the existence of these kinds of heterogeneous living areas. Within the spirit of that time, there even appeared the "other" from the state of Chu known as "man from Hanyin" who refused to make use of the contemporary technology of a shadoof to irrigate his fields upon which Zi Gong, who saw "that this efforts were great but his rewards little" felt "fully ashamed and was not able to face him" (*Zhuangzi*, ch. 12).[8] Today's world of globalization and abundant high technology would cause the sensitive Confucians to be aware that without this kind of heterogeneity or separation they would not be able to win for themselves a true place to live in the world in the present or the future. Regarding this, the experience of Amish "separation" is extremely precious to creating a new state of affairs for the continuity of the three traditions because although China, the United States and

Canada differ in some significant ways, they are mostly the same when it comes to their pursuit of modernity, advanced technologies, and "hard power." And a wise ruler, be they Chinese, American, or Canadian, will allow for and even encourage the emergence of these kinds of special zones or lifestyles because this is precisely an expression of one aspect of a country's healthiness. That is to say, if they are able to connect with the path of the "mandate of heaven" then it is also a revelation of the legality of the present political authority.

Second, these two aspects both strive to bind together religious belief and family ethics. For us, loving God or respecting Heaven is inseparable from the family. The Amish do not accept the slogans so often heard in other religious churches, such as "assurance of salvation," or "[faith provides you with] eternal security," as if God's grace can leave behind the human world presently being lived in and be had through some transcendental method. Their attitude toward religion is that they need to realize their own salvation through the ethical practice of "living hopes." Therefore, "it makes no sense to them to separate ethics from salvation or to speak of one dimension and not the other" (*The Amish*, 72). Here, "ethics," first of all, implies the ethics and morality of the family. The Amish thus do not believe in some up-on-high systematized religious church; instead they want to select their own priests, and moreover, they hold sacred religious ceremonies in their own homes on a rotating basis. They all live in a community composed of several tens of families (Gmay or Gemeinde) and these families to a great extent are all related through kinship. This extended family "provides care, support, and wisdom for all stages of life" (*The Amish*, 203). Therefore, "the family is the primary social unity in Amish society" (194) and "It is difficult to exaggerate the importance of the extended family in Amish society" (203). This kind of family oriented toward Christian beliefs makes it so that the Amish community zone is different from other Christian groups and is even closer to the Confucian community of the Confucian special zone.

Therefore, we have discovered that the way of filial reverence that marks Confucian culture is to a large degree also encouraged and practiced in the Amish community. "The words of the fifth commandment, 'Honor thy father and thy mother,' are heard frequently in Amish circles" (*The Amish*, 196). When a parent becomes too old to live on their own, they will move near one of their already married children and thus obtain the support of their descendants. They thus rarely seek assistance from assisted living homes or other facilities.

Third, both sides are contextualized and affective existential communities. *The Amish* describes them as a kind of "high context culture" (*The Amish*, 18). This kind of vitalized communal living is one of the elements that attracts young people to stay behind. In order to fully realize this kind of contextualized living, the members of the social community must not move around a lot, but instead must settle on their land and seriously consider any moves so as to guarantee the directness, frequency, and locationality of social interactions. This is one reason the Amish community refuses to use gas-powered vehicles and has always used horse carriages for travel. The result is a more conservative Amish community. There are also differences among the various Amish communities whereas some are conservative and others more relaxed, and those areas that are best at preserving traditional technologies and lifestyles retain the most young people (163). Contrary to the pessimistic predictions of many of those who research the Amish, the Amish population has increased from around 6,000 since the year 1900 and was 274,000 in 2012 (4).

Fourth, both sides maintain an appropriate use of technology. That is also to say that to maintain and expand their own lifestyle and beliefs, they must oppose the fettering of the oppressive wave of modern advanced technologies on human ways of living. They must selectively employ those technologies that are appropriate to their needs. This is what is meant by "appropriate use of technology." Regarding these two aspects, the technologies that are used will in turn create—when blindly chasing efficiency—and even restrict the lifestyle of those who use them. It is just like what an Amish leader as said: "The moral decay of these last days has gone hand in hand with lifestyle changes made possible by modern technologies" (*The Amish*, 315). Therefore, the Amish have always acknowledged that mechanization or technologization will destroy the family and the village community and will open up the possibility for distant means of production and cultural influence. You can drive your advanced harvester to go help your neighbor bring in the harvest, but if everyone uses these kinds of machines, the mutual help required for this way of living itself will be reduced. You can use your cellphone to call your parents, but if using your cellphone has turned communication with parents into no more than long-distance communication through sound or images, then the meaning and emotions of communal living and direct communication with one's parents has been lost. The result is that the social community and the big family are reduced to a smaller family, and the smaller family is reduced again to the individual. Thus, we are all controlled by commercial companies, media, and political parties; our lives and even our collective knowledge is manipulated by their technologies and ideologies.

Some advanced Amish communities try to leniently accept new technologies and respond to this rapidly changing world, but "diversity has its limits." As soon as there is an acceptance of the loss of the guidance of the old regulations and the ability of "negotiation" created through this with the new technologies, there will be catastrophic consequences. "Although Beachy Amish members have continued to dress somewhat plainly and even retained the Pennsylvania Dutch dialect for a generation or so, their embrace of the car, along with their technological and doctrinal innovations, put them outside the Old Order fence" (46). The reason for this is like what an Amish leader has said: it is because if someone has their own car then they will leave the family and the local church for the city to look for opportunities, and this will bring moral decline. In their view, protecting Amish beliefs and the community morals has been entirely made into a lifestyle; that is, it is an intimate and stable lifestyle inseparable from the family and land. When the Amish reject telephones, televisions, and the electric grid, they are, above everything else, making a consideration from the perspective of the existence of their living community—the absolute necessity of morality, faith, and family.

Fifth, both sides think that subsistence agriculture is the most appropriate economic method for protecting the lifestyle they cherish: "Over the generations, the Amish have developed a strong conviction that the small family farm is the best place to raise children in the faith" (*The Amish*, 275–276). However, since the 1950s, due to the pressures of new technologies, especially the increase in the costs brought about by the commercialization of agriculture (these Amish family farms have not, after all, cut all ties with the external world of agriculture), the agricultural communities of the Amish encountered great difficulties that led to a decrease in Amish families undertaking agriculture. A few families have already adopted high-tech equipment like vacuum milking tools and cold storage containers. Fortunately, in this century, other than some agricultural villages that have adopted traditional business methods, there has been an emergence of new, low-tech agricultural practices, such as in milk production, the marketing of agricultural products, organic farming, rotational grazing systems, and greenhouse cultivation. All of this has brought about an agricultural renaissance for the Amish community. It can be seen from this that the agricultural prosperity that can maintain one's own faith is internally related to which technologies are employed. The Confucian special zone needs to use traditional and green technologies to develop its own agricultural industry.

Confucian Lessons for the Amish

Standing within the position of the Confucian special zone, we have a sincere sense of admiration for the moral wisdom, courage, and the historical uniqueness of the Amish community that "criticizes the world expending great effort without faltering." We must continue to think deeply following the above points to completely absorb and broadly promote them. However, it seems there are still some things that we can learn to prepare for the future implementation of a Confucian special zone that is also some advice that we can provide for our Amish friends.

First, although the Amish have identified a sensitivity regarding the moral consequences of modern technologies, and have even adopted a gradual transformative resistance, *their overall response to technological problems is, however, excessively passive.* They have not organized long term efforts to create an appropriate technological grid that can satisfy the needs of their lifestyle. For example, they have in the past remodeled commercialized personal computers so that they do not require connection to an electrical grid but can operate from a battery, preserving their calculating and document storage capacities while losing their capacity to go online and play video games. This is a pretty good response. However, if you cannot buy an appropriate computer on the market that can be remodeled (e.g., there were many computers that were much more complex and expensive than the Intel 286 at that time), then this kind of adaptive strategy becomes implausible. A better strategy is perhaps to create one's own calculating and document storing machine, that is an improved abacus and typewriter, so that communal needs can be responded to at their foundation. The Amish resistance and remodeling of modern technology has always been difficult, and now there is a new threat, such as acceptance of cellphones and solar power by some Amish. These hide dangers to the community. Therefore, when the author of

The Amish discusses whether the Amish can tame modern technology, he says the answer is "uncertain" (*The Amish*, 334).

Next, the Amish should establish their *own* high-level institutes for education and research, so that they can establish the creative and preservative capacities gone over above. Historically speaking, the Confucians have possessed an effective web of education and examinations, however, this education and the exams contained very little that had to with agriculture or craftsmanship. The Confucian special zone also has to reform these, they have to study and plan for all that they need. Of course, this "need" is not limited to what is right before their eyes or some objectified need. "Do not make use of this with purposive intent but place yourself in what is common. As for what is common, it is what is made use of; as for what is made use of it, it is what is continuous without obstructions; as for what is continuous without obstructions, it is what obtains. Being comfortable in what obtains is about all there is to it" (*Zhuangzi* Ch. 2). (Precisely because one does not seek the usefulness of a rope, one will thus be able to reside in its common functionality. The so-called common functionality is the creative applicability of knowledge in one's timely and situational living. This application will bring about a mutual merging of all kinds of different lifestyles and it is understanding this merging that can be considered to be the obtainment of fundamental meaning, that is the appropriate obtaining of life's needs. There is no excess here, and neither is there any lack, and thus one has entered into the subtleties of human living and come close to *dao*.)

Again, in order to guarantee the realization of the above two things, and also in order to preserve the endurance of one's own unique lifestyle, there should be a clearer distinction between mainstream society and the Amish or the Confucian special zone. This is an even more effective realization of the principle of separation. This also implies that the Amish community should establish their special zone to allow the structure of their own way of life to not be impeded by external transportations that transverse their lands. We know that the Amish have always relied on collective buying power to purchase land and win for themselves a living place, and thus the periphery of their communal area is completely open to mainstream society, so much so that they interact with the outside world on individual family bases and not as an entire society. This kind of complete state of defenselessness can be maintained through daily life and with a low population. But in the face of the advancement of technology in the past half-century, the economic activity of the Amish has more and more suffered the influence of mainstream society leading to ever greater problems. For example, in the 1950s and the 1960s, the government implemented a regulation requiring milk products be designated as one of two kinds thus forcing some Amish sellers of milk to adopt mechanized milk producing equipment and cold storage containers. As of 2002, some Amish complained that the old social regulations impeded their economic activities, even forcing some of them to abandon agriculture (*The Amish*, 280). Why is it that some of these old regulations did not impose on them earlier but now they do? It is because of external transformations in the economic environment that raised the prices of seeds, fertilizer, equipment, animal care, and more. The costs of agriculture production in a community not cut off from mainstream society also rose, forcing some families to adopt modern technologies or be left behind.

Therefore, in order to avoid the ever greater attraction brought about by the high-speed development of mainstream society, there must be complete separation between one's own community and the economic activity of mainstream society, and an isolated living area governed by oneself must be established. Previously, the separation between the Amish and mainstream society was mainly in terms of religious belief, technology, and natural economics. Now, there seems to be a need to implement a complete administrative and economic separation. Otherwise, there will be no means to preserve their own special characteristics. The Amish opposition to bureaucratization is correct, but they cannot allow this opposition to prevent them from setting up the required administrative structures such as a leadership institution for the entire Amish community (the Amish have always made their own special zone the basic unit and have no united institutions scattered across different communities) and one or more large connected special zones. In comparison to the disaster effected by the assault of external mainstream society, it is worthy for the Amish to allow for the isolation of their own small communities, and even to establish institutes for their own high-level education and study so as to win for themselves opportunities to continue to exist.

Conclusion

The theory of the continuity of the three traditions and its practice reveal that the governmental form of a civilized nation can and even should be diverse and multifaceted or harmonious without a forced uniformity. There is no single thing that is most optimal; there is only the communal glory and harmony of a multilevel heterogeneity. In the unfortunate circumstances of today's world, it is imperative for the Confucians to create and develop a timely spirit of the continuity of the three traditions to win for themselves a place within which to exist and to also win for China a new justice of the Way of the Heavenly of the continuity of the three traditions for the modern era. Therefore, the establishment of a Confucian special zone is the new situation in which the Confucian essence can be developed. In order to do this, learning as much as possible from the Amish community experience and fully incorporating it in the creation of their own community is a precious opportunity for the Confucians. It is also especially worthy to absorb the Amish, in order to protect their lifestyle of familial morality and faith while resisting modern technology, though there remains room for improvement regarding this endeavor.

Chapter 10

Can Confucianism Accept a Matriarchal Family?

Learning from the Matriarchal Mosuo of Southwestern China

Matriarchal families and societies occupy a position in human history that cannot be ignored. However, regarding the society that we often see or is recorded in written records, patriarchy is undoubtedly the most dominant. The society born from and extended by Confucianism is also patriarchal, and in comparison to the West, Confucianism has its own characteristics in how it views the sexes and patriarchy due to the special characteristics of the intellectual tradition and civilization of China.[1] In recent decades, a popular theory that appeared in the West and is present in China thinks that, in the history of humanity, there was first an enduring matriarchal society after which patriarchy appeared and produced classes and the state during its developmental process. From the perspective of scientific and anthropological evidence, this theory has been subject to great doubt and even been rejected.[2] However, in the academic world of China and even within general ideology, it retains a strong influence. Other than this, if Confucianism wants to regain a chance for survival in the present and future world, it must respond to the important question of the role of women, including their roles (e.g., wife, daughter-in-law, daughter, citizen) in the family and society and also the position of women in ethics and its worldview. There are paths to this response. The first is to seek the appropriate Confucian method

128 | Family and Filiality

for dealing with women within the greater framework where patriarchy and modernism conflict. The second is not limited to the patriarchy but must consider the relation between Confucianism and women from the perspective of matriarchies, patriarchies, and even more intersecting viewpoints. This chapter attempts to take the second path, to discuss the characteristics of a matriarchal family and society and whether or not Confucianism is able to accept this kind of existential structure—and if it can, in what sense can it do so?

A Brief Introduction to the Mosuo People's Household and Society

A classic example of a matriarchal family and society in modern China is found in the Mosuo 摩梭 social group who live on the border of Yunnan and Sichuan. I visited Daluo Water Village 大落水村 on the banks of the Lugu Lake 泸沽湖 in August of 2016 and had a deep fireside conversation in the home of a Mosuo named Ge Ze'er 格則爾 that was quite revealing. Afterward, I visited related museums and Mosuo villages and upon returning continued to read books, reports, and related research about the Mosuo people. I subsequently formed a few opinions on the historical position of this matriarchal society.

The Structure of the Household

If the organizational method of this matriarchal family is to be described in one saying, it should be said that its normal or ideal form is this: a communal house organized by each of the women in a family and all of their children. In other words, in each house, everyone is related through blood, where there are no sexual relationships. The second clause excludes the father and his kinship network. The key to this matriarchal family is thus not that women manage the household, as others have emphasized; rather, the key is *the child-birthing and child-rearing of the women* because the brothers of the mother—referred to as "uncle" (*jiujiu* 舅舅) by the father's side—can also manage the household (*Guodu* 國度).[3] The physical labor and ability to manage affairs outside of the household are also important (*Guodu*), but if a generation has no daughters, there is also no child-birthing or child-rearing and therefore this family will come to an end. Obviously, if there are no men, the life will also be difficult for this family.[4] Mosuo families thus happily anticipant the coming of their descendants; the birth mother *and her sisters* are equally happy, and both care for and cherish their descendants so that all children refer to women older than them as "*ami* 阿咪" ("mommy"), while sometimes referring to them as "big mama" (*damama* 大媽媽) or "little mama" (*xiaomama* 小媽媽), depending on their ages (*Guodu*, 7–11). Although there is no "disparaging of the men," when mature girls get married, their mothers will arrange an upstairs room for them, a treatment that men do not receive as they must leave the household when they marry. Just the same, if the sisters give birth to too many children, causing a danger of splitting the family, then the nature of the family is to restrict pregnancies, to the point that women give birth to only one child, if any at all. Therefore, the population of the entire family increases quite slowly and basically maintains a balance (*Guodu*, 71). We can say that all of this preserves the extension of this matriarchal household and harmonious and stable foundation. This is the key to understanding Mosuo households, societies, customs, and culture.

In order to protect the family principle of "everyone is affectionate and there is no sexual love," sex between men and women or Mosuo spouses must be solved with a "not at home" (*fei jiaju* 非家居) method. This is not a meeting-up in the wild but instead indicates that the Mosuo have a certain marriage custom. "Walking marriage" (*zouhun* 走婚) in the Mosuo language is "*ti sese* 替色色" or "*sese* 色色," which means "to move back and forth" or "to come and go" (*Guodu*, 135). *Ti* has a spatial connotation. *Tisese* means that the man moves to the upstairs room of the women to consummate their marriage. This is obviously premised on mutual recognition, happiness, and the woman's acceptance. At the same time, it also implies that this action is generally undertaken at night and the man returns home before either side wakes up for breakfast. This is the method by which women become pregnant, and then they give birth in their own homes, thereby establishing a kind of husband–wife relationship with the man. Generally speaking, something akin to a wedding ceremony is held when the baby is a month old, where they "exhibit month-old alcohol" (*bai manyue jiu* 摆满月酒), publicly revealing the spousal relationship between the mother and father.

However, it should be pointed out that there are two or three stages to "walking marriage" and their confusion leads to many misunderstandings of the Mosuo people. The first stage can be called the "dark walking" (*anzou* 暗走) where the relationship between the two lovers (*axia* 阿夏) is kept secret, especially the family of the woman, and that takes place only in the dark. This can occur outside (*Yanjiu* 研究, 101)[5] or in the upstairs room of the woman. In this stage, sex between the two partners has a great deal of freedom and flexibility. The second stage can be called "bright walking" (*mingzou* 明走) and begins with the man formally visiting the woman's mother—"respecting *guozhuang* [a kind of circle dance]" (*jing guozhuang* 敬鍋莊) where both sides have dinner together in the main or mother's house. Here, the man presents gifts to the woman and her elders (*Guodu*, 137; *Yanjiu*, 102,) thus forming a certain bond between them. The third stage can be called "regular walking" (*changzou* 常走), which begins with the public presentation of the baby (*Guodu*, 138). The birth of the baby allows for the deepening of the relationship between the two and possible stability: "At the time when the baby is presented, each family on the woman's side in the village hold a party for the mother and the man's side will prepare and pay for it. It is the most grand and public ceremony for the relationship between the two involving all of the households in the village, and where the two partners are no longer 'lovers' (*axia* 阿夏) but become '*chumi* 处咪' (similar to 'wife;' *Guodu*, 137) and '*hanchuba* 汗处巴'" (similar to "husband;" *Guodu*, 138).

Many people think there are no rules to Mosuo "walking marriage" and that it was just satisfaction of desires leading to the Han and other ethnic groups to consider it something derogatory as a "licentious custom" throughout history. But this is only because they confused the first stage with the latter two. The outdoor meetings of the first stage are, strictly speaking, not "walking marriages" but only "testing of the waters" or "dating" to see if they "have had feelings for each other through normal interactions at work or festivals" (*Guodu*, 105) and is a relatively naturally sprouting of love that can be produced in any agricultural village. It is the preparation for the second and third stages that is the most characteristic of the Mosuo's "walking marriage." According to Ge Ze'er, there are some elder "walking marriage partners" who still love each other in old age so much so that when one dies, the other follows not too long after.

Even if "walking marriage" where the two sides do not live together is not on the same level as patriarchal marriage or do not belong to the same paradigm, the former is ultimately based on the passions and fate of the two sides (*Guodu*, 106) and not on the law, however, that does not mean there are absolutely no rules or rituals. Other than what was just rehearsed above, "walking marriages" between blood relatives is also prohibited, nor are they allowed to take place with a family of a bad reputation, and must take into consideration the attitude of the mother (*Guodu*, 107) and other factors. We can imagine that this kind of ritual will only be at full play within the original social ecology of the Mosuo—the relatively self-sufficient agricultural economy and stable and harmonious village society. The mobility brought by caravans in the past, modern school and work, the cultural revolution, and today's commercialism and travel fads all do harm to the original ecology of "walking marriage."

Why Are There Patriarchal Families? The Advantages of the Mosuo Household

The matriarchal families and society of the Mosuo are not leftovers of a group marriage system; instead, it is a choice that this ethnic group has made throughout history and under the pressure of neighboring patriarchal societies. The reason they made this choice is that this kind of parent–child or kin relationship is unique, making it irreplaceable by a patriarchal system.

Simply speaking, there are two advantages to the matriarchal Mosuo household: (1) in principle, every person lives their entire life with relatives whom they share a relation with,[6] so it is easy to empathize and care for them; (2) sexual partners only rely on, or mostly rely on, their passions when interacting and there is no great connection to the family, wealth, or position of either family where such connections are almost entirely irrelevant in the traditional village way of life, therefore, the degree of naturalization or purity of emotions of sexual interactions is relatively high. We can use the two phrases of "affectionate love" (*qinqin* 親親) and "sexual love" (*aiai* 爱爱)[7] to describe these two characteristics. We can imagine that people are naturally, enduringly, and continuously cared for by their family in this kind of lifestyle and that there are no "outsiders" who can step in or break apart the family to create trouble with them. Nor is there pressure to create a family on one's own or is there much pressure or complexity to the forms of sexual interaction. There is no great obstruction to not performing a "walking marriage" in comparison to patriarchal families where there is much pleasure and little suffering in these kinds of interactions. Therefore, the Mosuo social group presents a tranquility, self-sufficiency, and gentleness. It is lacking much of the conflicts, tensions, crimes, and spiritual imbalances of a patriarchal society. In short, it is a kind of life that allows people to obtain happiness and satisfaction relatively naturally and easily.

The Disadvantages of the Mosuo Household

Now, what are the disadvantages of this matrilineal household and the "walking marriage" system it adopts? It seems to be cause for perplexion that a system such as this which naturally satisfies people is present in only a tiny percentage of human ethnic groups. When I was at Daluo Water Village in the summer of 2016, what lingered in my mind was this question that I could not have even imagined in a dream before coming to Lugu Lake. This matriarchy avoids the troubles regarding the wealth of the different relations and identities of all kinds of aunts, sisters-in-law, stepmothers, parents-in-law, and even husbands and wives, as well as the public and private. Moreover, it uses a natural method to release and train sexual impulses. What it particularly brings to the table is not a destruction of the modern individual social relations and promiscuity of sexual relationships but a stable social structure and a kind of order to the sexual passions alongside a moral and social atmosphere of assistance, tolerance, enjoyment, and peace. It also even brings an economic ability to resist poverty (*Guodu*, 70–71) and to naturally stabilize their population. In its traditional society, other than the distinction between marriage forms and the "selection of worthy and competent people," the degree of harmony, even closing in on the "great unity" (*datong* 大同) described in the *Liyun* 禮運 chapter in the Confucian *Liji* 禮記 caused the historically Mosuo people, including the modern Mosuo who experienced the attack of "legal marriage recording" of the Cultural Revolution to always reminisce about it and have tried to return to it. But why has it not attracted the world outside of the forty thousand Mosuo people?[8] In other words, why do they not take the Lugu Lake as a model and expand concentrically outward?

The reason I can think of now primarily has to do with the safety of the ethnic group and structure of their culture. First, it is difficult to form effective alliances between families because in-law relations are not developed. In comparison to the kinship web and political alliances established by the patriarchal system of "taking a wife from a family with a different name by marrying those far away and taking seriously sexual differences (*fuyuan houbie* 附远厚别)," the close-distance "walking marriages" of this matriarchal family structure lead to a blandness in relationships among relatives on the father's side. The necessary costs of this "family where everyone has a blood relation is that no one has sexual relationships." This kind of ethnic group is easily cheated, attacked, and occupied by other ethnic groups, and in the worse cases, even annihilated. Second, even though this household society "values women but does not devalue men," it certainly takes "women as the root and men as the branches" (*Guodu*, 16) and the men basically take care of household chores and, for them, becoming the family uncle or "*awu* 阿烏" is "the climax of male status and authority" (*Guodu*, 70).[9] Therefore, the absence of a motivation on cultural and political levels to allow men to collaborate in doing something outside the household and working on behalf of the household has led to the underdevelopment of education, a lack of culture, a lack of their own writing system, and lack of a political spirit. During the time this was all part of a "a peach blossom spring,"[10] none of this was a problem and was even an advantage: "Small state, few people . . . savoring their food, appreciating their costumes, settling in their homes, and enjoying their customs. Neighboring states are within sight of each other, the sounds of dogs and chickens within earshot of each other, and all their lives the people do not travel back and forth" (*Laozi* 老子, 80). However, as soon as they faced the oppression and incursion of other ethnic groups and modernity, it became excessively passive and dangerous.

Xiao Shuming 肖淑明, a Han women who has lived most of her life in this way, is the last "princess" (*wangfei* 王妃) of the Mosuo leader. In 1942, she married into the household of the leader, and after a convoluted life has already entirely accepted Mosuo culture. She "summarized five important characteristics and three weaknesses of Mosuo culture: 'amiable with others, warmhearted to guests, good and just, honest and sincere, and hardworking, but at the same time they are timid, dependent, and do not expand'" (*Guodu*, 130). Actually, these three weaknesses, if the world was peaceful and tolerant would be reasonable and not considered a weakness in such a regional social group. "I make foolish the minds of the people, simplicity upon simplicity! The common people are clear on things, only I am confused; the common people are observant, only I am muddled . . . I am different from others in that I value feeding the mother (i.e., the *dao* 道)" (*Laozi*, 20). However, even if this is not entirely an era where the strong eat the weak, it is also certainly not a tolerant world, and even the "mother" will be somewhat left behind.[11]

Is the Mosuo Household a Family?

Is There Marriage?

We can already sense from the above description that the existence and characteristics of the matriarchal household society of the Mosuo raises a series of profound questions for us. First of all, is this household community (*yidu* 衣度) a family? This is obviously determined by how we define "family." If we define it in the popular way of as "family is a human community constituted through relations of marriage, care, or adoption," then it seems that because it lacks the element of "marriage," therefore it is not a true family (as in *Yanjiu*, 13, 47). Some researchers have used "matriarchal family" (*muxi qinzu* 母系親族) to refer to it because of this (*Yanjiu*, 47). However, as was seen above, the function of the "raising the month-old child" is similar to a wedding because it publicly reveals the husband-wife relation in the Mosuo sense between the man and the woman. It takes the parent–child relationship as the main constitutional factor and in comparison to when common wedding ceremonies are held, it is a rather late event. Moreover, the binding in the third stage of this kind of "walking marriage" already tends toward stability, but because a common residence for the husband and wife is lacking, in comparison to the stability of traditional patriarchal marriages, it is still not enough (but the rate of divorce in the United States is almost 50 percent of all marriages; as marriages decrease, perhaps its stability will be lower than the third stage of "walking marriages"). However, its function is certainly marriage because, in an anthropological sense, marriage just refers to the acceptance and acknowledgment by the social group of sexual intercourse, communal living (not excluding the situation where the couple is together only at night), and generation of descendants between a man and a woman. Precisely because there is this function, not being able to present a month-old child is a very embarrassing and shameful affair for the Mosuo.

Are There Fathers?

Of the popular misconceptions corrected by Zhou Huashan 周華山, three are directly related to our problem. That is, popular investigative reports and ethnographic descriptions think that "many Mosuo do not know who their father is; that the Mosuo do not have the term 'father;' and children on the father's side can intermarry" (*Guodu*, 40).

Now, do the children in this matriarchal family "not know their fathers"? This is not so. In most cases, sons and daughters know who their father is because "the father plays a necessary role at four events, that is, the child's coming of age ritual, the Spring Festival, the presenting of the month-old child, and funerals" (*Guodu*, 59). The so-called "month-old alcohol" (*manyue jiu* 滿月酒) refers to when the newborn is about one month old; the father treats the family or neighbors of the birth mother by bringing gifts and chickens, goats, or oxen. Each family in the village will send an adult women to attend, and the host gives gifts to the guests, and then each guest in turn treats the father and mother to gifts. Even villages without the "month-old alcohol" ceremony have something similar. The identity of the biological father is made public to the whole village through these methods. If the month-old child is not presented, that means there is a problem in explaining who the "father" is, or that a stranger (such as someone from a different place or a caravanner) left without returning, or that the mother cannot identify the father. These are all embarrassing and shameful matters for the mother and her family (*Guodu*, 56, 61). Since the whole village knows who the father of the child is, then even if the child's family does not tell the child, neighbors and other villagers surely will. Other than this, at the child's coming-of-age ritual and at every Spring Festival, the father will participate or have a special showing, and if the father is sick then the child will visit him. Therefore, in normal living conditions, most Mosuo people know who their father is. Zhou Huashan consulted many Mosuo over the age of fifty, and only 8 percent (four people) could not confirm who their father was (*Guodu*, 56). This is also a modern state of affairs resulting from having experienced land reform and the Cultural Revolution. We can imagine that in a traditional and more stable and natural Mosuo village that the percentage of people who knew their fathers would be even higher.

When the Mosuo refer to their fathers they use "*abo* 阿博" when in their presence and "*ada* 阿達" when not (*Guodu*, 51), and more often than not they use "*awu* 阿烏" (uncle) in order to preserve to the bonds of the family. For example, Xi'na Erche 溪娜兒車 (twenty-six years old) explained why she uses "*awu*" to refer to the three fathers of her siblings by their shared mother: "Of course I know who the father is, how could

I not know? Every year I received his gifts during the Spring Festival, and I will visit his hearth at every coming of age ritual, and I must visit his house on the first of the new year every year. I normally refer to him as '*awu*' just like I do my brothers' fathers when they come to my home. We three sisters [there are actually two brothers, but Mosuo tend toward using feminine words] don't think that we 'belong' to different fathers, we basically don't have this concept, we three sisters are related, if we all refer to our own fathers as *ada*, *abo*, or *baba*, then it would be difficult for us to sympathize with each other" (*Guodu*, 52). It is because of this kind of situation that the term "*awu*" became so common, and the existence of this phenomenon allows some sloppy investigators wearing colored glass like [the nineteenth-century anthropologist] Lewis Henry Morgan to believe that the Mosuo do not have a term for fathers, and even that the Mosuo only know their mothers and not their fathers. Therefore, should we not doubt whether or not the historical legend of "knowing the mother but not the father" was produced along these lines?

However, the relationship between children and their biological father here is very different from that in patriarchal families, because children live and work all their lives in the home of their mother's kin—in the Mosuo language this is called "*yidu* 衣度." It includes four parts, among which the "mother's house" (*muwu* 母屋) is most important—and their relationship with their biological fathers is rather distant. We can generally compare it to the relationship between cousins and their uncles in patriarchal societies. However, a few scholars recognized that it is untenable for "one's own biological father . . . to not actually be a relative, there is a complementary authority and duty between 'father' and 'son'" (*Guodu*, 59).

Zhou Huashan refers to the seventy-seven-year-old Abu Che'er 阿布車兒 to explain that the father plays a role before the child is born: "After 'walking marriage,' the man and woman are relatives so if the woman becomes pregnant, then the man should not travel far away. The child in the womb should hear its father's voice from time to time. Even if they (the biological parents) separate later, even if they meet on the road, they should greet each other amiably and there should not be a coldness between the child and its father because of the separation between the parents" (*Guodu*, 59). The local people have a saying to describe the role of the parents in Mosuo life: "Blood is given by the father, but the bones are the mother's" (*xue shi fuqin gei de, gu queshi muqinde* 血是父親給的，骨卻是母親的) (*Guodu*, 58). This means that the essence of the mother is as one, therefore, the phrase "*gengu* 根骨" (lit. "root bone") in the Mosuo language expresses that the root of the matrilineal line does not change, but the father can flow and even be replaced (like blood transfusions in a hospital). But the father nonetheless still participates in the structuring and development of the child's life. Zhou Huashan summarizes: the Mosuo "know and recognize their fathers, but don't treat them like family" (*Guodu*, 56).

Are There Husbands?

Are there husbands in the Mosuo world? This is an extension or a premise of the above question. If "husbands" are established through formal marriage ceremonies and continuous communal living before a child is born, then there are no husbands and thus no spouses. However, if husbands are formed through a functional wedding ritual *after a child is born* (month-old alcohol) and some kinds of daily *connection between parent and child* and kin relationships—a positive relationship is of mutual assistance and a negative one a taboo against "walking marriage"—then the Mosuo have husbands and wives. There are actual marriages in patriarchal societies and also situations where the mother and father live separately (such as the case of pre–Cultural Revolution China and Cultural Revolution China). None of this affects the existence of the husband-wife relationship, even if it is irregular. But the system of the Mosuo household structurally excludes the communal living of the spouses over a long period of time only allowing short periods during night "walking marriages." This situation greatly weakens the parent–child relationship and the connection between the families of both spouses, causing the "*awus*" or uncles on the father's side to equally replace the "non-sexual" functions of the father or related functions such as the daily labor provided thereby, managing the affairs outside of the household, and educating and protecting the children. From this we can know that for the Mosuo, although the identity of the father or the husband is constituted through some "month-old alcohol" or coming of age ritual, they still fulfill many important functions. Moreover, these functions are often taken up by many *awus* or uncles. However, if we adopt the perspective of the Mosuo matriarchy, husbands and fathers in patriarchal households and societies thus combine the normal functional roles of *adas* and *awus*. It is just that what can be said to be normal, different, or irregular can only be done so from the perspective of a certain model.

Are There Incest Taboos?

Among past researchers, few have affirmed the universal existence of a "remnant of group marriage" in the Mosuo, an expression of which is where "walking marriages" can take place between brothers and sisters with the same father but different mothers, and because they only know their mothers but not their fathers, they fall into group marriages or blood marriages. Besides, these researchers also claim the existence of mothers and daughters sharing husbands, fathers and sons sharing wives, sisters sharing husbands, brothers sharing wives, uncles and nephews sharing wives, and walking marriages between the children of brothers and sisters (*Guodu*, 44).

Yet Zhou Huashan has discovered that normal Mosuo people have severely negative reactions to such claims, for example: "Wawosang Na'asi 瓦窩桑娜阿斯 (102 years old) said: "*Aiya*! The Mosuo aren't domestic animals, we're people. How could mothers and daughters or sisters share husbands? I would absolutely not give my daughter to a male blood-relative . . . these things were not acceptable during my grandmother's time . . .'" (*Guodu*, 45). Mr. Wang (forty-five years old), a teacher in a Mosuo elementary school, said: "My daughter and the children of Jiaya (Mr. Wang's cousin) absolutely cannot have 'walking marriages,' even if it is the daughter of the previous husband of the second wife of my mother's second brother, they cannot have a walking marriage with me or my children! Nor can they have 'walking marriages' with children from a patriarchy."[12] Zhou Huashan provides many persuasive examples, and even finds many examples from previous reports that were mistaken as evidence, and moreover, also provides evidence through the shyness of culture of the Mosuo people and has the agreement of knowledgeable Mosuo. All of this can be considered very strong evidence.

Summary

Therefore, we can affirmatively say that the traditional existential structure of the Mosuo household is a kind of family. Its existence actually causes us to re-investigate the definition of "family." As long as the father is known, then there is no necessity to exclude the temporality of the pre-marriage parent–child relationship. Therefore, we maintain: "*The family is constituted through the life-long mutual recognition of parents and children, brothers and sisters, incest taboos, and the existential source of the extension of generations.*" The "incest taboo" here guarantees that the family possesses the important function of formal marriage, that is exogamy and heterosexual interactions, however, it loses the requirements for a pre-child birth marriage ceremony and continuous communal living. Thus, it can tolerate the delayed functionalized marriages and families of "walking marriages." "Lifelong mutual recognition of relatives" and the "generational extension" based thereon is thus the special characteristic of human kin relationships and obviously have incest taboos as their premise.

Measuring up the Confucian Concept of Family in an East–West Comparison: The Importance of the Father and the Complementarity of the Parents[13]

Confucianism appeared in a patriarchal family and society and also participated in molding the Chinese family and society with its own special characteristics causing it to be different from Western families and societies. Therefore, if we want to understand Confucianism, we must especially understand the role of the father in this tradition.

THE MEANING OF THE FATHER

Let us first adopt a broad anthropological perspective. Three requirements for being a father are (1) marriage with the mother and generation of descendants, (2) participation in the education of descendants, and (3) spiritual influence to form and maintain descendants. However, our understanding of these must be flexible. Present research more and more emphasizes the last requirement.

The appearance of humanity gave males new life. Because there appeared all kinds of forms of marriage within the human community—no matter if it was an elastic monogamy or a "moderate polygyny,"[14] therefore, in principle, it is the same for each male and each female, they can both participate in the child-rearing. There is not just a double extremism of the male—whether it be the male is singular and the female many or the exclusion of males from participating in reproduction—but there is a transformation and refinement into fathers having their own families, so that they can obtain the acknowledgment and even mutual protection of the community and, first of all, other men or fathers (*The Father*, 13).[15] This is the *beginning of virtue* in humanity.

140 | Family and Filiality

Broadly, the appearance of fathers implies the appearance of a real family. The first meaning of the term "real family" is the lifelong intergenerational recognition of relatives, even if it is hidden or non-objectified recognition. "Natural selection didn't work to the advantage of human beings by making their children strong: we know, indeed that infants grew ever more defenseless and dependent as apes turned into men. Natural selection increased the strength of the new family, which in all probability was already monogamic and patricentric, and thus without precedent among higher mammals" (*The Father*, 42). And real families and fathers thus imply the appearance of a special human characteristic, that is the appearance of profound temporal consciousness. Its particular expression is this: in comparison to other animals, including other advanced primates, humans have a more far-reaching and vivid imagination, memory, and ability to plan: "The appearance of the father coincided with the invention of postponement and the ability to formulate projects. It was a construction that took place in time, no less than an act that constructed time" (39). Some arguments say that the father and family appeared in the paleolithic era (3 million to 10,000 thousand years ago) (11), some say that the structural system of the father's identity was an important element in the appearance of civilization (approximately 8,000 to 9,000 years ago) (50). It seems the former theory is more tenable. The appearance of the father and true families cannot be later than the period of maturity of us modern *Homo sapiens*, that is that period approximately 40,000 years ago when technological inventions were constantly happening. Since then, the basic structure of the intelligence of the human brain has also experienced great change. Therefore, the father marks the appearance of human nature and profound cultural consciousness, and it's much earlier than the appearance of civilization. Conversely, some civilizations twist and stifle our human nature.

Fathers in the Eyes of the Greeks and Romans

Homer's epics and Hesiod's *Theogony* have been seen as the marker of the formation of the Western father. Because of the Greek mode of thought that is dualistic and formal as well as focused on "force," these epics and legends have reflected their relatively rigid view on the relationship between the two sexes. They excessively elevated the man and the father, while lowering the woman and the mother, therefore, they also necessarily did harm to the real father. For example, in the *Iliad*, when Hector, who was real a father, faced Achilles, who only represented the principle of force, he was killed and his body dragged behind a chariot. Before the battle in which he was killed, he returned to the city from the battlefield to find his family, and when he saw his own son, he went to hug him with a fatherly impulse, but his son was scared by the helmet that he wore. This symbolizes a distance between the father and son that does not exist between the son and the mother (*The Father*, 88). And this image of the father as tending towards the principle of force produces a separation from the image of the mother. Therefore, there was tendency to lower and denigrate the woman in Greece, such as the criticism of the feminized "Pandora" in the *Theogony* as well as the high praise of the father in Greek myths and even philosophy that thought the man or the father was the true origin of children and that women or the mother are only used as "wet-nurse that gathers seeds" (124). And Aeschylus's three-part *Oresteia* describes the public execution of the protagonist's mother as revenge for his father—the mother, Clytemnestra, killed her own husband, King Agamemnon, and the female god of vengeance seeks a blood-debt for this and is stopped by fatherly gods, including the masculine Athena. The philosopher Aristotle said along these lines that: "The woman cannot spread seeds, seeds come from the father" (quoted from Aristotle's *The Generation of Animals* in *The Father*, 120).

Although the Roman poet Virgil's *Aeneid* is not as famous as the two Homeric epics, however, it is the most fatherly work in ancient Western literature because it created the image of the father in the balanced and well-rounded character of Aeneas. Moreover, it also uses the obedience of his son and succession of his descendants to complete this character. The image of Aeneas escaping from danger in the city of Troy directly expresses this kind of fatherliness at the key moment in the family and even the blood of the ethnicity. He carried on his shoulders the deity of the family and divine father Anchesis and pulled by the hand the small child Ascanius in a fatherly manner in his charge out of the burning city running with blood. This turned the heroic male warrior into the father who established the Roman ethnicity and civilization! "While fleeing from death they are again united by a process of rebirth, by way of Aeneas's hands, which lend their support to both the following and preceding generation . . . For ancient Rome, the arms of the hero who had founded the city—the right arm that guides Ascanius, the left arm that steadies

Anchises on his shoulders—were symbols of the highest ideals, much as Christians see the open arms of Christ" (*The Generation of Animals* in *The Father*, 142). Therefore, Emperor Augustus ordered a statute depicting Aeneas's *escape* with the child erected in the center of the plaza in Rome. However, in the end, Aeneas's wife or mother of his children were not there, she followed behind and died trying to escape. The women that Aeneas later encountered were either all passionate and emotional or they were passive. Regardless, in Roman civilization, especially the first period, the father had abundant significance and a high stature. The father's acknowledgment of the "lifting up" ritual of the identity of his son as his heir (lifting the child above his head) was not only legally effective, but also a moral and divine extension of the family and succession of faith. However, the position of women in this culture was very low, and its later elevation followed the slide in population. That this Roman civilization was a political reality for almost one thousand years shows that it had a strong life in the ancient world of the West.

The Way of Filial Reverence and the Father in Chinese Culture

Fatherhood in China was molded by ancient Chinese culture and Confucianism in a broad sense, and while it shares similarities with the West—especially the Roman father represented in Aeneas—there are, however, large and profound differences. The two largest differences are (1) the *yinyang* mode of thought of the ancient Chinese, and (2) the basic reciprocity of the filial reverence promoted by the Confucians in the structure of the family, including fatherhood. The *yinyang* mode of thought (not an interpretation of the term "*yinyang* 陰陽") in the *Yijing* 易經 (*Book of Changes*) was already expressed by using the images in the *Yijing* during the age of the mythical hero Fu Xi. It thought that the original relations between complementary differences and oppositions and complementary necessities and supplements are the source of human lives and the world. Its main embodiment is the relationship between husbands and wives and parents and children within the family. Therefore, the *Yijing* "Xugua" 易經・序卦 has this passage: "There is the heavenly and the earthly and then there are the ten thousand things. There are the ten thousand things and then there are men and women. There are men and women and then there are husbands and wives. There are husbands and wives and then there are fathers and sons. There are fathers and sons and then there are rulers and ministers." The "heavenly and earthly" here is one kind of *yinyang* expression from which are born the ten thousand things, men and women, husbands and wives, fathers and sons, and rulers and ministers.

The relationship between the sexes will certainly be focused on with an *yinyang* perspective on the world and human lives,[16] however, it will not satisfy this relation among animals because just as the above indicates, they have yet to fully embody the complementary and opposite structure of *yinyang*. Therefore, human men and women cannot stop at the male–female relation of the most advanced mammals, this only expresses sexual differences where the male controls or abandons the female. Instead, it must combine complementary and opposite husbands and wives in a community and work together to raise children in order to truly realize fathers or fatherhood. A key here is that in the mutual interdependence and inter-constitution of *yinyang*, one side cannot be higher than and oppress the other, as is expressed in Pythagoras's table of opposites.[17] Viewing the relationship between husbands and wives from an *yinyang* perspective, then, neither side of the relationship will be favored more than the other because that would betray the mutual complementary of the *yinyang* opposites and create a solitary *yin* and solitary *yang*. Neither is it a strict monogamous system because that would betray the "generation upon generation" (*shengsheng* 生生) of the mutual interaction between *yin* and *yang* and the resulting characteristic of constant change along the flow of time. Moreover, the interdependence of *yinyang* does not equal the equality of *yin* and *yang*. According to the Confucians, due to the essentials of *yinyang* being "occurrence" ("The great virtue of the heavenly and earthly is to generate" *Yijing* "Xicixia" 易經 • 繫辭下). *Yinyang* can also be explained in different ways—such as thinking that *yang* represents generation and *yin* represents maintenance, or that *yin* is like birth in the mother and *yang* is like evoking and manifesting—therefore, there was a tendency to elevate *yang* over *yin* in the post-Han dynasty Confucians, but Daoism, ever since Laozi, had a tendency to elevate *yin* over *yang*. Both of these accepted the basic structure of the complementary opposites of *yinyang* and left sufficient space for the other. In this way they were very much unlike Greek thought that, as a rule, praises the male and denigrates the female or respected the father and oppressed the mother. Neither did they resemble Christianity's equality in the face of God that loses the characteristic modes of husbands and wives and fathers and mothers. In Confucian culture, differences between men and women are functional or play certain roles. The men manage affairs outside the home, and the women manage affairs inside the home. Each has that which they manage, and they are complementary opposites. If the man or husband does good in the world, the women or wife in the home will also be praised. Confucius edited the *Book of Poetry* (*Shijing* 詩經) that begins with the ode titled *Guanju* that praises the love between King Wen of the Zhou and his concubine Taisi (according to Zhu Xi's 朱熹 commentary in his *Shijizhuan* 詩集傳). Therefore, the *Zhonyong* 中庸 says: "The way of the ruler has its beginnings in husbands and wives, in reaching its utmost extent, observe the heavenly and earthly." If there is no transformation of the heavenly and earthly and *yin* and *yang* into men and women, especially if there is no transformation of men and women into husbands and wives, then there would be nowhere for rulers to begin. Therefore, this way of the ruler that begins from husbands and wives, when it is fully developed, necessarily opens up human nature (benevolence or *ren* 仁) and communicates with the heavenly and earthly.

The Way of Filial Reverence is an extension of *yinyang* to an embodiment of intergenerational time. If a family of two generations or one of many generations is not one of individual relations but is instead one of relations of complementary *yinyang* opposites, then the generation of the parents and that of the children will not be primarily of physical time. Instead, it will be directly embodied in phenomenological time by the parents and children. In this way, it is not that the past "will not come again" or that the future has "yet to come," but that both interdependently and complementarily produce the affectionate life of the present, pulling the distant past and ancestors into the not-yet-formed future of the descendants. Regarding this, "the family is the origin of human time" (Levinas, *Totality and Infinite*, 306).[18] In this way, children and the future and parents and the past are an interwoven and complementary original relationship that gives rise to human meaning, and as children grow up, they will not weaken their relationship with their parents in the way that Western philosophers such as Kant have said causing it to degenerate into a contractual relationship and through this devolve towards an animal relationship without a life-long recognition of relatives. Instead, it causes this *yinyang* relation of "familial affection" (*qinqin* 親親) to ultimately spiral in on itself. Therefore, when one's parents are old, children will care for their parents in the same way their parents cared for them when they were young, returning to care for their weakening parents, realizing the intergenerational balance between rightness and kindness within affection of the *yinyang* relation, as well as the original justice contained therein. The *Zhongyong* quotes Confucius's words: "The Way is not far from people. The *Poetry* say: 'Using an axe to chop wood for axe handles, the model is not far.' Holding an axe handle while chopping wood for an axe-handle, if you squint, then it appears far off. Thus, the gentleman uses people to govern people." The Way of Filial Reverence is this affectionate version of "using the way of humans to govern humans themselves" (Zhu Xi's comment to the above quote).

From this it can be seen that in comparison to Western fatherhood, no matter if it is that of Greece, Rome, or Christianity, the fatherhood of ancient China or Confucianism, due to the construction and protection of *yinyang* is fundamentally richer, more balanced and more capable of transformation and thinking of others regardless if it is the relationship between husbands and wives or fathers and son. With this kind of benevolent and right fatherhood formed through fatherly kindness and child filiality, the relationship between husbands and wives in China is not one of just command and subservience. Neither can it imagine the Greek denial of the mother's function regarding the children. Therefore, the mother has her own space of existence and ultimate life meaning in managing affairs within the household (the necessity of this "managing affairs of the household" during contemporary times is another problem we will not discuss here). The father–son relationship is non-subjectively, temporally, and familially formed through the intergenerational switching of places. Therefore, Chinese culture based on this kind of parenthood and Way of Filial Reverence is the most enduring and flexible among ancient civilizations and is able to expand beyond being conquered by other ethnicities. When the state is destroyed the family is not and neither is the civilization destroyed because the fatherhood that guides this civilization has the capability to change with the times. This is something that Western fatherhood lacks. However, it is not the universalized divine fatherhood that transcends the family of Christianity, either. For example, Kang Xi 康熙 (r. 1661–1722) represents the authority of the Manchurians who conquered the Chinese, yet they did not or were not able to change Chinese culture with their shamanism. Conversely, from the way they thought to the way they lived, they thoroughly became Confucian and willing to be changed and formed by Confucian fatherhood because they saw a family, political, and civilized life that was more harmonious and better fit human nature.

How Would Confucians View Matriarchal Families?

Confucianism maintains a view on the family as having an *yinyang* and temporal nature. It not only adjusts the husband–wife and parent–child relationships within the family, but also softens the relationship between patriarchies and matriarchies. This is also the *yinyang* relationship that they see as the structure of the family. Therefore, the matriarchy and the patriarchy in the Confucian perspective is very different from the rigid separation of the Western concept of the family (this leads to a strict theory on historical stages and a theory on a remnant matriarchy). With the premise that it acknowledges that both sides have important differences, it searches for a new relationship that is co-existential and complementary. The above discussion has shown that the matriarchy and patriarchy do not represent backwardness and progressiveness, there are no absolute hierarchical values. Instead, different social groups make their own choices based on the characteristics of their environment and bodily needs. Therefore, there is no *a priori* reason for the Confucians to exclude a matriarchal family.

The differences in the two sides are clear, manifested in the following ways: (1) whether or not the mainline of the family follows the father or the mother; (2) whether it is the biological father or an uncle who is the main male figure (i.e., the male who participates primarily in the raising of the children is the "father"); (3) the position of marriage—does marriage precede the birth of a child or follow afterward? Is it a tight bond or a loose one? Is it forcibly exclusive of others or is choice involved?; (4) the position of the in-laws—is it clear and important or ambiguous and unimportant? Are they reliable in times of need?; (5) simply speaking, are there any "outsiders" in the family, particularly "adults of a different sex who came from somewhere else"? Does "sex" or do "physiological and social genders" enter into the family?

The similarities between both sides are (1) both cherish the family and kin relations; (2) both have incest taboos; (3) both carefully raise children; (4) both respect, care for, and pay last respects to parents or other family elders as well as perform rituals for their ancestors; (5) both have adult men and adult women, but their relationship has an "inner/outer" distinction; (6) both self-consciously take up and carry on family traditions (*Yanjiu*, 44).

According to our view on the "family"—that is, "The family is constituted through the life-long mutual recognition of parents and children, brothers and sisters, incest taboos, and the existential source of the extension of generations"—patriarchies and matriarchies are both authentic families. The root of Confucianism is the family, filiality and deference, and benevolence: "Filiality to one's parents and deference to one's brothers, these are the roots of benevolence!" (*Analects* 1:2). "Be affectionate to your relatives and then benevolent to the people. Be benevolent to the people and then love all things" (*Mengzi*, 7A). Matriarchal families have affection for relatives and matriarchal societies have benevolence for the people (explained here as the atmosphere of love and mutual assistance between members of society) and love for all things (*Guodu*, 12), therefore, it also satisfies them. Thus, even if there are big differences in the way the "father" is embodied in matriarchal societies and the patriarchal clan and family of Confucianism, however, these differences are weak in comparison to the differences between patriarchies and matriarchies found in the West. A change in their interdependent survival and even their transition—this can be seen in the history of the Mosuo people (such as the experiences during and after the Cultural Revolution) is also possible. And these differences do not betray core Confucian characteristics, that is, the ultimate principles mentioned above of being affectionate to one's relatives, filiality and deference, being benevolent to the people, and loving all things.

Therefore, in a Confucian social group, there is no need to exclude matriarchal families. Patriarchies and matriarchies can be allowed to co-exist and to be chosen by contemporary people in their local areas as long as it respects the fundamentals of Confucianism. As for "ritual" adjustments, they should be achievable through hard work and long-term mutual adaptations. Historically, Confucius once asked Laozi about ritual (*Shiji* "Kongzi Shijia" 史記・孔子世家), there has always been a harmonious relationship of "mutual complementary opposites" between Confucianism and Daoism. Therefore, the Confucians who relatively emphasized "*yang*" and the Daoists who relatively emphasized "*yin*" not only peacefully interacted with each other, moreover, they drew on each other to communally create a bidimensional spirit of Chinese civilization and cultural ecology that is more abundant and livelier than a unidimensional one would be. They also created the requirement for the entry of Buddhism.

This kind of tolerance regarding the family system has these kinds of advantages: (1) the Confucian community is better able to adapt and survive. Such as when internal stability and self-sufficiency is needed, it can obtain the support of the matriarchal family (this obviously does not imply that all families must become matriarchal); and when external alliances with in-law relations and more complex societies are made, the patriarchal tradition can show its power. (2) It causes members of society to have a great consciousness of the "other," thereby increasing peace and tolerance. (3) It alters the *prejudices* against Confucianism of the external world, such as "female discrimination," "lack of freedom in the young," "eventual loss of population control," and "intellectual autocracy." (4) It embodies the principle of *yinyang* within the system.

We are situated within a new tide of high technology that is greatly transforming of human lifestyles, especially the forms of the family. This tide of new technology has silently initiated a quest to alter and improve humanity itself—including physiology, psychology, child-rearing, intelligence, and ethics. Looking from this future-oriented perspective, the human family, as a totality, is situated in a raging storm. It is in danger of having its place as the main lifestyle of humanity being replaced by technology, capitalism, and ideologies. Therefore, theories that resist this kind of a "theory of a technological *ubermensch*," such as theories that wish to restore the intellectual power of Confucianism, must expend energy in protecting and adjusting the structure of their own families that they rely on for existence and that of modern humanity. They must also abandon the old policy of "excluding Buddhism and Daoism," open their eyes, and absorb every element that can be useful to the family (diversity in forms of the family is one expression of its energy). The matriarchal family has its own good existential characteristic and internal superiority, therefore its reasonable, legal, and plural position should be accepted and even cherished by the Confucians.

Chapter 11

Family Relations and the Way of Filial Reverence in *Harry Potter*

The story in *Harry Potter* told by J.K. Rowling in a series of seven books was a great success in both its literary and cinema formats.[1] However, it was a cause for controversy in the Western worlds of religion and education.[2] Critics examining this story in search of the reason for its success had different answers. But very little research has been done in exploring its success through the perspective of the parent–child relationship of the protagonist, Harry Potter, especially his filial behavior. This chapter will show that this is a research path that can provide a deeper understanding. The great majority of Western literary successes do not take the parent–child relation as their foundation in the way that *Harry Potter* does. The literary works that do, such as Shakespeare's *Hamlet*, more often than not do not make its positive meaning a prominent feature. Yet I think that the praise expressed by *Harry Potter* for the parent–child relationship and the way of filial reverence is the key to the intercultural success of this series of books.

I will begin this chapter by reviewing the critiques of these books in the Western world in order to find the threads of a few problems. Then I will prove this chapter's main thesis: the motive power of the plot of this series of books comes from its treatment of the parent–child relationship and its filial consciousness, and that its artistic success and philosophical significance are thereto related. Therefore, other than directly displaying the position of this relation and consciousness within these books, I will also probe their presuppositions, that is, a consciousness of existential time or intergenerational time. This kind of consciousness is expressed through the differing views that Harry Potter and Voldemort have regarding the relation between death and immortality. Related analysis shows that this kind of consciousness is an important expression of human nature. Thus, "Harry Potter" and "Voldemort" respectively represent an affirmation and a negation as well as a protection and destruction of this kind of relationship. The moral teaching contained in this story subtlety criticizes the modern orientation to seek immortality through high technology.

The Reason for the Success of *Harry Potter* and Its Intellectual Tendencies

Attempts to Explain the Success of *Harry Potter* and Their Insufficiencies

Much discussion has taken place on *Harry Potter* in the critical and even the academic worlds of the Western world. Christine Schoefer represents a common explanation for the unusual success of this book. According to Schoefer, *Harry Potter*'s charm comes from the "glittering mystery and nail-biting suspense, compelling language and colorful imagery, magical feats juxtaposed with real-life concerns" (*Reading Harry Potter*, x–xi).[3] The phrase "real-life concerns" can be understood to mean a projection of modern life problems. For example, in book three of *Harry Potter*, the "boggart" that each of Professor Lupin's students face appears in the form of that which they feared the most. This expresses that which children fear the most in their everyday lives. Some explanations take issue with *Harry Potter*'s magic (the world of magic and the school of magic) and the fantastical realm created through the story of the ascendence of an orphan child to a world hero in addition to the beasts from Greek legend such as centaurs, unicorns, dragons, phoenixes, and others (*Reading Harry Potter*, 3). Other than this, the "childish nature"—it allows readers to return to childhood full of a happy imagination or to win back an interest in life from the rigors of adulthood—of the story as well as its "theory of justice" have also been seen as points of attraction.

Although these factors contributed to these books' success, they are not unique at all. For example, many critics have noted the relation of *Harry Potter* to C.S. Lewis's *Chronicles of Narnia* and J.R.R. Tolkien's *The Lord of the Rings*. Other than the element of the "orphan child," all of the other reasons for the success of *Harry Potter* can also be found in these two series. Actually, it is very possible that Rowling was heavily influenced by the fantasy novels of her predecessors Lewis and Tolkien. Obviously, these reasons cannot explain why *Harry Potter* has achieved its unique degree of success.

If we truly cannot see where *Harry Potter* is special, we will be unable to see its place within the literary world. For example, K.M. Smith thinks *Harry Potter* belongs to the tradition of "public education schools" because it uses a common model, and J. Zipes also argues that because of *Harry Potter*'s "repetition" Rowling should be "lump[ed] in with the 'predictable happy-end school' of fairy tale writers" (*Reading Harry Potter*, xviii).

The Religious Significance of *Harry Potter*: Rowling's Explanation and Its Limitations

In his book review in the *New York Times*, Michael Winerip says, "Though all this hocus-pocus is delightful, the magic in the book is not the real magic of the book."[4] Even more important than the magic is its vivid depiction of its characters because they become unforgettable three-dimensional beings.[5] This opinion is insightful but lacks detail. Certainly, this book expresses the "magic" of a "magical world," but if that is all there is, then after the initial freshness readers will quickly slip into the fantastical magic of "strange forces and chaotic spirits." It will be just like reading some trailing steps of the Chinese novel *Fengshen Yanyi* 封神演義 ("Investiture of the Gods"). Thus the key to the success of *Harry Potter* is how it vividly and realistically portrayed its characters.

These books certainly have some connections and structures that project into the real world. Other than the "boggart" mentioned above, its projections in terms of technology, institutions, government, morality, and even religion all drew the attention of reviewers. For example, its rather religious projections drew the opposition of some religious people. Prior to becoming Pope Benedict XVI, Cardinal Joseph Ratzinger had also criticized the books.[6] And Joseph Chambers wrote: "Without question, I believe the *Harry Potter* series is a creation of hell helping prepare the younger generation to welcome the Biblical prophecies of demons and devils led by Lucifer himself" (*Critical Perspectives*, 14).[7] Contrary to this, some Christians avidly supported *Harry Potter*. For example, in *Looking for God in Harry Potter* (2006), John Granger maintains that the key to understanding the book is understanding its internal harmony with the story of Christianity (*Critical Perspectives*, 16). And according to Shawn Adler's report, after all seven books in the series were published, Rowling herself said at a news conference that she always saw the series as based in Christian themes such as its view on life after death and the power of love to overcome death. The reason she did not make this connection clear was because she wanted to prevent readers from predicting how the narrative would unfold (*Critical Perspectives*, 16).[8] Although the thoughts and statements of the author are important, their authority are not as powerful as the work itself where there is any kind of separation between the two. That Rowling wanted to conceal the connection with Christianity until the final book was published is revealing in itself. She intuitively and accurately perceived that "Christian themes" would harm the artistic charm of her books. This shows that the inner life or meaning structure of this novel did not allow for this kind of evident connection as it was being told. Even if after the final book was published and these themes only appear on two tombstones where they were dimly projected and even satirically so (more on this below).

An Explanation of the Parent–Child Relation: Contract Theory and Psychological Analysis

Now, do the books themselves directly display the vividness and liveliness of their characters? Of course. Moreover, even though this display has a Western religious significance, it is nevertheless religiously or ethically neutral. It passionately and completely displays a parent–children relationship and a filial consciousness, which will be argued for below. There are places of comparison with Confucian theories on human nature and life. And that this display was to a certain degree unconscious or unforced just goes to show how fundamental this relationship and consciousness are and how they are desired by human nature and art so much so that an author with Christian tendencies, in order to increase the attractiveness of her book, could only suppress her religiosity while at the same time appealing to it.

At present, it can be seen that in most reviews of *Harry Potter* only a few involve Harry's relationship with his parents, his family situation, and even the question of filiality. As far as I am concerned, this is a serious lack. Of those who refer to the parent–child relationship, there are a few who appeal to family contract theory. For example, John Kornfeld and Laurie Prothro maintain that Rowling's novel views the ultimate principle of the family as a kind of covenant more powerful than the law. That is to say, members of a family must help and support each other unconditionally. Whoever violates this duty will no longer share in the benefits of the family. The Dursleys did not follow this covenant, and thus in Harry Potter's mind, they were not family. Therefore, Harry had to search for family elsewhere (*Critical Perspectives*, 128). Voldemort's father abandoned his mother, who was pregnant at the time, and never cared for his son. This led Tom Riddle—young Voldemort—to kill his father and grandfather. Afterward, he found a new family among his Death Eaters (128).

Another essay that discusses the parent–child relationship in *Harry Potter* utilizes a psychoanalytical theory—either Freud's or Jung's—in child developmental psychology. For example, Alice Mills thinks that, according to Jung's theory that the subconsciousness possesses a complementary capacity to balance consciousness, Voldemort is the evil wizard who killed Harry Potter's parents. For the subconsciousness of the child, he is the "dark double of Harry's father": "The struggle between Harry and Voldemort can thus be interpreted as an Oedipal power struggle between the son, ignorant of the whole truth about his past, and the monstrous father-figure, out to destroy his son before his son kills him" (*Reading Harry Potter*, 4).

Ronnie Carmeli, in his *Four Modes of Fatherhood: Paternal Contributors to Harry Potter's Psychological Development*, uses Freud's "Oedipus complex" to understand the psychological development of Harry Potter. He thinks there are four figures who stand in for Harry's deceased father and help him overcome mental depression and other problems. They complete the process of internalizing fatherhood and of leaving behind the Oedipal complex.[9] These four are Remus John Lupin, Sirius Orion Black (godfather), Albus Dumbledore, and Severus Snape. The appeal of this essay is that it acknowledges the important function of the role of the father in Harry's development. However, it has a similar problem as the one above. It relies too much on psychological analysis and always tries to divide Harry's love for his mother and father, thus making the psychological complex overly convoluted. It even sees Voldemort as a "father figure." This is to belittle the identity of the "father," and neither does it accord with the "subconscious" produced when reading *Harry Potter*. Moreover, Carmeli fails to notice that the role of Harry's father cannot be fully replaced by any person or group.

The Parent–Child Relationship in *Harry Potter*

The Original Existentiality of Blood Relations

How should we treat the parent–child relationship in *Harry Potter*? It is not simply a contractual relationship; neither is it limited to Harry's psychological development. It must be much more fundamental. Simply speaking, it is not the Christian theme of "love" that pervades the plot in these books from beginning to end. Instead, it is the love of the parent–child relationship that serves as the hidden driving force of the plot. This is expressed in all kinds of ways and is evident at important moments.

The name of the first chapter of the first book is "The Boy Who Lived" (the Chinese title is "The Boy who Lived through Great Difficulty"). Although the title clearly means that Harry Potter survived the magical attack of the evil Voldemort, the fact that he survived still has to do with his parents, James and Lily Potter. His parents gave birth to him so he could live in this world; his mother protected him by casting an ancient spell to protect him from Voldemort's magic so that a child of only one year of age, facing the "Avada Kedavra" spell of Voldemort, could survive, and to cause this spell to turn itself on its spellcaster. The whole book begins with the story of survival in the face of death. Moreover, the parents whose corporeal body is no more still protected him and completed him through nonobjectified and indirect methods. Other than the instances discussed below, there is a fact touched upon at the beginning of each book and at the ends of most chapters: Harry Potter has to live with his aunt and uncle, who do not love him.

Some critics treat this fact with a completely negative attitude, even to the point that they see it as the distortion of Harry's psychology to where he wants to get even with Voldemort—it was he who killed Harry's parents, which led him to live with his despicable relatives. Voldemort is thus seen as a "more powerful fantasy version of Mr. Dursley" (*Critical Perspectives*, 5). This is a confusion in principles that comes from a fundamental ignorance of the parent–child relationship in *Harry Potter*.

An important dialogue occurs in chapter 37 of book 5 (*Order of the Phoenix*) in the *Harry Potter* series. The explanation finally provided for this fact comes from he who has the most right to speak on it, Albus Dumbledore—the principal of the school of magic and, in a certain sense, Harry's spiritual teacher. Dumbledore first describes that after the death of Harry's parents, thinking of an uncertain future where Voldemort still threatened Harry Potter, and of his henchmen who might look for revenge, at the same time recognized that of all the ways in which he could protect Harry Potter, only one would be effective against the powerful magic of Voldemort:

> "But I knew, too, where Voldemort was weak. And so I made my decision. You would be protected by an ancient magic of which he knows, which he despises, and which he has always, therefore, underestimated—to his cost. I am speaking, of course, of the fact that your mother died to save you. She gave you a lingering protection he never expected, a protection that flows in your veins to this day. I put my trust, therefore, in your mother's blood. I delivered you to her sister, her only remaining relative."
>
> "She doesn't love me," said Harry at once. "She doesn't give a damn—"
>
> "But she took you," Dumbledore cut across him. "She may have taken you grudgingly, furiously, unwillingly, bitterly, yet still she took you, and in doing so, she sealed the charm I placed upon you. Your mother's sacrifice made the bond of blood the strongest shield I could give you." (book 5, ch. 37)[10]

This is this book's ultimate protection; to use philosophical terminology, it is its "existential" protection. It relies entirely on the kin relationship activated through the love between parents and children. This is something that requires the entire series to digest and display. It transcends the death of the individual bodies (objects) as well as the individual psychologies (subjects). Yet it does not lose its lively corporeal bloodline. "He [Voldemort] shed her blood, but it lives on in you and her sister. Her blood became your refuge. You need return there only once a year, but as long as you can still call it home, whilst you are there he cannot hurt you" (book 5, ch. 37).

Precisely due to this ultimate cause, the first line of the whole series reads, "Mr. and Mrs. Dursley, of number four, Privet Drive, were proud to say that they were perfectly normal, thank you very much" (book 1, ch. 1). It must be recognized that while "Mr. and Mrs. Dursely" are the most boring people in the series, they are the first to appear because they hint at Harry's lifeline: and *every chapter* that discusses Harry Potter does so by beginning with the "Dursleys." This formal repetition is necessary in the same way repetition is necessary in poems and music because it hints at the continuation of the bloodline contract.

Moreover, this book constantly expresses how poorly the Dursleys treat Harry Potter—how they discriminate against him, are stingy toward him, even how they abuse him, how stupid and uninteresting they are, and how against the world of magic they are. This is because the more unthinkable and unlikable this family is, the more it is able to lay out and reduce the family to its most important basis: Harry Potter can receive ultimate protection and some kind of cultivation only within this family. After all, it is within this family that the one-year-old Harry, in urgent need of someone to care for him, grew to the age of eleven. And by the time he appeared at the Hogwarts School of Witchcraft and Wizardry, he was "alive and healthy" (book 5, ch. 37). Although he lived through ten dark and difficult years, he had not been spoiled rotten (obviously), and neither was he lacking in personality, intelligence, physicality, or character. Conversely, he had accumulated much innate and acquired capacities, which allowed him to appear so brilliantly throughout the seven books in the series. We can say that, for Harry Potter, the Dursleys were bad (*yin*) and that Hogwarts was good (*yang*). But where is there a good without some bad? Therefore, after reaching eleven, Harry Potter had to return to the "dark and difficult" home of the Dursley's every summer. Yet, while we can accept the unfair treatment of Harry Potter by the Dursleys, we cannot accept the humiliation of our own parents (such as that expressed by aunts and uncles) because that threatens the foundation of this relationship.

Therefore, that the Dursleys were the worst reveals that the family is existentially prior to any kind of subjective or objective quality. The family is so unavoidable and penetrates the depths of the origins of life so thoroughly that no matter what kind of distortions or alterations it undergoes, as long as blood relations still exist, so does the family. This is the important information that *Harry Potter* gives us in our era of the declining family. It is a gospel; it is what all of its readers will feel even if they do so unconsciously or peripherally. All love and hate for this book (such as the public resistance of some churches) has nothing to do with its "magic" but comes from what it has to say on the family.

Why Did Harry Potter Not Become a Second Voldemort?

There are many important links and similarities between Harry Potter and Voldemort that cause him to be, at least latently, very dangerous. First, there is a direct link in terms of their bodies and even their consciousness. This is because when Voldemort first tried to kill him, he was counterattacked and harmed by his own magic. Thereupon, a small piece of Voldemort was knocked off and entered Harry (book 2, ch. 18). This is why Harry is able to speak the language of snakes, just like Voldemort. There is also a mental connection between Harry and Voldemort. This is developed in book five to such a strong degree that Voldemort could temporarily control Harry's mind, causing him to desire attacking Dumbledore. At the time when the "wand chooses the wizard," the wand that Harry received was the twin of Voldemort's wand. This led the wand maker Ollivander to exclaim "Curious!" and then predicted that Harry would "do great things" (book 1, ch. 5). Moreover, there are some very important similarities in character between Harry and Voldemort: determination, creativity, and even their complete defiance of regulations, such as those of the school of magic. This is why the Sorting Hat originally sent Harry to the House of Slytherin, the house established by Voldemort's ancestors. This is all even more clear in the final book in the series: Harry Potter is actually one of the Horcruxes that ensures Voldemort's immortality. This is to say that Voldemort's death and Harry Potter's death are closely connected. Even Dumbledore saw this relationship with concern, alarm, and even fear.

Now, why did Harry Potter not become a second Voldemort or follow in his footsteps? Why was he the complete opposite of Voldemort? We can say that Harry was good and that Voldemort was evil, but we should say that Harry dared to and was willing to die while Voldemort feared death and that in his pursuit of immortality brought about his own death. Their philosophical, ethical, and even religious significances are the topics of the following section. However, what created this fundamental difference in their existential ways of being? There are many possible answers, but the most important one is to be found within the parent–child relationship because it is this that is so fundamental and that can shape who a person is.

In terms of the parent–child relationship, Harry Potter and Tom Riddle (Voldemort) are also similar: they are both orphans in the general sense. However, they are dissimilar in that Harry's parents died in his very first year alive. This is not insignificant. Another difference is that Harry Potter never lived in an orphanage; instead, he lived in his aunt's house. And even though the way his aunt treated him was possibly worse than living in an orphanage, as noted above, this fact is also not insignificant. As far as the attitudes of Harry and Tom toward their own relationship with their parents goes, we can say they are vastly different. Harry's is the "good in the bad" (*yang* in the *yin*), while Tom's is the "bad in the bad" (*yin* in the *yin*). Even though he still did not know the truth about his parents by the age of eleven, his love, longing, imagination, and acceptance of them blazed like an unstoppable fire. There is already a clear expression of this in book one. He saw in the Mirror of Esired ("desire") his "deepest, most desperate desire." For Harry, this was his parents and other members of his family. Rowling's depiction of Harry's enchantment in front of the mirror is vivid and moving. He saw that his mother "was crying; smiling, but crying at the same time . . . He had a powerful kind of ache inside him, half joy, half terrible sadness. How long he stood there, he didn't know" (book 1, ch. 12). And in the last book of the series, when Harry is on his way to die, at the moment of the greatest despair and when he used the resurrection stone, those whom he asks to walk with him toward death are his parents and their friends. In this moment of passionate, enchanting, yet bitter love, we can finally see sparkling, upstanding, and emotional Harry Potter grow up.

But Voldemort, although he resembled his father, had nothing but coldness, revulsion, and harshness for their relationship. He thought little of his deceased mother and took revenge on his father and grandparents by killing them. He even laid the blame for this crime on his uncle and let him die in the prison of Azkaban. His inhumanity began in his lack of familial affection. If he had a mother's love or at least felt loved, Tom Riddle would never have become Voldemort. However, it is not the case that there was some kind of family contract that would perceive Voldemort's father abandoning him as a breach of contract. It is just that Tom Riddle's father had already lost the identity of father (there are other reasons), and therefore Voldemort murdering him was not an instance of patricide. Actually, this kind of patricide did the greatest harm to Tom Riddle because this is when his spirit began to split in two.

Therefore, although it was entirely correct for Dumbledore to tell Harry that "it was [his] heart that saved [him]" (book 5, ch. 37), it is even more important to know that this heart was saved through the love between parent and child—compassion and filiality. Regarding this, we find another reason for placing Harry in the care of his aunt: "protection." This protection should be understood in terms of both the body and time. The "survival" in the "the boy who survived" becomes even more profound when understood this way. Dumbledore always told Harry that Voldemort was powerful because he did not understand love, and he thus believed that love was his greatest weakness. Moreover, love was also Harry's greatest advantage. This explanation can be hard to understand when applied to Harry Potter. For a great deal of other people, it is either pedantic or unfathomable. However, Dumbledore was right in the end. When you have finished reading all seven books in the series and have reflected on the story, perhaps you will come to realize where Dumbledore was right. Nonetheless, it must be pointed out that the reason he was correct was not because this "love" was a universal abstract or a divine love, nor was it the love among friends, teachers and students, or couples; instead, it could only be the love between parents and children of the same bloodline. Without the explanation in book five, chapter 37, Dumbledore would probably have been misunderstood by most readers. Such misunderstandings will also occur when people do not want to find the key for understanding the entire series.

Therefore, no matter if it is Harry Potter or Voldemort, their intercommunication and shared life and death nevertheless relied on that fiery and impervious love that turned the demonic into the divine. Neither Quirrell nor Voldemort could stand the enduring strength of Harry's body and mind, thus, "In the end, it mattered not that [he] could not close [his] mind [to Voldemort]" (book 5, ch. 37).[11] The brilliance of this novel lies in the fact that it uses the power of love in every detail to depict every situation as lifelike and believable as possible. Moreover, is it possible that Harry's super-intuition has nothing to do with his passionate, fearful, and troubled relationship with his parents and other family members? Intuition originates in a spontaneous temporal sense, and the broken yet continuous bloodline represented by the parent–child relationship is best suited to activating and cultivating this sense.

The Author's Methods for Deepening and Activating the Love and Consciousness between Parent and Child

This series of books used as many methods as possible to activate and preserve the consciousness of the parent–child relationship. Other than the many ways mentioned above in which the "boy" was able to survive, two more ways can be generally divided into positive and negative categories.

There are many methods that positively strengthen the significance of familial emotions. First, the basic existential layout of this series of books is molded through family traditions broadly defined. In terms of the plot, it mainly involves the families of the Potters, the Weasleys, the Malfoys, and the Marvolos. In terms of Hogwarts, there are four large houses that take the names of each of their four great founders, among which the houses of Gryffindor and Slytherin are especially important. In this world of magic, the relationships between people all begin with family traditions broadly defined and are formed through individual personality. This is very similar to historical mode of existence in human history up to the present today. There are seven books with a total of 198 chapters, including an epilogue. The first chapter, as mentioned earlier, begins with "the boy who survived," and the epilogue ends with a look into the future of the intergenerational transmission of the three great families. In summary, the existential structure of this "world of magic" is a premodern and even postmodern world. None of the lives and glory of the people, their transmission of technical arts, or value judgments are modern or universal. They all have a tendency toward familial transmission. Among which, the magic arts conjure up a traditional art and an anticipation for the future. The mainstream of Western religion excludes it, and those who praise modernity ignore it. However, those who respect living traditions enjoy it because their distance from modernity is transformed by the novel into a "fissure" (as Heidegger would say) that inspires beauty and interest.

Second, this series often brings up all kinds of markers and qualities that indicate similarity between the families in order to maintain the continuity of the familial bloodline in the reader's perspective. The lightning scar on Harry's forehead is an acquired mark, but other than indicating the failed attempt on his life, it also indicates the function of his mother's love in protecting him. The shape and color of Harry's eyes are the same as his mother's, so whenever this is brought up it is a reminder that strengthens his bloodline. Harry's hair, the way he plays Quidditch, and his sense of adventure are all similar to his father. This association is also repeatedly mentioned be it through the Mirror of Esired, his classmates' (such as Hermione's) discovery, or the cold sarcasm of Professor Snape. Again, Harry's parents never left life at the school. Whether it was the scrying bowl and his parents' friends and enemies,

Family Relations and the Way of Filial Reverence | 161

every detail of their personality and history was vividly displayed in Harry's mind and the space of the reader. When Hagrid met the eleven-year-old Harry Potter, he had a strong air that revived a memory that "caused Harry to return to his parents and their world." On a lonely island with rain and thunder, right before the day Harry was about to celebrate his birthday, this giant brought a warm fire, tasty sausages, and opened a letter that would start his new life, especially an entirely new image of Harry's parents and a fresh meaning for Harry's life. Hagrid also gave Harry his first birthday cake, which indicated the great significance of his birthday that year. Moreover, the appearance of Lupin, Sirius, Pettigrew, and the Marauder's Map all brought Harry's father alive in their battle for life and death. The honest feelings between Sirius Black, Harry's godfather, represented a reunion of sorts between Harry and his father. The death of his godfather in book five made Harry lose control to the point that he exploded in anger in Dumbledore's office. This led to their very important conversation. And the grief and emptiness that Harry felt then were even greater than when Dumbledore died.

Third, his parents and godfather all showed up at key times to save him, inspire him, comfort him, and accompany him. In the third and fifth books, his godfather saved him with no concern for his own safety; in book four, chapter 34, his parents' ethereal bodies appeared to help him against Voldemort's death magic; in book seven, chapter 34, his parents, godfather, and their friends all sacrificed themselves for him.

In addition, there are also instances of where second-level, third-level, and fourth-level family relations are displayed. For example, Ron's relationship with his family affected Harry, the relationships between Neville Longbottom and his family, the influence of Hermione's "mud-blood-loving" family in the world of magic, the difficulties Hagrid faced due to his mixed blood background, and the new families formed among the classmates at Hogwarts.

As for the negative methods, Voldemort's affectionless life was already mentioned above, and the role of Professor Snape is also interesting. His open derision and general ill-will toward Harry makes Harry and the reader continually rekindle their family consciousness until the very end when it is revealed that it was his unending love for Harry's mother Lily that made him secretly protect Harry. Dumbledore also used this to place an important figure at Voldemort's side. In the end, Harry used Snape's name for his second child, thereby expressing the fact that his line will be continued through that of the Potters. Draco's family has the role of the antagonists, but they are not in as much decline as the Marvolos because Draco's mother still lives. It was thus not possible for Draco to be as cruel as Voldemort when he faced off against the already helpless Dumbledore. All of this separated the Malfoys from Voldemort, so that even though they were the losers, their family line continued on. Of these examples of the primacy of the family, none is greater than the defense of the positive image of the family. Do not the family tragedies of Dumbledore and Crouch also have a value for the defense of the family?

Let me conclude what was said above about *Harry Potter* by using a few parallelisms: dead families cause people to lose themselves; unfortunate families cause people to be unfortunate or suffer harm; living families allow people to keep living on; families full of love allow people to be saved and to have glory; and the loving family of life and death causes people to ascend, to return to liveliness and magnificence.

Why Is Harry a Great Filial Son?

Carrying Out the Will of One's Parents

It is possible that some people will think it strange and unclear when we say that Harry Potter was a filial son. Can an English wizard, an orphan, be said to be a filial son?

Let's first talk about "filiality" (*xiao* 孝). Just as the Chinese character expresses, filiality is the respect, support, and care of the children's generation for the generation of their parents. This is the unique capacity and essential quality of modern humans. There is only a 1 percent difference between humans and chimpanzees, but the latter are not capable of being filial. Chinese Confucian culture can be said to be a culture of filiality in a broad sense. And the Confucians have excavated the profound meaning of filiality. According to a quotation of Confucius in the *Liji—Zhongyong* 禮記・中庸, "As for filial reverence, it is carrying out the will of one's parents and describing their deeds . . . Treating them in death as one would in life and treating them in poverty as one would in prosperity, this is the pinnacle of filial reverence." Obviously, as long as one's parents are still alive, filial sons and daughters must behave and think in a directly filial manner. When their parents have died, filial reverence has an equally important—if not even more important—expression. That is, sons and daughters must carry on the work of their parents and embody everything they did in life so that death does not impede their life and that poverty does not obstruct their prosperity. This is the "pinnacle of filial reverence." According to this principle, King Wu of Zhou and the Duke of Zhou were both filial sons because they carried on and realized the aspirations of their father King Wen to cultivate himself, order his family, govern the state, and bring peace to the world.

In these terms, Harry Potter is obviously a filial son. Although he was not with his parents and could not care for them and respect them, those things that his parents greatly loved and despised were those things that Harry greatly loved and despised. The unfinished work of his parents—to resist evil and to pass on the Potter lineage—were completed by Harry. More specifically, the closest friends and colleagues of Harry's parents were, under certain unavoidable circumstances, the followers and friends of Harry as well. And, in turn, Harry was just as warm-hearted and kind to those who followed him. At the highest level was Dumbledore, at the middle level were Sirius and Remus, and at the bottom level was Hagrid. Even the traitor Pettigrew, who was forced to sell out Harry's parents, considered whether he would kill James Potter if he were there. He even considered giving the knife over to his two cohorts so they could do the deed, but in the end, he took pity on them and let them go. This is a classic example of "carrying out the will of one's parents . . . serving them in death as one would in life." How filial was Harry Potter!

REVENGE (1): SIGNIFICANCE AND INSTANCES

However, there is an even more important reason why Harry Potter is a filial son. This is that he achieved revenge for his parents who were killed by evil. This point is not entirely the same as "carrying out the will." This is not something that most people think of while one's parents are still alive; there is usually not a specific "will" in this sense. Other than this, we will have different answers even if we consider that "if one's parents are still alive, then their children will not desire to get revenge for them." Some parents will not agree with their children seeking revenge out of consideration for their child's safety. However, according to a Confucian principle, this kind of revenge is unconditional and does not necessarily require the assent of one's parents.

This principle can be called the "theory of great revenge." It is expressed in a story from the *Chunqiu Gongyangzhuan* 春秋公羊傳 (Gongyang Commentary to the *Spring and Autumn Annals*). Its basic meaning is that if a father or a ruler is unjustly killed, then sons or direct male descendants can seek revenge for their father and ministers can seek revenge for their ruler. This is still the case even though they must get revenge against another ruler or someone else in power.

There are two classic examples in the *Chunqiu Gongyangzhuan*'s treatment of these affairs. These include the summer of the fourth-reign year of Duke Zhuang where Duke Xiang of Qi eliminated the state of Ji in revenge for his ninth-generation ancestor. Another well-known event happened in the winter of Duke Ding's fourth-reign year where Wu Zixu helped Wu Shi defeat the state of Chu and whipped the corpse of King Ping of Chu in revenge for his father. Duke Xiang of Qi was an evil ruler, but because the reason he gave for sending his army to eliminate the state of Ji was revenge for his ancestor, he was praised by the *Gongyangzhuan*. The commentators of the Gongyang family and the *Chunqiu* used their excessive praise of these bad people to show clearly how fundamental and immovable the "theory of great revenge" is.

This is the revenge of a lord against another lord for the murder of his ancestor. Wu Zixu's revenge was against a lord who killed his father. Is this acceptable? According to some Confucian ideas that came later, such as some opinions and theories found in the *Zuozhuan* (Zuo Commentary to the *Spring and Autumn Annals*), this is unacceptable because the sovereign represents the will of *tian* and thus an even higher principle. So even if the wrong person is killed, it is not the fault of the individual person himself. However, according to the *Gongyangzhuan* and original Confucianism, if one's father is unjustly killed by a ruler then one should seek revenge.

Wu Zixu's getting revenge for the death of his father against King Ping of Chu is recorded to have happened in the eleventh month of winter of the fourth-reign year of Duke Ding. The *Chunqiu* records: "In winter, during the eleventh month, on the *gengwu* day, Cai Hou went with Master Wu to do battle with Chu in Baiju. The state of Chu was utterly defeated." This story mentions a "Master Wu." During the Spring and Autumn period, the state of Wu was considered to be uncivilized, and therefore to refer to the ruler of Wu as "Master Wu" showed especially high praise. Thus, the *Gongyangzhuan* further explains:

Why was the lord of Wu called "master"? He is of the Yi and Di peoples yet had concern for the middle kingdoms. What did he do about his concern for the middle kingdoms? Wu Zixu's father was executed in Chu, thus he took up his bow and went to Chu, offering his services to Helu of the state of Wu . . . Since serving one's ruler is like serving one's father, how is it acceptable to get revenge for one's father in this way? If one's father is not executed justly, then a son can seek revenge.

The state of Wu was uncivilized, so its ruler should not have been referred to as "master." However, the state of Wu "had concern for the middle kingdoms," that is, had concern for the state of Cai. In addition to this, Wu Zixu's father was unjustly and cruelly killed by King Ping of Chu. This is why he went to King Helu of Wu to wait for his chance to get revenge. Finally, the state of Cai turned to Wu for assistance, and Wu Zixu's chance had arrived. However, "Since serving one's ruler is like serving one's father, how is it acceptable to get revenge for one's father in this way?" Serving one's father is no different than serving one's ruler, so how could he seek revenge for his father? The answer is that if one's "biological" father is unjustly killed, that he should not have been killed in the first place and in fact was harmed by an evil-doer, then in such a situation it is acceptable to seek revenge. Wu Zixu's revenge is a historically shocking event that left a deep scar on Chinese culture. A twentieth-century poet wrote: "Preserving the grand courage of Zixu, after three years returning to kill the King of Chu."[12]

I think that the first reason Confucianism brought up the theory of great revenge is not because they "praised shame" or for some quest for historical justice (as Jiang Qing 蔣慶 thought). Instead, it was to bring to light the parent–child relationship, especially the originary position of the way of filial reverence and to allow it to transcend all ritual regulations. Its purpose was to use a flashing blade to proclaim the ultimate value of the life of the father. Ministers seeking revenge for their rulers is derived from sons seeking revenge for their fathers. This is similar to how a minister's dedication to his ruler is a derivation of a son's filiality to his father. After the Han dynasty, this thought that saw "filiality" as more important than "dedication" was suppressed, and the Gongyang's tradition of great revenge almost disappeared entirely. And by the modern New Culture Movement, Confucianism was seen as the voice that assisted sovereigns, lacked its own value, and as being entirely corrupt. In 1993, through the excavated texts discovered at Guodian in Hebei province, people "suddenly" discovered a new aspect of original Confucianism. Among these excavated texts, one is titled "Six Virtues" (*liude* 六德), which reads: "Break ties with your ruler on behalf of your father; do not break ties with your father on behalf of your ruler. Break ties with your wife on behalf of your brothers; do not break ties with your brothers on behalf of your wife. Find fault with your friends on behalf of your ancestral clan; do not fault your ancestral clan on behalf of your friends."[13] This could not have said it any clearer: "Break ties with your ruler on behalf of your father; do not break ties with your father on behalf of your ruler." These two relationships are not equal. These three relationships all emphasize family relations, especially that between parent and child. This is the relation of most importance. Li Ling 李零 says that it is a saying "not seen in the ancients nor in those who came after" (*Guodian Chujian* 郭店楚簡, 138). Actually, it is already there in the texts mentioned above, but, wearing the colored glasses of the New Culture Movement, it is hidden from sight.

Why are these relationships not equal? Because the positions and meanings of "rulers" and "fathers" in the existential structures of people's lives are different.

> Distinctions are produced between males and females; familial affection is produced between fathers and sons; duty is produced between rulers and ministers . . . If males and females are not differentiated, then fathers and sons will not be affectionate; *if fathers and sons are not affectionate, then rulers and ministers will lack a sense of duty*. This is why the former kings, in educating the people, *began with filial reverence and fraternal deference*. The ruler, in being *one with this*, there will be nothing left behind. This is why former kings, in educating the people, did not cause them to worry for their *person* or lose their *body*. *Filial reverence is the root*. (*Guodian Chujian* 郭店楚簡, 132; my emphasis)

The most important thing in the passage remains the relationship between parent and child. Why? Because males and females or husbands and wives are differentiated (see chapter 5). They are differentiated in order for there to be affection between parents and children. And the sense of duty of rulers and ministers relies on the affection between parents and children as its source. "Filial reverence is the root." Filial reverence is the foundation of Confucianism. It is the foundation of the state and of ritual and music. Therefore, the education of the people by the former kings began in filial reverence and fraternal deference. It is the original "person" (*shen* 身)[14] and "body" (*ti* 體) of all culture; it is the profoundest successor of all interhuman values and morals.

Revenge (2): Was Harry's Killing of Voldemort Self-Defense or Revenge?

Harry's killing of Voldemort was actually getting revenge for the evil that killed his parents seventeen years earlier. According to the theory in the *Chunqiu* and Confucian notions on filiality, he is undoubtably a filial son. However, some might argue that Harry did not kill Voldemort out of revenge but in self-defense. There is some sense to this argument in light of some of the key plot points. For example, there was a prophecy interpreted by Voldemort as meaning that between him and Harry, only one of them could survive (book 5, ch. 37). Thereupon, Voldemort gave his all in trying to kill Harry. And if Harry could not kill Voldemort, he would not be able to stay alive. Therefore, his feat of killing Voldemort was first understood as self-defense and not necessarily revenge for his parents, even though he certainly saw Voldemort as his enemy and wanted revenge.

However, after carefully reading the series we will see that this interpretation is untenable. Indeed, it was clear that when Harry faced Voldemort and his various forms that if he did not fight, he would die. But according to the surrounding text, Harry was basically the first to move. If he had not thrown himself into the mix on his own, most of the situations he found himself in would not have occurred. We can see this is the case simply by examining the important plot points in the first, second, fifth, and sixth books. For example, if he (with Ron and Hermione) were not persistent in regard to the sorcerer's stone, "Nicolas Flamel," and even "Snape's scheme," then even if they made a few slight mistakes and gave it their all at the key moments, they would not have encountered Voldemort and Quirrell's attack. In other books, sometimes Ron and Hermione did not believe that Harry could "discover the enemy's situation." But Harry's sharp intuition never ceased, and whenever he

168 | Family and Filiality

had to act, no matter how dangerous or terrifying, he never hesitated in the way that Hamlet did.

Regarding whether Harry actively tried to kill Voldemort, an important conversation between Harry and Dumbledore in the second half of chapter 24 in the sixth book provides a determinative answer. Dumbledore, in order for Harry to see clearly his own intentions and to see just how powerful a force "love" is, expresses an anxiousness rarely seen in the series. He calls Harry's name twice: "Harry, Harry, [the reason the prophecy was effective was] only because Voldemort made a grave error, and acted on Professor Trelawny's words!" Voldemort's decisions precisely facilitated this potentially empty prophecy: he created his most formidable foe (Harry), and due to his initial failure, he gave Harry a power that could defeat him—such as his sympathy with snakes and the ability to speak their language. Up to this point, Harry was still unclear on what made a difference in all of this. He still thought that going to kill Voldemort of his own intent and killing Voldemort out of self-defense "were a single thing." Dumbledore urgently told him this was not the case. If he was acting out of self-defense, then that power he obtained from Voldemort would turn him into one of his followers and to even make Harry manipulatable by him. But if he sought revenge out of his own intention, he would possess the power told of in the prophecy, and Voldemort would be completely unable to stop him. What is the motivation behind this activity and passivity? The conversation continues:

> [Dumbledore said:] "It is Voldemort's fault that you were able to see into his thoughts, his ambitions, that you even understand the snakelike language in which he gives orders, and yet, Harry, despite your privileged insight into Voldemort's world (which, incidentally, is a gift any Death Eater would kill to have), you have never been seduced by the Dark Arts, never, even for a second, shown the slightest desire to become one of Voldemort's followers!"
>
> "Of course I haven't!" said Harry indignantly. "He killed my mum and dad!"
>
> "You are protected, in short, by your ability to love!" said Dumbledore loudly. "The only protection that can possibly work against the lure of power like Voldemort's! In spite of all the temptation you have endured, all the suffering, you remain pure of heart, just as pure as you were at the age of

eleven, when you stared into a mirror that reflected your heart's desire, and it showed you only the way to thwart Lord Voldemort, and not immortality or riches. Harry, have you any idea how few wizards could have seen what you saw in that mirror? Voldemort should have known then what he was dealing with, but he did not! But he knows it now." (book 6, ch. 24)

This long passage is just an annotation and explanation of Harry's line in the middle. Harry thinks that "he killed my mum and dad" is a very natural and ultimate answer, but he had failed to notice that he had already overcome the power worship that many other wizards fall victim to (even the young Dumbledore). Obviously, the ambiguous "power of love" talked about by Dumbledore comes from the "ability to love." And Harry's ability to love is rooted in the parent–child relationship indicated by his "mum and dad." Moreover, Dumbledore has unconsciously ignored a related fact here: what Harry saw in the magic mirror was first the "method for how to beat Voldemort" and then it was his mother, father, and relatives. This is how he finally saw that "method." It is as if Dumbledore could not understand the source of this love in the most key of moments. Does this have to do with the family tragedy he faced when he was young?

At this point, Harry had already provided the reason for why he and Voldemort fought. But he was too pure to notice that he was still doubtful of the momentum created by the prophecy that gave him no other choice. Dumbledore had only one last thing to say:

"But, sir," said Harry, making valiant efforts not to sound argumentative, "it all comes to the same thing, doesn't it? I've got to try to kill him, or—"

"Got?" said Dumbledore. "Of course you've got to! But not because of the prophecy! Because you, yourself, will never rest until you've tried! We both know it! Imagine, please, just for a moment, that you had never heard that prophecy! How would you feel about Voldemort now? Think!"

Harry watched Dumbledore striding up and down in front of him, and thought. He thought of his mother, his father, and Sirius. He thought of Cedric Diggory. He thought of all the terrible deeds he knew Lord Voldemort had done.

A flame seemed to leap inside his chest, searing his throat.

"I'd want him finished," said Harry quietly. "And I'd want to do it."

Dumbledore spoke correctly: if Harry did not go to kill Voldemort of his own will, he would "never rest until [he had] tried." And the phenomenological "imagination" advised by this wise principal eliminated the existential prediction and passive state of mind created by the prophecy. This allowed Harry to consciously live in the situation that he occupied. The first thing he thought of or vividly experienced were still his mother, father, and the death of his godfather. And then it was the terrible deaths of his classmates and acquaintances. Thereupon, a fire was lit. This fire burned away everything that was irrelevant, including the explanation of self-defense. It directly called to him to kill Voldemort and get revenge for his parents! At the same time, it called for him to avenge his friends and bring justice back to the world! There was simply nothing more to be discussed, and thus he calmed down and made a "predetermined decision" to live with his fate, which appeared to leave him without a choice and which in fact did not require a choice and was, after all, a choice that was necessary and inevitable. Precisely due to this decision to seek revenge for his parents, Harry forgot his own self. When he learned that he unconsciously became one of Voldemort's Horcruxes, he did not feel that all of Dumbledore's preparations—including his plan to sacrifice himself—had clouded his eyes. Instead, he chose to face death in darkness and loneliness—("I am willing to go with you to die"—*Shangshu* 尚書). His path forward was not clear, and Voldemort would necessarily die when he did, but as long as he died first, he could expect Voldemort to die too. Thus, he went to die. This is true revenge—great revenge! According to the Gongyang *Chunqiu*, he was a truly consummate person who forgot about gains and losses and abandoned his life for his moral duty. According to the Confucian theory of filiality, he was a great filial son because he carried on the will of his parents and brought peace to the world.

Voldemort also discussed revenge, the revenge he desired to achieve against his father for abandoning him and his mother.

"My father lived there. My mother, a witch who lived here in this village, fell in love with him. But he abandoned her when she told him what she was. . . . He didn't like magic, my father . . .

"He left her and returned to his Muggle parents before I was even born. Potter, and she died giving birth to me, leaving me to be raised in a Muggle orphanage . . . but I vowed to find him . . . I revenged myself upon him, that fool who gave me his name . . . Tom Riddle . . ." (book 4, ch. 33)

This is completely opposite to Harry's revenge. His father did not kill his mother. Tom killed his father out of personal anger. According to the Confucians, this is a great crime that goes against *tian* and breaks from its mandate. What "revenge" is there in this? From here, he could see only the Death Eaters whom he created as his "*true* family." Some reviewers do not see the difference between Harry and Voldemort here. They think that both are orphans and take Hogwarts as their nuclear family, and so on. Yet they ignore a key difference: they treat their fathers differently. Therefore, the meaning behind their "revenge" is vastly different.

Immortality or Life Even in Death?
The Theory of Time in Harry Potter's Time Consciousness

Pursuing Immortality: The Mark of Black Magic

Above, we saw that the biggest difference between Harry Potter and Voldemort was the love for one's family. The presupposition for this love is a kind of time consciousness.[15] The structure of this consciousness has an internal relation with the artistic measure of human beings. We also talked about the so-called "filial consciousness" in terms of "carrying on the will," "describing the deeds," and "revenge." All these have a full sense of time consciousness. This is the interweaving represented by the intergenerationality between the generation of the parents and that of the children or the succession of the past by the future. We cannot provide a full analysis of time consciousness here and can deal with it only in terms of a single issue: that the temporal presupposition between family and love necessarily involves the phenomenon of death and related ideas thereon. Confucius said: "Not knowing life, how can you know death?"

172 | Family and Filiality

(*Analects* 11.12). This does not mean that one should not think about death; rather, it means we cannot depart the experience of life in the present to fabricate an afterlife and metaphysical foundation. From the perspective of the parent–child relationship displayed in this novel, its treatment of death directly influences its attitude toward the parent–child relationship. This is why we cannot but analyze it.

Voldemort's greatest trait, or his strongest desire, is his personal transcendence of death. All of his important actions are for the most part driven by this motivation: in order to seek immortality, he created the evil horcruxes and killed with abandon; because of the prophecy that told of who will live and who will die, he went to get rid of an infant; in order to obtain another body, he went to every extreme. Yes, he was also greedy for power and authority. This was his character. Yet, for him, the search for power and eternal existence existed alongside each other. Moreover, the latter was the basis for the former. (This point made it so he could not be fully equated to those of the "will to power," referred to by Nietzsche.) Therefore, the seven books of the *Harry Potter* series began with the "sorcerer's stone" and ended with the "Deathly Hallows." Both are means to seek immortality in which can be seen the question of whether "to die or to live?" For me, there is no more fundamental a question.

The sorcerer's stone was created by Nicolas Flamel so he could be immortal. It appears that what he did was good and with no bad intentions, but Voldemort could use it to obtain a normal and even immortal body. Therefore, how to hide it became a headache for Dumbledore and his wizards. They robbed the underground vault of Gringotts Bank with all of its defenses for the stone, and the underground cave at Hogwarts with all of its protective spells was also unable to prevent the infiltration of black magic. It was only through the magic mirror, Harry, and Dumbledore's cooperation that they were able to protect it. Afterward, Dumbledore and Flamel discussed how to destroy this stone because its capacity to grant immortality was useful to black magic and the possibility of death was actually on the side of the good.

Historically, the Deathly Hallows were three treasures used by three brothers to triumph over the Master of Death: the Cloak of Invisibility, the Elder Wand, and the Resurrection Stone. They do not allow their possessor to escape death at all; instead, they provide a kind of miraculous magic power, and the consequences produced greatly differ based on their characteristics and how they are applied. The Elder Wand is the most powerful and quickly causes the person wielding it to be killed; the Resurrection Stone seems to have the ability to bring people back from the dead, but it actually travels backwards in time and eventually causes its possessors to kill themselves; the Cloak of Invisibility is simply negative de-objectification, and thus "using it properly" allows people to avoid unusual deaths.

In the seventh book, Harry does not seek the Deathly Hallows because he wants to achieve immortality. Contrarily, he wants to use them to kill what is immortal, that is, the horcruxes and Voldemort himself. Thus, when faced with the choice of destroying the horcruxes or looking for the Hallows, he chose the former. Therefore, there was the second robbery at the underground vault of Gringotts. (This kind of symmetry is common in *Harry Potter*.) The former robbery at Gringotts was for the sorcerer's stone, while the second was for one of the horcruxes. Harry possessed two of the Hallows—the Cloak of Invisibility and the Resurrection Stone—but they were incapable of preventing the march toward death (that he did not die in the end was not due to their magic). Moreover, the Resurrection Stone called forth the ghosts of his parents and godfather so they could accompany him to death, and the Cloak of Invisibility covered Harry so that he could appear in front of the spell of death. Voldemort possessed the Elder Wand, and to a certain degree died because of it.

In conclusion, those things that grant people immortality, regardless of whether it is the sorcerer's stone or a horcrux, must be destroyed or else the immortality they grant must be revealed to be fake (the Hallows). And he who strives for immortality with all of his power (Voldemort) must be killed! Otherwise, this world will be without a flourishing process of life. In this very philosophical novel, "immortality" is a representation of evil, and a natural, sound, and heroic death (thus the "courage" of the House of Gryffindor must be understood in his way) is the presupposition and protection of human goodness and fortune. The principle here is this: immortality wants to overcome, control, and suppress living time whereas natural death participates in the construction and protection of this very time. Therefore, destroying the horcruxes and killing Voldemort are the release and free flow of life and time in the reader's experience. It is full of the interaction between good (*yang*) and bad (*yin*) and produces a profound aesthetic feeling. Flamel's wife thus abandons immortality in book one, and Voldemort finally receives death at the end of the final book (book seven). Although his death is not a sound one, it is still the death of a normal person. These books are a praise of natural death, especially heroic death and living time. Even the "seven" of the seven books in the series, in Greek philosophy—such as Pythagoras—represent time. And the seven horcruxes of Voldemort that overcome death are finally destroyed in the seventh book.

Harry Potter's View on Life and Time

Looking back on Harry, our filial hero, his attitude toward death and time is completely opposite to that of Voldemort's. Death was not something he wanted to overcome; instead, it was one of the motivations and sources for his life. As noted above, the death of Harry's parents was one of his later motivations, and the lightning scar on his forward represented the connection between life and death. Therefore, for him, life and death are not sharply demarcated, and his life and death are not sharply demarcated from the lives and deaths of others—especially his parents. This scar, along with the green light and screams in his nightmares, imply that he has experienced the threat of death and that, moreover, he will have to face it again in the present and the future. But this threat precisely excites a feeling for original time and is expressed as a fearless courage and penetrating intuition. Further, this intuition and courage causes him to despise the quest for absolute eternity and power.

Therefore, for him, death is not an absolute nothing, negativity, or separation. Instead, it is the more profound channel that connects the past with the future. Each time he encountered death, it would open for him an existential time that interwove past and future, especially the new gate of *familial generational time*. When he learned from Hagrid and others the truth about his parents, he began to live with his parents in an intergenerational time world of a continuous blood lineage. This time is more real and precious than the time of physics. Harry only recognized a non-absolute and non-individual immortality—that is, the immortality of the family and the lineage. Therein, even though the individual dies, it is still as if they are alive. In chapter 16 of book seven, he and Hermione read the inscription on his father's tomb in the graveyard in Godric's Hollow: "The last enemy that shall be destroyed is death." The novel does not indicate the source of this quote; it actually comes from First Corinthians 15:26 in the New Testament.[16] Some critics claim this reflects *Harry Potter's* Christian tendencies, and some have even reported that this is the view of Rowling herself. Yet, in the novel, when Harry read this line, his first reaction is exclusionary: "A horrible thought came to him, and with a kind of panic. 'Isn't that a Death Eater idea? Why is that there?'" Harry's reaction was natural. The literal meaning of this sentence is certainly the idea of Voldemort's to "destroy death" no matter what and achieve immortality. But Hermione immediately explains, saying: "'It doesn't mean defeating death in the way the Death Eaters mean it, Harry,' said Hermione, her voice gentle. 'It means . . . you know . . . living beyond death. Living after death.'" In this new explanation, the meaning of the inscription becomes much broader, broad enough to contain the views on death of both Harry and Confucian thought. After the death of an individual, through the love between parent and child, they continue to live within the memory and filiality of the family and lineage, and the family and lineage also continue to survive.

Therefore, Harry's love for his parents and even his godfather continued their work by "carrying on their will" and "describing their deeds." His friendship and consideration for his friends and lovers allowed life to be full of passion and renewal constituted in the present. Regarding those children who had the infinite kindness of their parents while growing up—then, those who love their parents will absolutely love their children; this is what is determined by the "logic" that three-dimensionally interweaves existential time or generational time. Although the "epilogue" is not very long, its meaning is nonetheless profound. Harry sends his second son off to Hogwarts running alongside the train that takes off from Platform Nine and Three-Quarters, waving his hands until the train was out of sight. Afterward, once he has stopped waving, he touches his lightning scar. At this point, the form of the time of a pulsating bloodline and gushing family lineage comes to completion. Therefore, this novel is not like other novels in that, at the narrative climax, it does not come to a sudden end when Harry kills Voldemort and becomes the hero and leader of the magical world. Instead, it adds some exchanges and final words. Regarding this novel that expresses a filial consciousness and familial temporality, this is necessary because living existential time does not "come to a sudden end" unless it is eternalized time.

This later interchange clearly expresses Harry's view on death, time, and power. It further displays the true meaning of the tombstone's inscription. In his exchange with Dumbledore's portrait—he was at least still alive in his eyes—he wanted to abandon the Resurrection Stone and the fabricated triumph over death; he wanted to keep the Cloak of Invisibility because it was a family treasure and because it did not conflict with a natural death; he did not want to possess the Elder Wand, a representation of power, and instead placed it in Dumbledore's grave—that is, he placed it next to the second person to own the wand so that its power would end with his (Harry's) own death. However, before he placed the Elder Wand, he used it once, for the first and last time, to restore his own original wand in order to experience the warmth and joy of a reunion with his own tradition. Afterward, he wanted to return to his own bed to sleep and eat a sandwich. That is all! Harry's purity is extremely moving and stimulates us to think on its deeper meaning.

This purity is the purity of existential temporality itself. That is, it is the human embodiment of time's purity. If, when death is unavoidable (such as in revenge), there is no means for a natural and sound death, then the flow of this time through "day and night" will be corrupted, obstructed, and enslaved. Time is certainly impermanent, certainly temporary, and certainly untamable. Therefore, it can be the source of meaning and the nest of life. But time is also continuous, not preformed or limited, and thus it can embrace remembrance, longing, order, cyclicality, possibility, and endurance. And death is just the cleaner of time that gets rid of its objectified excessive growths and that connects and lets it cross over, such as when a death in the present completes the past and brings about the future, and thus each moment interweaves past and future. Precisely because it is like this, death in the present is not substantial; it is preserved in the just now and stored in memory. Therefore, it can always meet us again in the future with a different appearance. After all, there is no absolute unity to guarantee the eternity of the past or the present to walk toward the future (the so-called laws of history or plan of salvation); being forgotten or misrecorded is always a possibility, and so is to die and not be reborn.

This is how death expresses existential time, especially the fundamentality of familial time. It denies that there is a higher substantial existence above this. The time acknowledged by Harry is just this kind of time, this kind of life. He challenges and rejects all attempts to establish an absolute authority above this. And in terms of this, he is more thorough and persistent than even Dumbledore. His battle with Voldemort, philosophically speaking, was the battle of familial and existential time with timeless eternity. It is that traditional time and artistic time that has been unjustly and severely harmed; it is a revenge against the quest for modernity and high technology of a transcendent time. When Nietzsche said "God is dead!," he was not aware of an even more deadly threat: the threat of the "death of the family." It is because the death of the family strips away the possibility for a sound natural death that it makes us unable to hear the musicality of the world and humanity—the "pipes of *tian*" (*tianlai* 天籟), "pipes of earth" (*dilai* 地籟), and "pipes of humanity" (*renlai* 人籟)—Oedipus to go mad, and Apollo to lose the strings to his lyre and become a spaceship that went to the moon. When Harry went to battle for this kind of time, he gave us a stronger aesthetic feeling than that in *Star Wars* because this feeling is the artistic embodiment of existential time.

In conclusion, all of Harry's motivations to exist, believe, feel, and to act emerge out of the interweaving of death and new life. He wants to recover the connection between traditional and actual life to let that undying singularity die. Therefore, the "sorting hat" cannot be destroyed. When it was burned by Voldemort and in danger, a great change occurred. The treasure of Gryffindor, a sword, was pulled from it and was used to destroy one of the horcruxes and to preserve the diversity of the tradition and indeterminacy of spontaneity. In this way, Rowling probably felt that if she did not add something about the denial of the Deathly Hallows or his plans for separation, then the end of these books would be unacceptable because this is when Harry had possession of all three of the Hallows (he could find the Resurrection Stone) and appeared to be the most powerful wizard and capable of triumphing over death. Thereupon, even though Harry was extremely tired and worn out, he still had to proclaim in front of the portrait of his teacher and once head of the school of magic and his friends: he was going to abandon everything that did harm to natural death and existential time. Afterward, it was sleep, food, and the transmission between parents and children and between families that takes place in our daily lives. "All was well" (book 7, epilogue).

Conclusion

The reason *Harry Potter*'s attitude toward death is so important is because it directly connects to people's theory of time. Is it a finite and existential theory of time an infinite and transcendental theory of time? Which theory of time we choose and our treatment of the parent–child relationship, especially the attitude of filial consciousness, have an internal connection. It is only within the first kind of theory of time that the parent–child relationship and filial consciousness has its ultimate meaning. And what we can see in Harry himself is the magnificent expression of this ultimate magic. That the *Harry Potter* series received such great praise and success is thus not a surprise. At this point, do we not realize our own human natures first and foremost within familial affection and the way of filiality?

Notes

Chapter 1

1. All quotations from the Bible follow the King James version.

2. Søren Kierkegaard, *Fear and Trembling—Dialectical Lyric by Johannes de silentio* (henceforth *Fear and Trembling*), translated by Alastair Hannay (Middlesex, New York: Penguin Books, 1985).

3. Zhang is playing on the multiple meanings of the Chinese word "*shi* 世," which can mean "world," "era," or "generation."

Chapter 2

1. *Qingnian Zazhi*, di 1 juan di 1 hao, Shanghai: Qunyi Shushe, 1915 (the fourth year of the Republic of China) Sept. 15. Since the second publication on Sept. 1 of 1916, its name was changed to *Xin Qingnian*. (Publication info for Chinese texts have been left in *pinyin* to reduce confusion. For example, the *juan* 卷 here can mean "volume," but so can *ce* 册 or *shang* 上. —Translator.)

2. Quoted from *Zhongguo Jindai Qimeng Sichao* 中國近啟蒙思潮, zhong juan (shortened to *Qimeng Sichao*), Ding Shouhe (ed.) (Beijing: Shehuikexue Wenxian Chubanshe, 1999).

3. For a more thorough discussion of this concept of Kant, refer to my essay "Kant on the Parent–Child Relationships and Its Problem," in my *Deguo Zhexue, Deguo Wenhua yu Zhongguo Zheli* 德國哲學，德國文化與中國哲理 ("German Philosophy, German Culture, and Chinese Philosophical Thought") (Shanghai: Shanghai Waiyu Jiaoyu Chubanshe, 2012), 49–61.

4. Jane English: "What Do Grown Children Owe Their Parents?," in *Having Children: Philosophical and Legal Reflections on Parenthood*, ed. Onora O'Neil and William Ruddick (New York: Oxford University Press, 1979), 352–354.

5. For an essay and explanation related to this, please see the last part of the essay listed above, "Kant on the Parent–Child Relationships and Its Problem."

6. Conrad P. Kottak: *Anthropology: The Exploration of Human Diversity*, 12th edition (herein abbreviated as *"Anthropology"*) (New York: McGraw-Hill Companies; jointly published by the Renmin University Press and McGraw-Hill, 2008).

7. See parts 1 and 2 of Wu Fei's 吳飛 unpublished *Tianlun Renxu—Xingzhilun Chuantong Zhong de Jiaguo Jiaolü* 天倫人敘—形質論傳統中的家國焦慮 (to be published by SDX Joint Publishing Company).

8. Westermarck: *Renlei Hunyin Shi* (*The History of Human Marriage*). Translated by Li Bi, Li Yifu, and Ouyang Jueya (Beijing: Shangwu Yinshuguan, 2002).

9. Refer to *Inbreeding, Incest, and the Incest Taboo: The State of Knowledge at the Turn of the Century*, ed. A.P. Wolf and W.H. Durham (Stanford, CA: Stanford University Press, 2005).

10. A tendency within modern cognitive science is to explain this special characteristic with the formula of pairing and computational probability (the Bayesian formula) discovered by English mathematician Thomas Bayes in the eighteenth century.

11. For more on this, see the next chapter.

Chapter 3

1. See Edward O. Wilson's autobiography: *Daziran de Lieren—Shengwuxuejia Weierxun Zizhuan* 大自然的獵人—生物學家威爾遜自傳, translated by Yang Yuling 楊玉玲 (Shanghai: Shanhai Kexue Jishu Chubanshe, 2000), chapter 17, *Shehui Shengwuxue Dalunzhan* 社會生物學大論戰.

2. Edward O. Wilson: *Sociobiology: The New Synthesis*, 25th anniversary edition (Cambridge, MA & London: The Belknap Press of Harvard University Press, 2000).

3. Edward O. Wilson: *On Human Nature* (Cambridge, MA & London: Harvard University Press, 1978), 208.

4. Refer to He Chuanqi 何傳啟: *Diliuci Keji Geming de Jiyu yu Duice* 第六次科技革命的機遇與對策 ("The Opportunity and Strategy of the Sixth Scientific Revolution"), in *Diliuci Keji Geming de Zhanlüe Jiyu* 第六次科技革命的戰略機遇, ed. He Chuanqi (Beijing: Kexue Chubanshe) 08-2011.

5. Robert Blyd and Joan B. Silk: *How Humans Evolved*, 5th edition (Los Angeles: W.W. Norton, 2009). This book maintains there were at least four kinds of hominids in Africa between 4 to 2 million years ago: *Australopithecus*, *Paranthropus*, *Kenyanthropus*, and *Homo sapiens*.

6. "Tool use" can be simply understood as the utilization of one external thing to make changes in the shape, position, or state of another external thing. In this way, the first thing becomes a tool, and "utilization" can be understood as the tool user possessing or carrying the thing before using it and therefore

has a responsibility for turning it into a tool. This is more or less the definition provided by B. Beck in 1960. See *Primates in Perspective*, ed. C.J. Campbell, A. Fuentes, et al. (New York: Oxford University Press, 2007), chapter 41, "Tool Use and Cognition in Primates," by Melissa Panger (665). Chimpanzees are also able to use simple tools, such as using blades of grass to pick up ants.

7. Conrad P. Kottak, *Anthropology: The Exploration of Human Diversity*, 12th edition (New York: McGraw-Hill Companies), 2008.

8. Some scholars have referenced the rumors of naturalists and even Japanese stories about primitive peoples who do not care for and abandon their elderly to deny that caring for the elderly is a human characteristic. This argument has a methodological problem because if people do not care for their elderly for a partial or short period of time, this does not mean that elder care is not a feature of their primary lifestyles. This is also a problem of interpretative perspective. Different cultures can have extremely different understandings of the same phenomena. For example, the sky burials of Tibet express a disrespect toward one's parents from the perspective of Han Chinese. However, in Tibetan culture, sky burials have a different interpretation. The conclusion that ancient humans "cared for and protected their elderly" arrived at through the extensive field work and archeological excavations of twentieth-century anthropology is more or less reliable and complete.

9. Lewis Henry Morgan: *Ancient Society* (Chicago: Charles H. Kerr & Company, 1907), part II, ch. 1, 47.

10. For instance, Claude Lévi-Strauss writes in his "introduction" to *A History of the Family*: "They [the contemporary scholars] agree, it is true, in their rejection of the old theory according to which a supposed 'primitive promiscuity' preceded the emergence of the family in the history of mankind. . . . The general tendency today is to assume that 'family life,' in the sense that we ourselves give to the phrase, exists in all human societies" (*A History of Family*, vol. 1, ed. André Burguière, Christiane Klapisch-Zuber, Martine Segalen, Françoise Zonabend. Translated by Sarah Hanbury Tenison, Rosemary Morris and Andrew Wilson (Cambridge, MA: The Belknap Press of Harvard University Press, 1996), 8.

An author of *A History of the Family* expresses the generally accepted view nowadays as "the family is a natural phenomenon, that is, like language, an attribute of the human condition and that, above all, it must be the same for all people in all societies" (Cambridge, MA: The Belknap Press of Harvard University Press, 1996), 10.

Wilson writes: "The building block of nearly all human societies is the nuclear family" (*Sociobiology*, 553).

11. Jared Diamond: *The Third Chimpanzee: The Evolution and Future of the Human Animal* (abbr. as "*The Third Chimpanzee*") (New York: HarperCollins, 1992).

182 | Notes to Chapter 3

12. A popular theory to explain the bipedalism of hominids is the "adaptation to open grasslands ecology theory." Due to several million years of climate change, some tropical forests in the eastern part of Africa turned into savannas and original hominins, in order to adapt to this new environment "came down from the trees" and evolved to have an upright stance and to walk on two feet because this kind of locomotion had several benefits: they could see above the grasses over long distances, they could carry prey for long distances, the evolution of the front limbs into hands, and it was beneficial for reducing radiation from direct sunlight so as to maintain body temperature (*Anthropology*, 104). Of course, there are other possible explanations.

13. Discoveries in recent decades show there are several million years between the developments of bipedalism, large brains, and the hunting of large prey animals. However, the "hunter theory" introduced below still has some influence. See Kristen Hawkes, "Mating, Parenting, and the Evolution of Human Pair Bonds," *Kinship and Behavior in Primates* (abbr. as "*Kinship*"), ed. Bernard Chapais and Carol M. Berman (New York: Oxford University Press, 2004).

14. Wilson writes: "[B]ecause men can breed at shorter intervals than women, the pair bond has been attenuated somewhat by the common practice of polygyny, the taking of multiple wives." Edward O. Wilson, *On Human Nature* (Cambridge, MA: Harvard University Press, 1978), 140.

15. *Primates in Perspective*, ed. Christina J. Campbell, et al. (New York: Oxford University Press, 2007).

16. Such expressions can be found in *Zengguang Xianwen* 增廣賢文, *Quanbao Qin'en pian* 勸報親恩篇, etc. Refer to *Zhongguo Gudai Xiaodao Ziliao Xuanbian* 中國古代孝道資料選編 (The Selections of Chinese Ancient Literature of Filial Dao), ed. Luo Chenglie (Jinan: Shandong University Press, 2003), 105, 112, 121.

17. Perhaps some people will think this kind of elder care is not undertaken by a single family but by an entire clan and as such should not be considered filial. But as argued above, it is useless to claim that early humans did not have families, and thus clans are composed of families.

18. *Handbook of Paleoanthropology*, vol. 11, *Primate Evolution and Human Origins* (herein referred to as "*Primate Evolution*"), ed. Winfried Henke and Ian Tattersal (Berlin, Heidelberg, & New York: Springer-Verlag, 2007).

19. Jane Goodall: *My Life with the Chimpanzees* (New York: A Minstrel Book, 1988).

20. Jane Goodall: *In the Shadow of Man* (London: William Collins Sons & Co. Ltd., 1971).

21. The term *yinyang* represents a complex element of Chinese philosophical thinking where the former, *yin*, references all that is feminine, wet, supple, shady, etc. and the latter, *yang*, refers to all that is masculine, dry, rigid, and sunny. *Yin* and *yang* are not fixed substances but represent the fluid modes of

becoming of all things as they connect and disconnect with each other over the natural courses of their lives. Thus, while a young man might be seen as *yin* in comparison to his elders who are *yang* in terms of age, however in terms of his vitality, he is seen as *yang* in relation to their frailty. —Translator

22. Meredith F. Small, "Our Babies, Ourselves," *Annual Editions: Anthropology 2002/2003*, ed. Elvio Angeloni (Guilford, CT: McGraw-Hill/Dushkin, 2002).

23. Zhang uses two terms here that can be technically translated in Kantian terms of "*a priori*"(*xiantian* 先天) and "*a posteriori*"(*houtian* 後天), but which in classical discourse really refer to what is "innate" and what is "acquired" in the similar sense to the "nature/nurture" debate common in the West. The phrase *houtian de xiantian guanlian* 後天的先天的關聯 might then be translated as "the innate connection of what is acquired." —Translator

24. Charles J. Lumsden and Edward O. Wilson, *Promethean Fire: Reflection on the Origin of the Mind* (Cambridge, MA: Harvard University Press, 1983), 79; Henry C. Ellis and R. Reed Hunt: *Fundamentals of Cognitive Psychology*, 5th edition (Boston, MA: McGraw Hill, 1993, ch. 4–5.

25. Eldon D. Enger and Frederick C. Ross, *Concepts in Biology* (New York: McGraw-Hill, 2003).

26. Diamond states: "The intense phase of parental care is unusually protracted in the human species and lasts nearly two decades" (*The Third Chimpanzee*, 133). We can imagine that during the formation of modern humans that the stage of development (advanced tools for hunting and gathering had already been invented) is more or less like this. But during the early and middle stages of this process, the situation is not like this at all. Obviously, these changes depend on changes in the ecology and the kinds of foods humans eat. When an ecology is beneficial, this will happen at a younger age, but it will happen later when the ecology is bad. The appearance of bipedalism will be even later during the stage when hunting is very important (because the techniques and physique required for hunting large pray has higher requirements), and for very early humans who at the very least mainly subsisted on plants, this age will be earlier.

27. Carline E.G. Tutin: "Reproductive Success Story—Variability among Chimpanzees and Comparisons with Gorillas," *Chimpanzee Cultures*, ed. R.W. Wrangham, W.C. McGrew, et al. (Cambridge, MA & London: Harvard University Press, 1996), 181, table 1.

28. The above has already mentioned another factor, that is, it is possible that humans are like chimpanzees in that they mature quicker if they are in "confinement" or a "state of civilization." This might resist to a certain degree the delay in child development due to the state of maturity in newborn babies. (According to anthropological evidence, this delay will become longer as humans continue to evolve. See *How Humans Evolved*, 264, 291–292.)

29. Patricia J. Ash and David Robinson: *The Emergence of Humans: An Exploration of the Evolutionary Timeline* (UK: Wiley-Blackwell, 2010), 239.

30. Aristotle, *The Politics of Aristotle*, edited and translated by Ernest Barker (London: Oxford University Press, 1946/1979), 5.

31. These terms are taken from the *Zhouyi* "Xicixia" (*Book of Changes—Appended Sayings*) that says: "When change is exhausted there is transformation, when there is transformation there is penetration, and when there is penetration there is endurance. This is how *tian* protects and there is nothing that is inauspicious (易窮則變，變則通，通則久，是以自天佑之，吉無不利)."

Chapter 4

1. Immanuel Kant, *Critique of Pure Reason*, translated by Paul Guyer and Allen W. Wood (New York: Cambridge University Press, 1998).

2. Martin Heidegger, *Kant and the Problem of Metaphysics*, translated by James S. Campbell (Bloomington: Indiana University Press, 1965).

3. Zhang references Ni Liangkang's 倪梁康 Chinese translation of Husserl's *Phenomenology of Time-Consciousness* (*Neishijian Yishi Xianxiangxue* 內時間意識現象學, Beijing: Shangwu Yinshuguan, 2010.) An English translation of this text can be found in *On the Phenomenology of the Consciousness of Internal Time*, translated by John Barnet Brough (Dordrect, Boston, & London: Kluwer Academic Publishers, 1991). The page numbers referenced here refer to the original German text as included in parentheses in Ni's translation.

4. Endel Tulving: "Episodic Memory and Autonoesis: Uniquely Human?," *The Missing Link in Cognition Origins of Self-Reflective Consciousness*, ed. H.S. Terrace and J. Metcalfe (New York: Oxford University Press, 2005), 3–56.

5. See Menzel's essay "Progress in the Study of Chimpanzee Recall and Episodic Memory," in *The Missing Link*, 188–224.

Chapter 5

1. Heinrich Zankl, *Phänomen Sexualität. Vom "kleinen" Unterschied der Geschlechter*. This text has no English translation, but Zhang references the Chinese translation, so the pagination refers to that version; see *Xingxianxiang—Guanyu Xingbie de "Xiao" Chayi* 性現象—關於性別的"小"差異, translated by ZhangYunyi 張雲毅 (Beijing: Shangwu Yinshuguan, 2001).

2. Lewis Henry Morgan, *Ancient Society* (Chicago: Charles H. Kerr & Company, 1985).

3. André Burguière, *Jiating shi* 家庭史, translated by Yuan Shuren 袁樹仁 (Beijing 北京: Sanlian Shudian 三聯書店, 1998). There does not appear to be an English translation of this French text. Therefore, I have translated from the Chinese. I request the reader's understanding. —Translator

4. Li Ling 李零: *Guodian Chujian Jiaoduji* 郭店楚简校读记 (Beijing: Beijing Daxue Chubanshe Press, 2002).

5. The term used for "deferential love" is "*ti'ai* 悌愛," where the former character is a Confucian term referring to "deference" of younger brothers for older brothers. —Translator

Chapter 6

1. Marc Shell: *The End of Kinship: "Measure for Measure," Incest, and the Ideal of Universal Siblinghood* (Baltimore & London: Johns Hopkins University Press, 1995), 12.

2. See *Inbreeding, Incest, and the Incest Taboo: The State of Knowledge at the Turn of the Century*, ed. A.P. Wolf and W.H. Durham (Stanford, CA: Stanford University Press, 2005).

3. How we define "humanity" will influence the answer to the question of whether "humanity has a history of incest." If we use the appearance of language as the most direct marker of humanity, even more scholars will answer this question in the negative. Conversely, if we view humanity as the genus "hominid," then humanity will have appeared three million years earlier and there will thus be more reasons to answer in the positive or the negative. However, Morgan most likely held the former opinion when he said humanity had a stage of incest because if he was not talking about *Homo sapiens* but hominids more broadly, then his theory does not help us much in understanding the social evolution of humanity.

4. Is completely asexual reproduction possible? Why was troublesome and dangerous sexual reproduction produced from convenient and safe asexual reproduction? Does this mean that sexual production is already contained as potential in asexual reproduction?

5. This fact conflicts with those people who believe in a period of human evolution that lacked incest taboos. Therefore, several scholars have either directly or indirectly denied, covered, or ignored it until twentieth-century investigations provided irrefutable evidence. This fact is among the motivating factors behind the transformations in anthropological and scientific thinking. Some scholars argue that incest has the advantage of preserving the good qualities of a certain species group. This is another question entirely. After expending a great effort, incest will have certain impressive results within a short period of time, such as that seen in the evolution of human beings, but in principle, long-term incest will produce many disadvantages.

6. J.H. Turner and A. Maryanski, *Incest: Origin of the Taboo* (Boulder, CO & London: Paradigm Publishers, 2005), chapters 6 and 7.

7. Plato: *The Symposium*, translated by M.C. Howatson (Cambridge: Cambridge University Press, 2008), 45.

8. Zhang notes that he references Zhang Zhuming 張竹明 and Jiang Ping's 蔣平 translation of the *Theogony* in their *Gongzuo yu Shiri-Shenpu* (Beijing: Shangwu Yinshuguan, 1997). The English translation referred to here is Glenn W. Most's *Theogony, Works and Days, Testimonia* (Cambridge, MA & London: Harvard University Press, 2006)

9. Scholars such as Barry Powell maintain that Gaia, Chaos, Tartarus, and Eros were the first gods to appear. But another scholar, Donna Rosenberg, sees Chaos as being the first to appear and that Gaia and the other gods were born therefrom. Powell also thinks that Gaia joined with Tartarus first to give birth to Uranus. But other mythologists think that Gaia gave birth to them on her own. I follow Powell's explanation here.

10. Ruth Fainlight and Robert J. Littman, *Sophocles: The Theban Plays* (Baltimore: Johns Hopkins University Press, 2009).

11. These and the following quotations are taken from *Presocratic Philosophers* (G.S. Kirk and J.E. Raven (Cambridge: Cambridge University Press, 1957), which Zhang cites from the Chinese text *Guxila Zhexue* 古希臘哲學 ("Ancient Greek Philosophy") edited by Miao Tianli 苗力田.

12. Fainlight and Littman, *Sophocles: The Theban Plays*.

13. David Ross, *The Works of Aristotle*, vol. 12 ("The Fragments") (Oxford: Clarendon Press, 1952), 144.

14. If we look to the "memory" that Plato speaks of through the mouth of Socrates in light of the distinction made in sections 3 and 4 of chapter 4 in the present book, then what he is talking about is "semantic memory" and not "episodic memory" because the key is the things that are remembered—that is, the Idea, rather than in remembering how a thing was experienced in the first place.

15. Zhang is playing with the fact that the "*jing* 經" here can mean both "warp" and "classical text." —Translator

16. The *Zi Xia Zhuan* 子夏傳 says: "*Yuan* means beginning; *heng* means penetration; *li* means harmony; and *zhen* means rightness." Cheng Yi's 程頤 *Cheng Shi Yizhuan* 程氏易傳 ("Cheng's Commentary to the Changes") says: "*Yuan, heng, li,* and *zhen* are four virtues. *Yuan* is the beginning of the ten thousand things; *heng* is the chief of the ten thousand things; *li* is the penetration of the ten thousand things; and *zhen* is the completion of the ten thousand things." From this we can see an explanation of the natural transformation of the seasons in addition to many other such phenomena. (We can also see the difficulty in translating this phrase into English. Regarding this phrase, Francois Jullien [*Book of Beginnings*, New Haven, CT & London: Yale University Press, 2015].) says: "What can we imagine to be the opening formula or the first sentence put forward? But first of all, once again, is it a sentence, strictly speaking? Just four Chinese sinograms follow one another side by side, without anything to indicate rection or relationships of coordination or subordination between them.

These four monosyllables are equal, without anything arranging or hierarchizing them, but in their own series they form a complete whole. In such a formula, is it even a matter of verbs, nouns, adjectives, or whatever function these words have? Nothing can mark it grammatically; there is no more morphological specification here than there is syntactical rection" (25–26), and he chooses to translate this phrase as "beginning expansion profit rectitude," or "just as good," he translates it as "to begin—to expand rapidly—to profit/to turn to good account—to remain sound (solid)" (26). —Translator)

Chapter 9

1. This chapter did not originally have section titles. They have been added for the reader's benefit. —Translator

2. Dong Zhongshu says: "Thus, at the same time those called august emperor numbered five and those called king numbered three. This was to bring to light the five beginnings and interconnect the three traditions. This is why the king of the Zhou promoted Shen Nong as one of the nine august emperors and changed Xuan Yuan's title to Yellow Emperor . . . [and] each of the emperors were assigned a small nation. Next came the descendants of Yu in Qi and those of Tang in Song who were each given five hundred square *li* and the title of duke. They were all made to dress in their own attire, practice their own rituals and music, claim to be guests to the former kings and pay tribute" (Su Yu 蘇輿 and Zhong Zhe 鐘哲: *Chunqiu Fanlu Yizheng* 春秋繁露義證 [Beijing: Zhonghua Shuju, 1992]), 198–199.

3. Zhang Guangzhi 張廣志: *Xizhoushi yu Xizhou Wenming* 西周史與西周文明 (Western Zhou History and Civilization) (Shanghai: Shanghai Kexue Jishu Wenxian Chubanshe, 2007), 126.

4. Matteo Ricci writes: "It would seem to be quite worthwhile recording a few more things in which [the Chinese] people differ from Europeans. To begin with, it seems to be quite remarkable when we stop to consider it, that in a kingdom of almost limitless expanse and innumerable population, and abounding in copious supplies of every description, though they have a well-equipped army and navy that could easily conquer the neighboring nations, neither the King nor his people ever think of waging a war of aggression. They are quite content with what they have and are not ambitious of conquest. In this respect they are much different from the people of Europe, who are frequently discontent with their own governments and covetous of what others enjoy. While the nations of the West seem to be entirely consumed with the idea of supreme domination, they cannot even preserve what their ancestors have bequeathed them, as the Chinese have done through a period of some thousands of years. This assertion seems to have some bearing upon what many of our writers maintain relative

to the initial founding of the empire, when they assert that the Chinese not only subjugated the neighboring nations but extended their sway even as far as India. After diligent study of the history of China, covering a period of more than four thousand years, I must admit that I have never seen any mention of such conquest, nor have I ever heard of them extending the boundaries of their empire . . . Another remarkable fact and quite worthy of note as marking a difference from the West, is that the entire kingdom is administered by the Order of the Learned, commonly known as The Philosophers." Matteo Ricci: *China in the Sixteenth Century: The Journals of Mattew Ricci: 1583–1610*, translated by Louis J. Gallagher (New York: Random House, 1953), 54 –55.

5. The poem #235 "Wen Wang" in the *Book of Poetry* says: "Although Zhou is an old state, its mandate is new."

6. Zhang Xianglong, *Chengli Rujia Wenhua Tequ huo Baohuqu de Liyou yu Fangshi* ("Reasons and Methods for Establishing a Confucian Culture Special Zone or Protection Zone") and *Qiju zhong de Jia Hezai?—Feigao Keji de Jianzhu Xianxiangxue Tantao* 棲居中的家何在？——非高科技的建築現象學探討 ("Where is the Family in Residing? A Phenomenological Exploration of Low-Tech Architecture), in my *Fujian Tiandi Xin: Rujia Zailin Yunyi yu Daolun* 複見天地心：儒家再臨的蘊意與道路 ("Seeing again the Heart of Heaven and Earth: the Path and Meaning of the Return of Confucianism) (Beijing: Dongfang Chubanshe, 2014), 129–162.

7. See Donald B. Kraybill et al., *The Amish* (Baltimore: Johns Hopkins University Press, 2013). See also John A. Hostetler (ed.): *Amish Society* (Baltimore & London: Johns Hopkins University Press, 1993).

8. This story goes like this: "Zi Gong was traveling south in Chu and on his way back to Jin he passed through Hanyin where he saw a man watering his fields by going into a well and drawing water with a bucket. His effort was great but his gain was little. Zi Gong said: 'There is an implement for this with which you can water one hundred paddies in a single day. Your effort would be little but your gains would be great. Do you not desire it? The farmer looked up and said: 'What kind of thing is it?' Zi Gong replied: 'Wood is carved into a lever that is weighted at the back but light in the front. You can collect a great deal of water by pulling it back and forth. It is called a water pulley.' The farmer blushed and laughed. 'I have heard it from my master that if one has a contrived implement then one will have contrived affairs, and if one has contrived affairs then one will have a contrived heart-mind. If a contrived heart-mind is one's breast, then one will be impure; if one is impure then one's concentration will not settle down; and if one's concentration will not settle down, then there will be no place for *dao* to reside. It is not that I don't know of this thing, it is that I'm unwilling to use it.' Zi Gong, with a face full of shame, looked down and did not reply."

Chapter 10

1. See my *Fuqin de Diwei—Cong Rujia he Renleixue de Shiyekan* 父親的地位—從儒家和人類學的視野看, in *Tongji Daxue Xuebao* 同濟大學學報, 2017, di 1 qi, 52–60.

2. A recent book that discusses this problem is Wu Fei's 吳飛 *Renlun de "Jieti": Xingzhilun Chuantong Zhong de Jiaguo Jiaolü* 人倫的"解體": 形質論傳統中的家國焦慮 ("The 'Dissolution' of Human Relations: Concerns for the Family and State in the Tradition Formalism") (Beijing: Sanlian Shudian, 2017).

3. Zhou Huashan 周華山, *Wufu Wufu de Guodu* 無父無夫的國度 ("The Nation without Fathers and Husbands") (Beijing: Guangming Ribao Chubanshe, 2010). A saying at the front of the book says: "The principle for choosing family is not sex, status, or age; instead, it is purely one's capabilities—see who best understands household affairs, who can best manage personal relationships, and who treats others fairly."

4. Common methods that the Mosuo use to overcome shortages of men and women include adoption and marriage solicitations.

5. Yan Ruxian 嚴汝嫻 and Liu Xiaoxin 劉小辛, *Mosuo Muxizhi Yanjiu* 摩梭母系制研究 ("Mosuo Matriarchy Research") (Kunming: Yunnan Chban Jituan, 2012).

6. We will not consider the matter of adoption here.

7. The former, *qinqin*, is a Confucian term that means "to treat family affectionately." The latter, however, comes from no classical texts but in modern Chinese colloquially means "to make love." —Translator

8. According to some scholars' investigations, other than the Mosuo people, there are a few other matriarchal societies with "walking marriages" in southwest China, such as the Ganzi 甘孜 and Zhabei 紮壩 peoples in Sichuan (*Yanjiu*, 241). In addition, there are vestiges of a matriarchal system in the Lahu people, some Wa people, the Blang people, the Dai people, and the Jino people (241).

9. In Mosuo society, the three roles prized by males include being a caravanner, a lama, and an "uncle" (*Guodu*, 199). However, the first two come from outside and do not represent the lengthy historical structure internal to Mosuo society. The religion of the Mosuo is called Daba, and their religious leader is a male referred to as "Daba 達巴," but this position is, nevertheless, not higher than that of an "uncle" (29).

10. This is a reference to a post–Han dynasty poem of the same name written by Tao Yuanming 陶淵明 (365–427 CE) describing a utopia hidden away from contemporary troubles. —Translator

11. If markers of "civilization" like modern cities, commercial economies, and individuality are degrading and denigrating those things that allow people

to live peaceful and content lives, and will do so as far as can be seen, then their integrity as a rational mode of existence should be seriously questioned.

12. These clear sayings represent the greater situation, but there are always boundary cases that arise due to the different needs of individuals. For example, during his investigation, Zhou encountered a situation where two sisters from the same family lineage shared the same husband in succession (*Guodu*, 48). There was also the case where "the mother of the boy's father was the sister of the mother of the girl's mother" (49). Although they were separated by two generations, the local people still found it morally revolting. We can imagine those investigators wearing ideologically tinged glasses would use this kind of situation to prove their point.

13. This section overlaps some of my *Fuqin de Diwei—Cong Rujia he Renleixue de Shiyekan* 父親的地位—從儒家和人類學的視野看, in *Tongji Daxue Xuebao* 同濟大學學報, 2017, di 1 qi, 52–60. Apologies!

14. Edward O. Wilson writes: "And because men can breed at shorter intervals than women, the pair bond has been attenuated somewhat by the common practice of polygyny, the taking of multiple wives" (*On Human Nature*, Cambridge, MA & London: Harvard University Press, 1978, 140) and "We are, first of all, moderately polygynous, with males initiating most of the changes in sexual partnership. About three-fourths of all human societies permit the taking of multiple wives, and most of them encourage the practice by law and custom" (125–126). Wilson's "moderate polygyny" should include our "elastic monogamy." For example, in China, where half of the world's population once lived, men were allowed to marry more than just one woman. However, this was not a polygynous system but rather an elastic monogamy because in addition to the wife, men could take multiple concubines. Moreover, there were many households that were monogamous; otherwise, the main philosophy could not have considered "widows and orphans" as abnormal and therefore expect the government to offer them assistance.

15. Luigi Zoja, *The Father: Historical, Psychological and Culture Perspectives*. Translated by Henry Martin (East Sussex: Brunner-Routledge, 2001).

16. See my *"Xingbie" zai Zhongxi Zhexue Zhong de Diwei jiqi Sixiang Houguo* "性別"在中西哲學中的地位及其思想後果 ("The Status and Intellectual Consequences of 'Gender' in Chinese and Western Thought"), in *Jiangsu Shehui Kexue* 江蘇社會科學, 2002, di 6 qi, 1–9. This essay is also in *Sixiang Binan: Quanqiuhua de Zhongguo Gudai Zheli* 思想避難: 全球化的中國古代哲理 ("Intellectual Refuges: the Globalization of Ancient Chinese Philosophy") (Beijing: Beida Chubanshe, 2007), ch. 14.

17. *Guxila Luoma Zhexue* 古希臘羅馬哲學 ("Ancient Greek and Roman Philosophy") (Beijing: Shangwu Yinshuguan, 1982), 32.

18. Emmanuel Levinas, *Totality and Infinity: An Essay on Exteriority*. Translated by A. Lingis (The Hague, Boston, & London: M. Nijhoff, 1979), 306. "As

a source of human time it [the family] permits the subjectivity to place itself under a judgement while retaining speech."

Chapter 11

1. According to the "Harry Potter" entry on baidu.com's "Baidu Encyclopedia," the *Harry Potter* novels have been translated into more than seventy languages and have sold over four hundred million copies in over two hundred countries and territories across the world. It is the best-selling non-religious book (http://baike.baidu.com/view/18045.htm#1). Its film adaptation is also extremely impressive.

2. Refer to some of the reports in the "religious debate" cited by Wikipedia (http://en.wikipedia.org/wiki/Religious_debates_over_theHarry_Potter_series). It has been criticized by Protestant, Catholic, and Eastern Orthodox Christians and Muslims. It was criticized the most for promoting magic because neither white nor black magic fits with belief in God. In the United States, during the 1990s, there was a debate on whether this series should be in public libraries. The *Harry Potter* series is one of the seven most challenged books. In 1999, thirteen states opposed it twenty-three times.

3. *Reading Harry Potter: Critical Essays* (herein *Reading Harry Potter*), ed. G.L. Anatol (Westport, CN: Praeger, 2003).

4. See: www.nytimes.com/1999/02/14/books/children-s-books-199338.html.

5. See: www.nytimes.com/1999/02/14/books/children-s-books-199338.html.

6. See: http://mtv.com/news/articles/1572107/20071017/index.jhtml

7. *Critical Perspectives on Harry Potter* (henceforth *Critical Perspectives*), ed. Elizabeth E. Heilman (New York: Routledge, 2009).

8. For S. Adler's report on this speech by Rowling, see www.mtv.com/news/articles/1572107/20071017/index.jhtml.

9. Ronni Carmeli, "Four Modes of Fatherhood: Paternal Contributors to Harry Potter's Psychological Development," in *Harry Potter's World Wide Influence*, ed. Diana Patterson (Newcastle on Tyne: Cambridge Scholar Publishing, 2009), 11–33.

10. Zhang notes that he is referring to the editions published by Arthur A Levine Books from 1998 to 2007. The translator refers to the same series.

11. Therefore, saying that Voldemort is the "dark double of Harry's father" or that he is a "father figure" is meaningless. There is no Oedipus complex here. Harry never hid or suppressed his desire to kill Voldemort. The bit of life given to him by Voldemort and that given to him by his parents are not comparable. Moreover, Harry can finally free himself from Voldemort, but he cannot free himself from his parents.

12. "*Liude zixu haoqi zai sannian gui bao chu wang chou* 留得子胥豪氣在，三年歸報楚王仇. "This line is from Yang Chao's 杨超 poem titled "Toward Justice" (*jiuyi shi* 就義詩).

13. Zhang quotes the original passage in Li Ling (2007) here, but I have referred to Scott Cook's translation in his *The Bamboo Texts of Guodian* (2013). This passage appears on page 780. —Translator

14. The term translated as "person" here is "*shen* 身." In the classical Chinese context, it not only refers to the "body" but also the "social self." —Translator

15. See my "Temporal Analysis of Filial Consciousness" (*Xiao Yishi de Shijian Fenxi* 孝意识的时间分析), in *Beijing Daxue Xuebao* 北京大学学报, 2006, vol. 1, 14–24. This essay has English and Bosnian translations.

16. In this book, Harry and Hermione see the words "Where your treasure is, there will your heart be also" on the tombstones of Dumbledore's mother and sister. The book does not indicate that this quote comes from the *Gospel of Matthew* 6:21.

Works Cited

Andelie Bierjiai 安德烈・比爾基埃 (Burguière, André): *Jiating shi* 家庭史 (A History of the Family), trans. by Yuan Shuren 袁樹仁, Beijing 北京: Sanlian Shudian 三聯書店, 1998.

Anatol, G.L. (ed.): *Reading Harry Potter: Critical Essays*. Westport, CN: Praeger, 2003.

Aristotle: *The Politics of Aristotle*. Edited and translated by E. Barker. London: Oxford University Press, 1946/1979.

Ash, Patricia J., and David Robinson. *The Emergence of Humans: An Exploration of the Evolutionary Timeline*. London: Wiley-Blackwell, 2010.

Blyd, Robert, and Joan B. Silk. *How Humans Evolved*, 5th edition. New York W.W. Norton, 2009.

Burguière, André, Christiane Klapisch-Zuber, et al. *A History of Family*, vol. 1. Translated by S. Tenison, R. Morris, and A. Wilson. Cambridge, MA: The Belknap Press of Harvard University Press, 1996.

Campbell, C.J., and A. Fuentes, et al. (eds.). *Primates in Perspective*. New York & Oxford: Oxford University Press, 2007.

Chen, Duxiu 陳獨秀 (ed.). *Qingnian Zazhi*, di 1 juan di 1 hao. Shanghai: Qunyi Shushe, 1915.

Cook, Scott. *The Bamboo Texts of Guodian*. Ithaca, NY: Cornell University East Asia Program, 2013.

Diamond, Jared. *The Third Chimpanzee: The Evolution and Future of the Human Animal*. New York: HarperCollins, 1992.

Ding Shouhe 丁守和 (ed.). *Zhongguo Jindai Qimeng Sichao* 中國近啟蒙思潮, zhong juan. Beijing: Shehuikexue Wenxian Chubanshe, 1999.

Ellis, Henry C., and R. Reed Hunt. *Fundamentals of Cognitive Psychology*, 5th edition. Boston, MA: McGraw Hill, 1993.

Enger, Eldon D., and Frederick C. Ross. *Concepts in Biology*. New York: McGraw-Hill, 2003.

English, Jane. "What Do Grown Children Owe Their Parents?" In *Having Children: Philosophical and Legal Reflections on Parenthood*, ed. O. O'Neil and W. Ruddick. New York: Oxford University Press, 1979, 352–354.

Fainlight, Ruth, and Robert J. Littman. *Sophocles: The Theban Plays*. Baltimore: Johns Hopkins University Press, 2009.

Goodall, Jane. *In the Shadow of Man*. London: William Collins Sons & Co., Ltd, 1971.

Goodall, Jane. *My Life with the Chimpanzees*. New York: A Minstrel Book, 1996.

Haiyinlixi Zankeer 海因里希·燦克爾: (Zankl, Heinrich): *Xingxianxiang—Guanyu Xingbie de "Xiao" Chayi* 性現象—關於性別的"小"差異. Translated by Yunyi Zhang 張雲毅. Beijing: Shangwu Yinshuguan, 2001.

Hawkes, Kristen. "Mating, Parenting, and the Evolution of Human Pair Bonds." In B. Chapais and C. Berman (eds.), *Kinship and Behavior in Primates*. New York: Oxford University Press, 2004.

He, Chuanqi 何傳啟. *Diliuci Keji Geming de Jiyu yu Duice* 第六次科技革命的機遇與對策 ("The Opportunity and Strategy of the Sixth Scientific Revolution"). In *Diliuci Keji Geming de Zhanlüe Jiyu* 第六次科技革命的戰略機遇, edited by Chuanqi He. Beijing: Kexue Chubanshe, 2011.

Heidegger, Martin. *Kant and the Problem of Metaphysics*. Translated by James S. Campbell. Bloomington: Indiana University Press, 1965.

Heilman, Elizabeth E. (ed.). *Critical Perspectives on Harry Potter*. New York: Routledge, 2009.

Henke, Winfried, and Ian Tattersal (eds.). *Handbook of Paleoanthropology*, vol. 11, *Primate Evolution and Human Origins*. Berlin, Heidelberg, & New York: Springer-Verlag, 2007.

Hostetler, John A. (ed.). *Amish Society*. Baltimore & London: Johns Hopkins University Press, 1993.

Husserl, Edmund. *On the Phenomenology of the Consciousness of Internal Time*. Translated by J. Brough Dordrect. Boston & London: Kluwer Academic Publishers, 1991.

Jullien, Francois. *Book of Beginnings*. New Haven, CT & London: Yale University Press, 2015.

Kant, Immanuel. *Critique of Pure Reason*. Translated by P. Guyer and A. Wood. New York: Cambridge University Press, 1998.

Kierkegaard, Søren. *Fear and Trembling—Dialectical Lyric by Johannes de silentio*. Translated by A. Hannay. Middlesex & New York: Penguin Books, 1985.

Kirk, G.S., and J. E. Raven. *Presocratic Philosophers*. Cambridge: Cambridge University Press, 1957.

Kottak, Conrad P. *Anthropology: The Exploration of Human Diversity*, 12th edition. New York: Renmin University Press and McGraw-Hill, 2008.

Kraybill, Donald B., et al. *The Amish*. Baltimore: Johns Hopkins University, 2013.

Levinas, Emmanuel. *Totality and Infinity: An Essay on Exteriority*. Translated by A. Lingis. The Hague, Boston, & London: M. Nijhoff, 1979.
Li, Ling 李零. *Guodian Chujian Jiaoduji* 郭店楚简校读记. Beijing: Beijing Daxue Chubanshe Press, 2002.
Lumsden, Charles J., and Edward O. Wilson. *Promethean Fire: Reflection on the Origin of the Mind*. Cambridge, MA: Harvard University Press, 1983.
Luo Chenglie 駱承烈 (ed.). *Zhongguo Gudai Xiaodao Ziliao Xuanbian* 中國古代孝道資料選編 (The Selections of Chinese Ancient Literature of Filial Dao). Jinan: Shandong University Press, 2003.
Morgan, Lewis Henry. *Ancient Society*. Chicago: Charles H. Kerr & Company, 1907.
Ni Liangkang 倪梁康. *Neishijian Yishi Xianxiangxue* 內時間意識現象學. Beijing: Shangwu Yinshuguan, 2010.
Miao Tianli 苗力田 (ed.). *Guxila Zhexue* 古希臘哲學 (Ancient Greek Philosophy). Beijing: Zhongguo Renmin Daxue Chubanshe, 1989.
Most, Glenn W. *Theogony, Works and Days, Testimonia*. Cambridge, MA & London: Harvard University Press, 2006.
PKU Department of Philosophy Foreign Philosophy Teaching and Research Office 北京大学哲学系外国哲学史教研室 (ed.). *Guxila Luoma Zhexue* 古希臘羅馬哲學 ("Ancient Greek and Roman Philosophy"). Beijing: Shangwu Yinshuguan, 1982.
Plato. *The Symposium*. Translated by M.C. Howatson. Cambridge: Cambridge University Press, 2008.
Ross, David. *The Works of Aristotle*, vol. 12 ("The Fragments"). Oxford: Clarendon Press, 1952.
Ricci, Matteo. *China in the Sixteenth Century: The Journals of Mattew Ricci: 1583–1610*. Translated by L. Gallagher. New York: Random House, 1953.
Rowling, J.K. 1997–2008. *Harry Potter* (1–7). New York: Arthur A. Levine Books.
Shell, Marc. *The End of Kinship: "Measure for Measure," Incest, and the Ideal of Universal Siblinghood*. Baltimore & London: Johns Hopkins University Press, 1995.
Small, Meredith F. "Our Babies, Ourselves." In Elvio Angeloni (ed), *Annual Editions: Anthropology* 2002/2003. Guilford, CT: McGraw-Hill/Dushkin, 2002.
Su, Yu 蘇歟, and Zhe Zhong 鐘哲. *Chunqiu Fanlu Yizheng* 春秋繁露義證. Beijing: Zhonghua Shuju, 1992.
Tulving, Endel. "Episodic Memory and Autonoesis: Uniquely Human?" In H.S. Terrace and J. Metcalfe (eds.), *The Missing Link in Cognition Origins of Self-Reflective Consciousness*. New York: Oxford University Press, 2005.
Turner, J.H., and A. Maryanski. *Incest: Origin of the Taboo*. Boulder, CO & London: Paradigm Publishers, 2005.
Tutin, Carline E.G. "Reproductive Success Story—Variability among Chimpanzees and Comparisons with Gorillas." In R.W. Wrangham, W.C. McGrew,

et al. (eds.), *Chimpanzee Cultures*. Cambridge, MA & London: Harvard University Press, 1996.

Weisitemake 威斯特馬克 (Westermarck, E.). *Renlei Hunyin Shi* (*The History of Human Marriage*). Translated by Li Bi, Li Yifu, and Ouyang Jueya. Beijing: Shangwu Yinshuguan, 2002.

Wilson, Edward O. *On Human Nature*. Cambridge, MA & London: Harvard University Press, 1978.

Wilson, Edward O. *Daziran de Lieren—Shengwuxuejia Weierxun Zizhuan* 大自然的猎人—生物学家威尔逊自传. Translated by Yuling Yang 杨玉玲. Shanghai: Shanghai Kexue Jishu Chubanshe, 2000.

Wilson, Edward O. *Sociobiology: The New Synthesis*. Cambridge, MA & London: The Belknap Press of Harvard University Press, 2000.

Wolf, A.P., and W.H. Durham (eds.). *Inbreeding, Incest, and the Incest Taboo: The State of Knowledge at the Turn of the Century*. Stanford, CA: Stanford University Press, 2005.

Wu, Fei. 吳飛 *Renlun de "Jieti": Xingzhilun Chuantong Zhong de Jiaguo Jiaolü* 人倫的"解體": 形質論傳統中的家國焦慮·(*The "Dissolution" of Human Relations: Concerns for the Family and State in the Tradition Formalism*). Beijing: Sanlian Shudian, 2017. (This text was also cited as the forthcoming *Tianlun Renxu—Xingzhilun Chuantong Zhong de Jiaguo Jiaolü* 天倫人敘—形質論傳統中的家國焦慮.)

Yan, Ruxian 嚴汝嫻, and Xiaoxin Liu 劉小辛. *Mosuo Muxizhi Yanjiu* 摩梭母系制研究 ("Mosuo Matriarchy Research"). Kunming: Yunnan Chuban Jituan, 2012.

Zankl, Heinrich. *Phänomen Sexualität. Vom "kleinen" Unterschied der Geschlechter*

Zhang, Guangzhi 張廣志. *Xizhoushi yu Xizhou Wenming* 西周史與西周文明 (*Western Zhou History and Civilization*). Shanghai: Shanghai Kexue Jishu Wenxian Chubanshe, 2007.

Zhang, Xianglong 張祥龍. "*Xingbie* zai Zhongxi Zhexue Zhong de Diwei jiqi Sixiang Houguo "性別"在中西哲學中的地位及其思想後果 ("The Status and Intellectual Consequences of 'Gender' in Chinese and Western Thought"). In *Jiangsu Shehui Kexue* 江蘇社會科學, 2002, 1–9.

Zhang, Xianglong. "Temporal Analysis of Filial Consciousness" (*xiao yishi de shijian fenxi* 孝意识的时间分析). In *Beijing Daxue Xuebao* 北京大学学报, 2006, vol. 1, 14–24.

Zhang Xianglong. *Deguo Zhexue, Deguo Wenhua yu Zhongguo Zheli* 德國哲學、德國文化與中國哲理 ("German Philosophy, German Culture, and Chinese Philosophical Thought"). Shanghai: Shanghai Waiyu Jiaoyu Chubanshe, 2012.

Zhang, Xianglong. *Chengli Rujia Wenhua Tequ huo Baohuqu de Liyou yu Fangshi* ("Reasons and Methods for Establishing a Confucian Culture Special Zone or Protection Zone"). In X. Zhang, *Fujian Tiandi Xin: Rujia Zailin Yunyi yu Daolun* 複見天地心: 儒家再臨的蘊意與道路 ("Seeing Again the Heart of

Heaven and Earth: the Path and Meaning of the Return of Confucianism"). Beijing: Dongfang Chubanshe, 2014a.

Zhang, Xianglong. "*Qiju zhong de Jia Hezai?—Feigao Keji de Jianzhu Xianxiangxue Tantao* 棲居中的家何在？——非高科技的建築現象學探討" ("Where Is the Family in Residing? A Phenomenological Exploration of Low-Tech Architecture). In X. Zhang, *Fujian Tiandi Xin: Rujia Zailin Yunyi yu Daolun* 複見天地心: 儒家再臨的蘊意與道路 ("Seeing again the Heart of Heaven and Earth: the Path and Meaning of the Return of Confucianism"). Beijing: Dongfang Chubanshe, 2014b.

Zhang Xianglong. *Fuqin de Diwei—Cong Rujia he Renleixue de Shiyekan* 父親的地位——從儒家和人類學的視野看. In *Tongji Daxue Xuebao* 同濟大學學報, 2017, 52–60.

Zhang, Zhuming 張竹明, and Ping Jiang 蔣平. *Gongzuo yu Shiri—Shenpu* 工作與時日·神譜. Beijing: Shangwu Yinshuguan, 1997.

Zhou, Huashan 周華山. *Wufu Wufu de Guodu* 無父無夫的國度 (The Nation without Fathers and Husbands). Beijing: Guangming Ribao Chubanshe, 2010.

Zoja, Luigi. *The Father: Historical, Psychological and Culture Perspectives*. Translated by H. Martin. East Sussex: Brunner-Routledge, 2001.

Index

Amish, 109, 117–126
Ancestors, 76, 105, 118, 144–145, 164
Aristotle, 59, 73
Augustine, 73

Body, 45, 55, 83–84, 155, 157, 167; conscious, 41; intergenerational, 49; temporal, 47
Buddhism, 147–148

Chen, Duxiu 陳獨秀, 13–14
Christianity, 31, 77, 99, 120, 142–143, 145, 152
Confucius, 24, 49, 95, 104, 113, 145, 147, 171; Confucianism, 24, 104–105, 110, 112, 127–128, 139, 142, 145–148, 164–167; Confucians, 112–119, 124, 126, 142–143, 162–164, 167, 170–171; Confucian classics; 105–107; Confucian culture, 120, 144–145, 162; Confucian essence, 126; Confucian fatherhood, 145; Confucian socialism, 12; special zone, 109–110, 113–118, 120, 123–124, 126; Neo-Confucians, 95, 111
Consciousness, 27, 35, 38, 49, 55–56, 59, 66, 75–76, 92, 103, 115, 140, 150, 153, 157, 159, 161; filial or of filial reverence, 49, 75–76, 149, 152, 171, 175, 178; originary, 10; temporal 17, 23–25, 51, 140; time, 31, 35–36, 39–40, 42–43, 45–46, 48–49, 55, 58, 63–65, 103, 149, 171; semantic consciousness, 65; of sexual differences, 92; of the other or others, 112, 114, 148
Culture, 11, 16–17, 22, 25, 28–29, 47, 71–72, 77–78, 113, 144

Daoism, 143, 147–148
Death, 150, 152, 155, 157–158, 161, 163, 170–177
Durkheim, Émile, 71, 73

Education, 27, 49, 69, 85, 104, 106, 113–114, 116, 118, 119, 124–125, 139, 167
Elderly and eldercare, 97–101
Evolution, 28, 32–35, 38–39, 43–47, 60–61, 64, 79, 98
Existence, 30, 36, 40, 52, 58, 72, 89, 148, 160; temporal, 4, 33, 72, 75–76; existential base, 22; existential experience, 113; existential meaning, 40, 58; existential mode, 59; existential source, 138, 147; existential

199

200 | Index

Existence (*continued*)
structure, 58, 76, 116, 128, 138, 160, 166; existential temporality, 4, 76, 176; existential time, 149, 174–177; existential value, 59
Existentialism, 36, 66
Experience, 7, 24, 53–54, 58–61, 65, 90

Family, 12–17, 21–25, 27, 30–32, 35, 37, 43, 48, 70–78, 80, 85–86, 92–93, 95, 97–98, 103–106, 112–118, 120–122, 127–131, 134–135, 138–142, 144–148, 152, 154, 156, 158–163, 166, 171, 174–175, 177; familial affection, 4, 8, 104–105, 112, 145, 166, 178
Fathers, 134–147 *passim*, 153, 158, 160–161, 164–166
Filial or filiality, 16, 37, 39, 75–76, 95, 103–104, 113, 144, 147, 149, 152, 162–163, 165, 167, 170–171, 175, 178; reverence, 14, 27–28, 36–37, 45–46, 48–49, 75–76, 104–105, 116–117, 120, 142, 144–145, 149, 163, 165–167; unfilial, 16, 98, 100
Flo (chimpanzee), 37–38, 98
Freedom, 15, 92, 114, 117, 130, 148
Fu, Sinian 傅斯年, 12, 14

Harry Potter, 149–178 *passim*
Heidegger, 51, 53, 57–59, 63–64, 66–67, 160
Hong, Xiuquan 洪秀全, 13
Hu, Shi, 11
Human nature, 3, 15, 18, 22–23, 25, 27–28, 31, 33, 35–36, 43, 47–48, 68, 76–79, 103, 105, 107, 114, 140, 144–145, 150, 152, 178
Husbands and wives, 23, 25, 30, 33–36, 40, 48, 104, 132, 134, 137, 143–146, 166

Husserl, 51, 55–57, 59–60, 63–67

Imagination, 51–58, 62, 65, 67, 170
Immortality, 106, 150, 157, 169, 171–174
Incest, 21, 22–24, 30, 69–86 *passim*, 88–89, 91–92, 95, 138–139, 146–147
Intergenerational, 36, 144, 160, 171, 174

Kant, 19, 51–53, 58, 64, 67, 99, 144
Kang, Youwei 康有為, 13, 98, 101
Kierkegaard, 1, 3, 6, 8, 10

Levi-Strauss, 21–22, 72
Love, 83–85, 88–89, 103–105, 131, 152–155, 158–162, 168–169, 171, 175
Lu Xun 魯迅, 14, 16, 18, 99

Marriage, 13, 20–21, 30–32, 72–73, 129–132, 134, 136–139, 146; gay, 98; walking marriage, 129–132, 134, 136–139
Marx, 72; Marxism, 15–16, 20; Marxist, 15
Matriarchy or matriarchal, 127–129, 131–135, 137, 146–148
Memory, 41, 45–46, 52, 60–68, 86, 91, 98–99, 140, 175–176; episodic, 60–68; intergenerational, 46; long- and short-term, 24, 41, 62; historical, 51; primary, 57; secondary 57; semantic, 51, 60–68
Merleau-Ponty, 40, 60
Morgan, Lewis, H., 20, 27, 31, 72, 86, 136
Mosuo 摩梭, 127–138 *passim*
Mothers, 42–43, 129–132, 135–143, 145, 153–155, 160

New Culture Movement, 11–16, 100, 166
Nietzsche, 12, 172, 177
Nothingness, 95, 174

Oedipus, 71, 82, 88; 153, 177

Panzee (chimpanzee), 63
Parents and children, 1, 4, 7–10, 12, 14–16, 19, 21, 25, 30–31, 35, 40, 45–46, 48, 67, 72–73, 75–76, 79, 86, 88–89, 95, 97–101, 103–104, 106–107, 112, 114, 118, 131, 134, 136–137, 144, 146, 149, 152–155, 157–167, 169, 171–172, 175, 177–178
Phenomenology, 36, 58–59; of body, 40, 60; phenomenological reduction, 7
Plato, 73, 77, 83–91
Primates, 29–30, 35, 42, 140
Protention, 55–58, 66–67

Reproduction, 69–72, 74, 79–80, 85–86, 88, 91, 139
Retention, 55–58, 63–64, 66–67
Revenge, 163–165, 167, 170–171, 176
Ricci, Matteo, 113

Sexualization, 70–71, 73, 76

Socrates, 88

Tan, Sitong 譚嗣同, 13
Technology, 22, 28, 100–102, 114–117, 119–126, 140, 148, 150, 177
Temporality, 9, 51, 58–59, 66, 76, 95, 106, 138; existential, 4, 76, 176; familial; 176; generational, 2; internal, 5
Three traditions (santong 三統), 109–113, 119, 125–126
Time, 3, 5, 6, 54–55, 58–59, 62–63, 76, 95, 140, 143–144, 149, 171, 173–178; genealogical, 5; (inter)generational, 5, 144, 150, 174, 175; internal, 10, 57, 60; living, 7, 10, 173–175; original, 51, 54, 174; originary, 6, 8, phenomenological, 55, 62; 144; physical, 62, 144; primordial, 51, 67; pure, 57–58; subjective, 62, transcendent, 177; timeliness, 7

Way of the Heavenly (tiandao 天道), 109, 111, 126
Westermarck, 22, 78; effect, 22–23, 78, 80
Wu Yu 吳虞, 14

Yinyang, 30, 70, 80, 92–95, 105, 117, 142–148, 156, 158, 173